DK BACKPACK BOOKS

1,001 FACTS ABOUT INSECTS

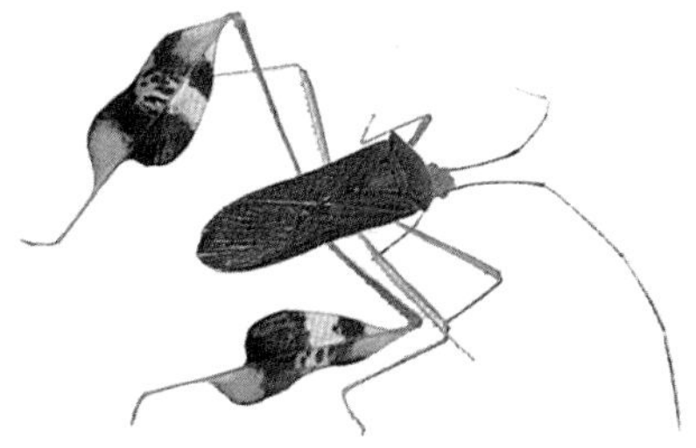

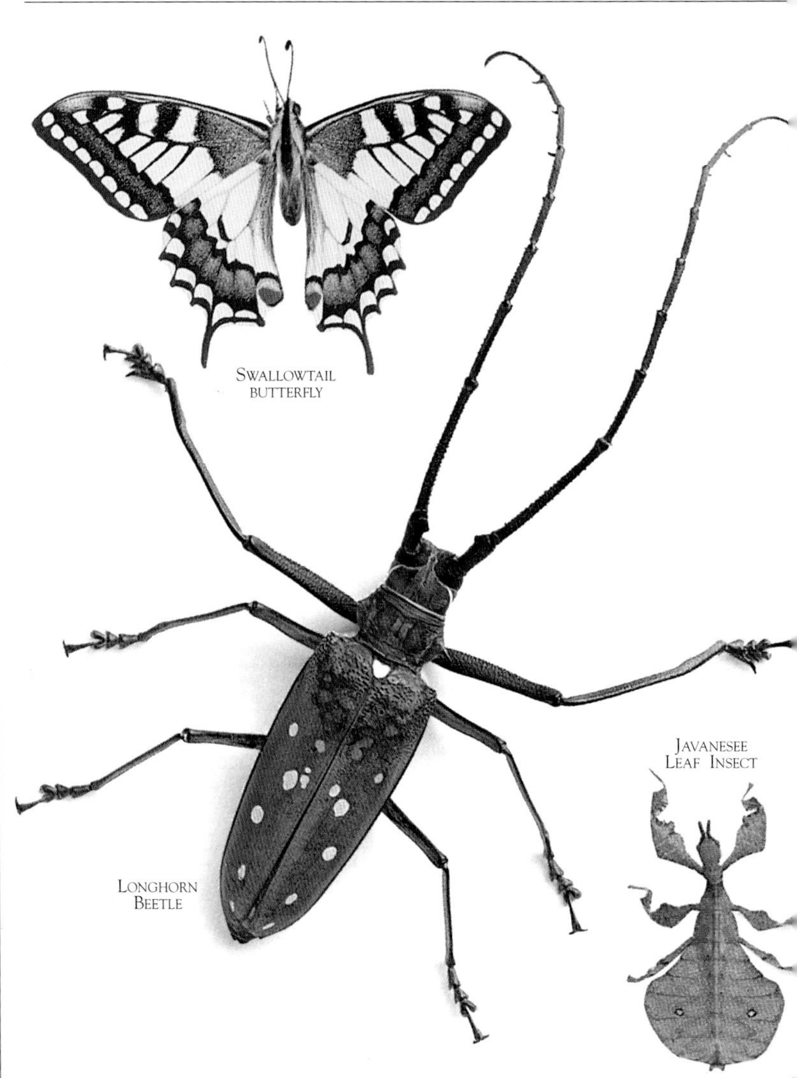
Swallowtail
butterfly
Longhorn
Beetle
Javanesee
Leaf Insect

BACKPACK BOOKS

1,001 FACTS ABOUT INSECTS

Written by LAURENCE MOUND and STEVE BROOKS
Additional material by BRYONY CLOSE and CHRIS MAYNARD

COCKCHAFER BEETLE

DESERT LOCUST

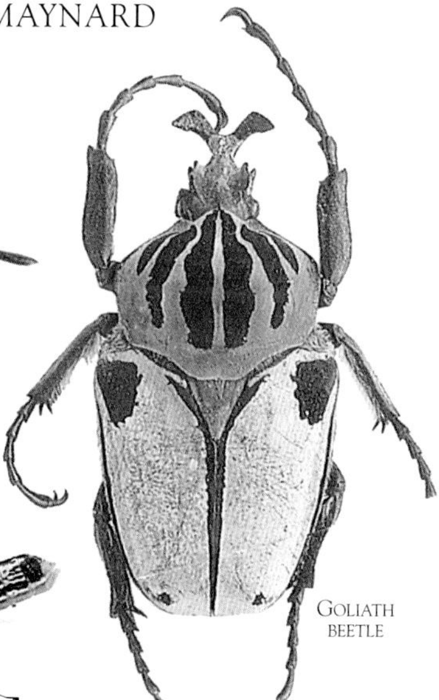

GOLIATH BEETLE

A DK Publishing Book

LONDON, NEW YORK, MUNICH,
MELBOURNE, and DELHI

Project editor Clare Lister
Senior designer Adrienne Hutchinson
Assistant designer Joanne Little
Senior editorial coordinator Camilla Hallinan
Senior design coordinator Sophia M. Tampakopoulos Turner
DTP Jill Bunyan
Category publisher Sue Grabham
Production Linda Dare
With thanks to the original team:
Art editor Ann Cannings
Senior editor Susan McKeever
Picture research Caroline Brooke

First American Edition, 2003

03 04 05 10 9 8 7 6 5 4 3 2

Published in the United States by
DK Publishing, Inc.
375 Hudson Street
New York, New York 10014

A catalog record for this book is available from the Library of Congress

ISBN 0-7894-9041-2

Color reproduction by Colourscan
Printed and bound in Singapore by Star Standard

See our complete product line at
www.dk.com

CONTENTS

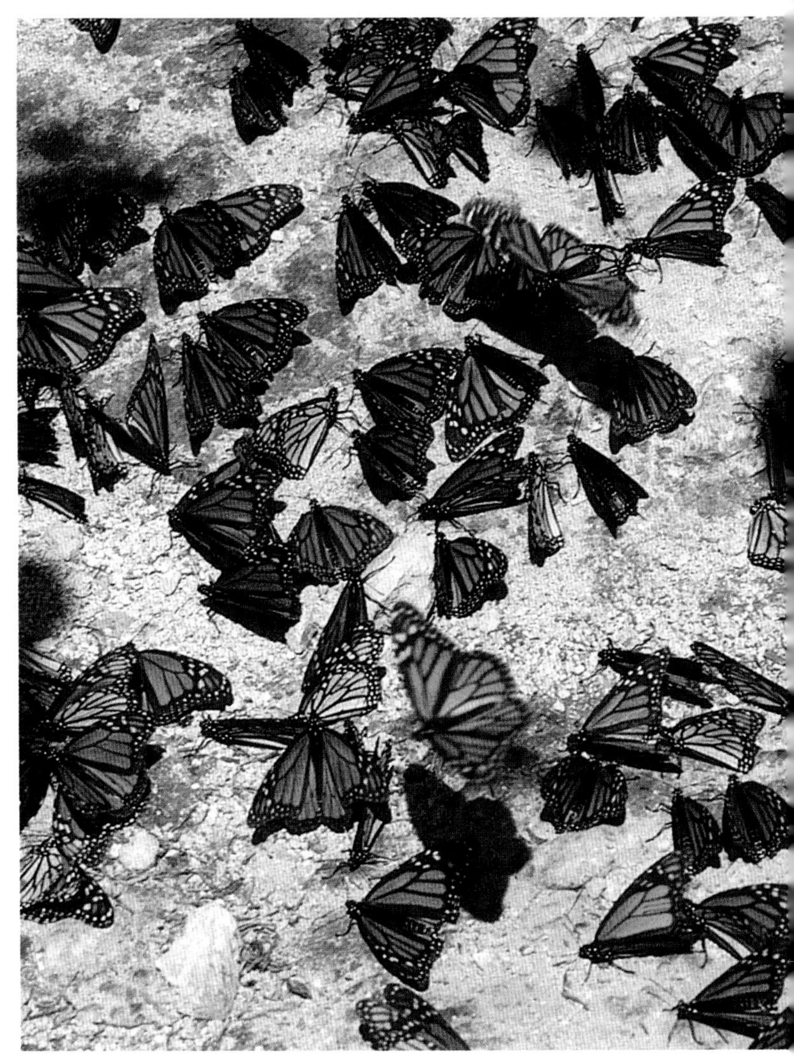

Introduction to Insects

WHAT IS AN INSECT?

THERE ARE AT LEAST five million insect species – they are the most abundant animals on earth. All insects have six legs, and their skeleton is on the outside of their body. This outer skeleton forms a hard, protective armor around the soft internal organs.

DISSECTED BEETLE

The antennae of insects can sense smells and vibrations in the air.

Eye

First part of thorax bears the front legs

Jointed front leg

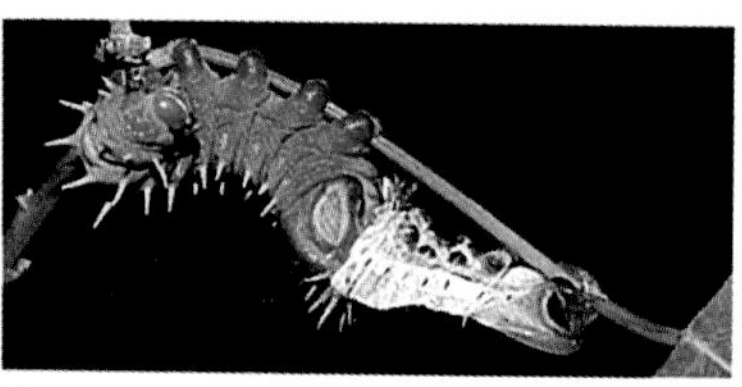

SHEDDING SKIN

A young insect is called a larva. As each larva feeds and grows, it must shed its hard outer skin, which is also called an exoskeleton. When the larva grows too big for its skin, the skin splits, revealing a new, larger skin underneath.

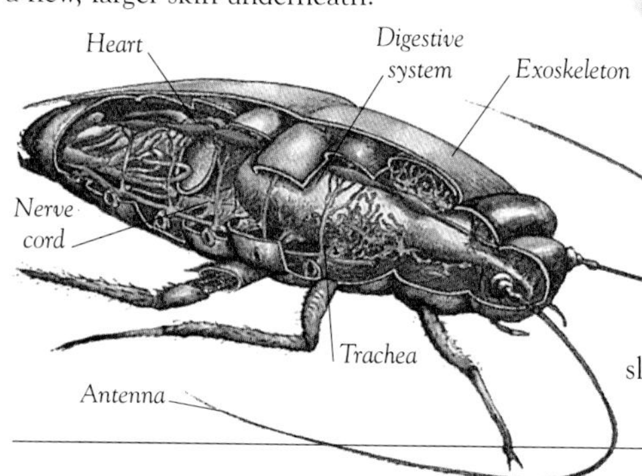

INTERNAL ANATOMY

A typical insect breathes through holes in its sides and distributes air around the body in tubes called tracheae. It has a nerv cord that runs beneath the digestive system. The heart, slender tube with several holes, pumps blood around the body.

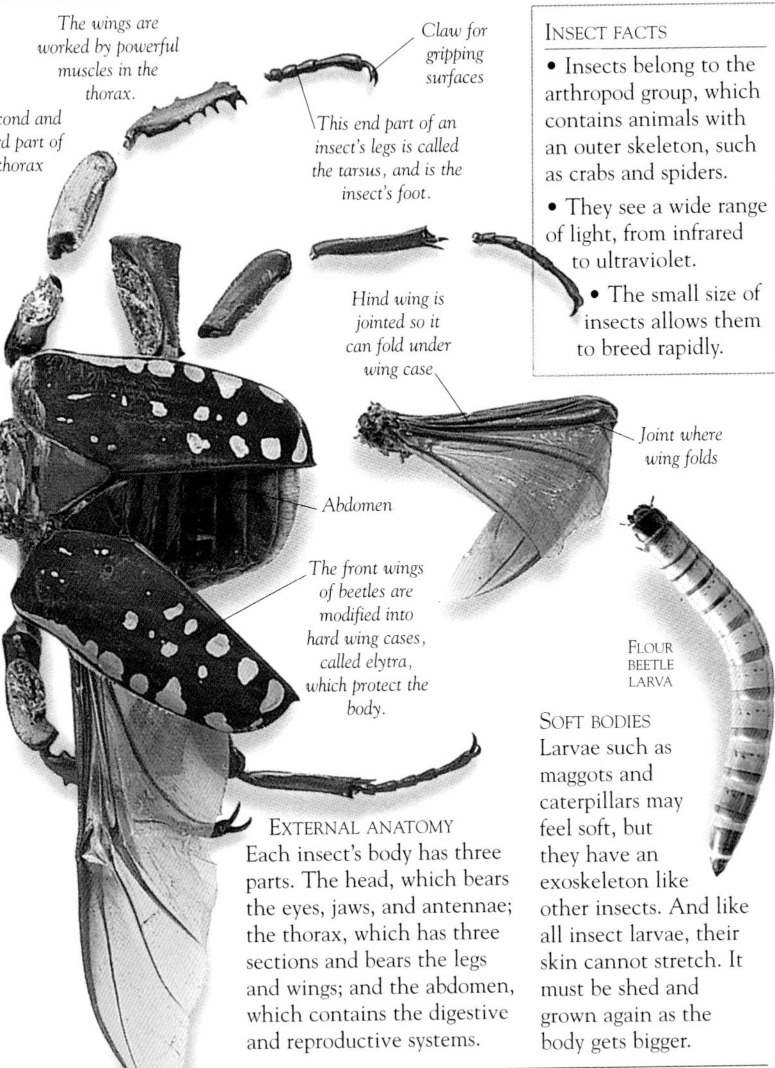
The wings are worked by powerful muscles in the thorax.
Claw for gripping surfaces
This end part of an insect's legs is called the tarsus, and is the insect's foot.
:ond and
'd part of
thorax
Hind wing is jointed so it can fold under wing case
Joint where wing folds
Abdomen
The front wings of beetles are modified into hard wing cases, called elytra, which protect the body.

FLOUR BEETLE LARVA

Insect facts

- Insects belong to the arthropod group, which contains animals with an outer skeleton, such as crabs and spiders.
- They see a wide range of light, from infrared to ultraviolet.
- The small size of insects allows them to breed rapidly.

External anatomy

Each insect's body has three parts. The head, which bears the eyes, jaws, and antennae; the thorax, which has three sections and bears the legs and wings; and the abdomen, which contains the digestive and reproductive systems.

Soft bodies

Larvae such as maggots and caterpillars may feel soft, but they have an exoskeleton like other insects. And like all insect larvae, their skin cannot stretch. It must be shed and grown again as the body gets bigger.

THE FIRST INSECTS

INSECTS WERE the first animals to fly. They appeared 300 million years ago – long before humans, and even before the dinosaurs. The ancient insect species are now extinct, but some were similar to modern dragonflies and cockroaches.

FLOWER FOOD
When flowering plants evolved 100 million years ago, insects gained two important new foods – pollen and nectar. Insects thrived on these foods. They pollinated the flowers, and many new species of plants and insects evolved together.

INSECT IN AMBER
Amber is the fossilized tree resin that came from pine trees over 40 million years ago. Well-preserved ancient insects are sometimes found in amber. This sweat bee is in copal, which is similar to amber but not so old.

FIRST INSECT FACTS

- The oldest known fossil insect is a springtail that lived 400 million years ago.
- Some of the earliest insects seem to have had three pairs of wings.
- The oldest known butterfly or moth is known from England 190 million years ago.

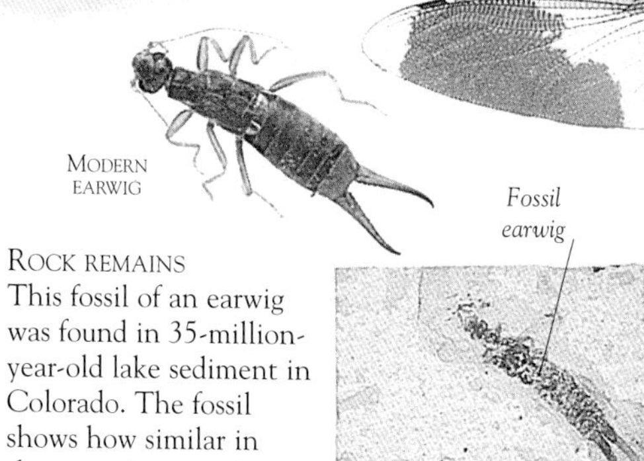

MODERN EARWIG

Fossil earwig

ROCK REMAINS
This fossil of an earwig was found in 35-million-year-old lake sediment in Colorado. The fossil shows how similar in shape ancient earwigs are to modern ones.

ssil Dragonfly

agonflies were one of the first types of ;ect. Fossils show that they have not anged very much in appearance er millions of years. Some cient dragonflies were very ge and may have had wing-ans of up to 3 ft (1 m). is dragonfly fossil ind in southern gland is of a small ecies. The ricate wing ins can be arly seen.

Modern dragonfly

One of the largest present-day dragonflies is this species from Borneo, with a wingspan of 6¼ in (16 cm). Although the larvae of modern dragonflies live in water, we cannot be sure that this was true of prehistoric dragonflies.

Agile fliers

Modern dragonflies are fast, agile fliers, and ancient dragonflies were probably the same. A prehistoric flying reptile would have had greater trouble catching a dragonfly than this fanciful engraving suggests.

Types of insect

We do not know exactly how many species, or types of insect there are, since scientists constantly discover new insects. But we estimate that about five million insect species exist. Each belongs to one of about 24 groups, or orders, which are defined according to body structure and larval development.

Jaws

Stag beetle

Hard wing cases meet midline.

Beetles, wasps, bees, and ants

About 400,000 species of beetles are described – they are the largest order of insects. Wasps, bees, and ants form the second largest order of insects, made up of about 200,000 species. The common feature in this order is a narrow "waist."

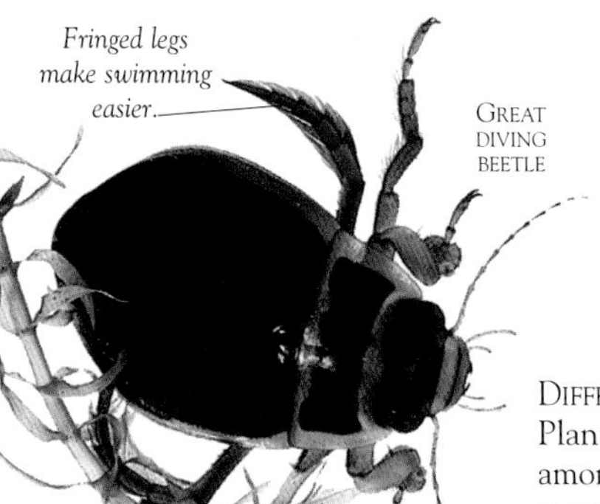
Fringed legs make swimming easier.
Great diving beetle

Beetles

Wings and jaws
The front pair of wings in beetles is hardened and forms a strong shield over the folded hind wings. Some beetles, such as stag beetles, have greatly enlarged jaws that look like horns.

Different foods
Plants, fungi, insects, and dead animals are among the wide variety of beetle foods. The great diving beetle lives in ponds. It is a fierce predator that hunts tadpoles and small fish.

ANTS, WASPS, AND BEES

WASPS

Adult wasps have a narrow "waist" and two pairs of transparent wings. The larvae look like grubs or caterpillars. Female wasps have an egg-laying tube that is often modified to form a sting.

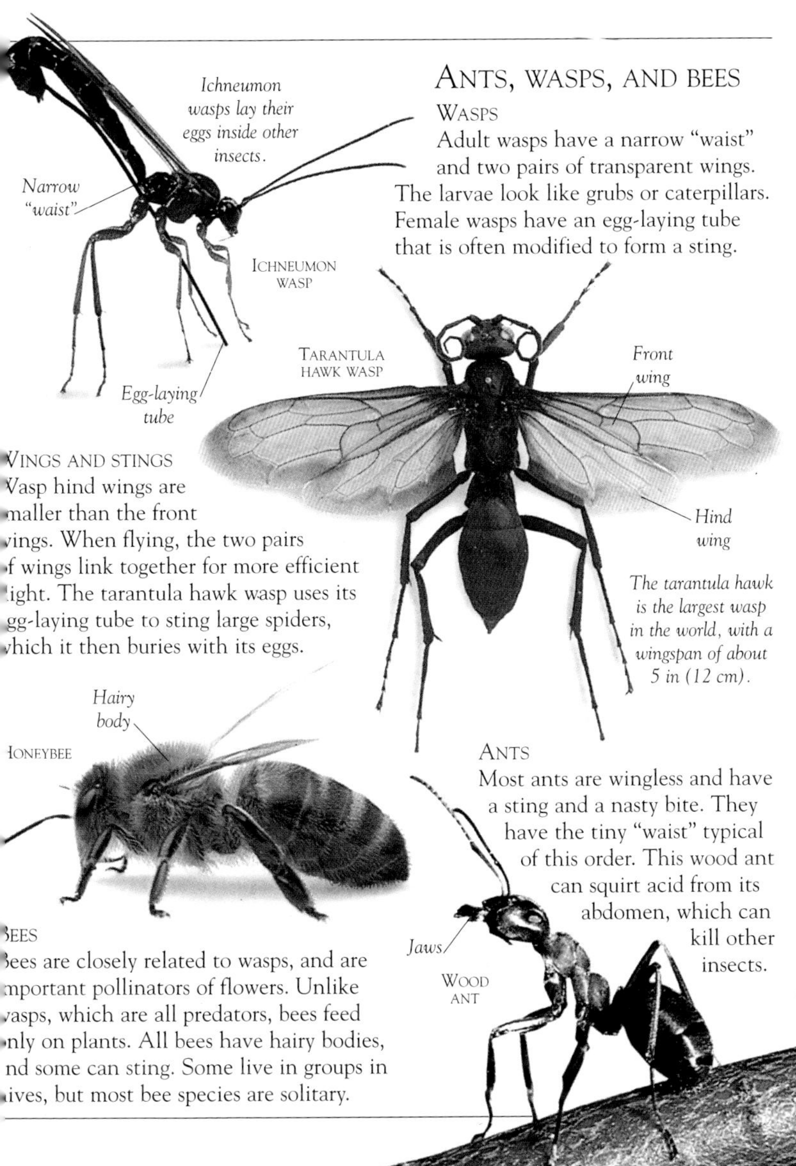

Ichneumon wasps lay their eggs inside other insects.

The tarantula hawk is the largest wasp in the world, with a wingspan of about 5 in (12 cm).

VINGS AND STINGS

Vasp hind wings are maller than the front vings. When flying, the two pairs f wings link together for more efficient light. The tarantula hawk wasp uses its gg-laying tube to sting large spiders, vhich it then buries with its eggs.

ANTS

Most ants are wingless and have a sting and a nasty bite. They have the tiny "waist" typical of this order. This wood ant can squirt acid from its abdomen, which can kill other insects.

BEES

Bees are closely related to wasps, and are mportant pollinators of flowers. Unlike vasps, which are all predators, bees feed nly on plants. All bees have hairy bodies, nd some can sting. Some live in groups in ives, but most bee species are solitary.

Butterflies, moths, and flies

Two common insect orders are the two-winged flies and the butterflies and moths. Flies are distinctive because their second pair of wings is converted into balancing organs, which look like drumsticks. Their young stages are maggots. Butterflies and moth have a coiled feeding tube, and their wings are covered in minut flattened scales. Butterfly and moth larvae are called caterpillars.

BUTTERFLIES AND MOTHS

CATERPILLARS

Although caterpillars' bodies are soft, they have an exoskeleton like other insects. Caterpillars grow at a very fast rate. They feed on leaves and have sharp jaws for slicing vegetation.

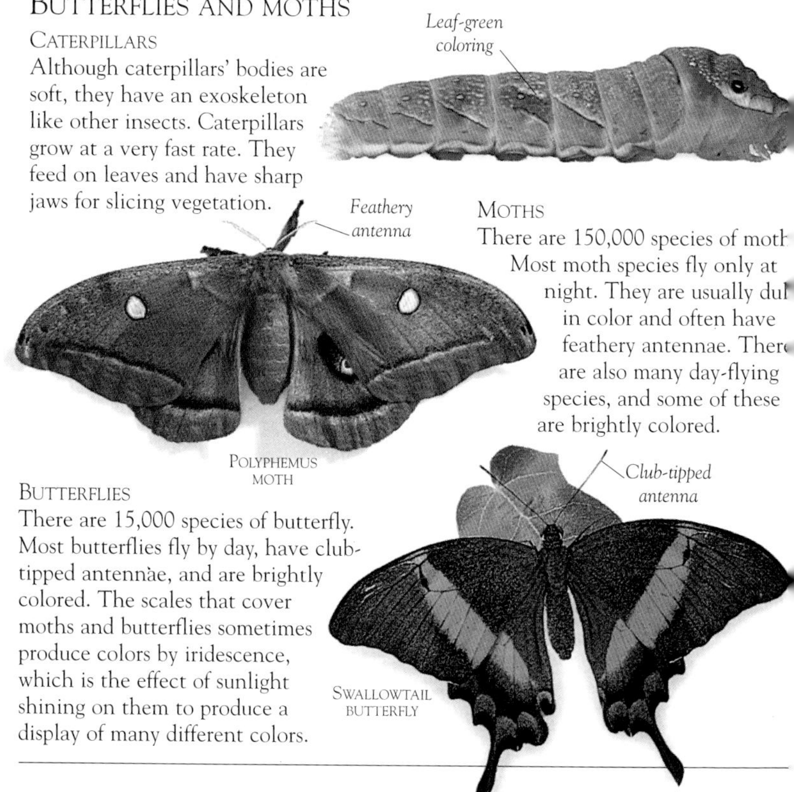

POLYPHEMUS MOTH

SWALLOWTAIL BUTTERFLY

MOTHS

There are 150,000 species of moth Most moth species fly only at night. They are usually dul in color and often have feathery antennae. There are also many day-flying species, and some of these are brightly colored.

BUTTERFLIES

There are 15,000 species of butterfly. Most butterflies fly by day, have club-tipped antennae, and are brightly colored. The scales that cover moths and butterflies sometimes produce colors by iridescence, which is the effect of sunlight shining on them to produce a display of many different colors.

Flies

Crane-fly

Crane-flies live successfully all over the world. The larvae of some species of crane-fly are known as "leather-jackets," because their skin is so tough.

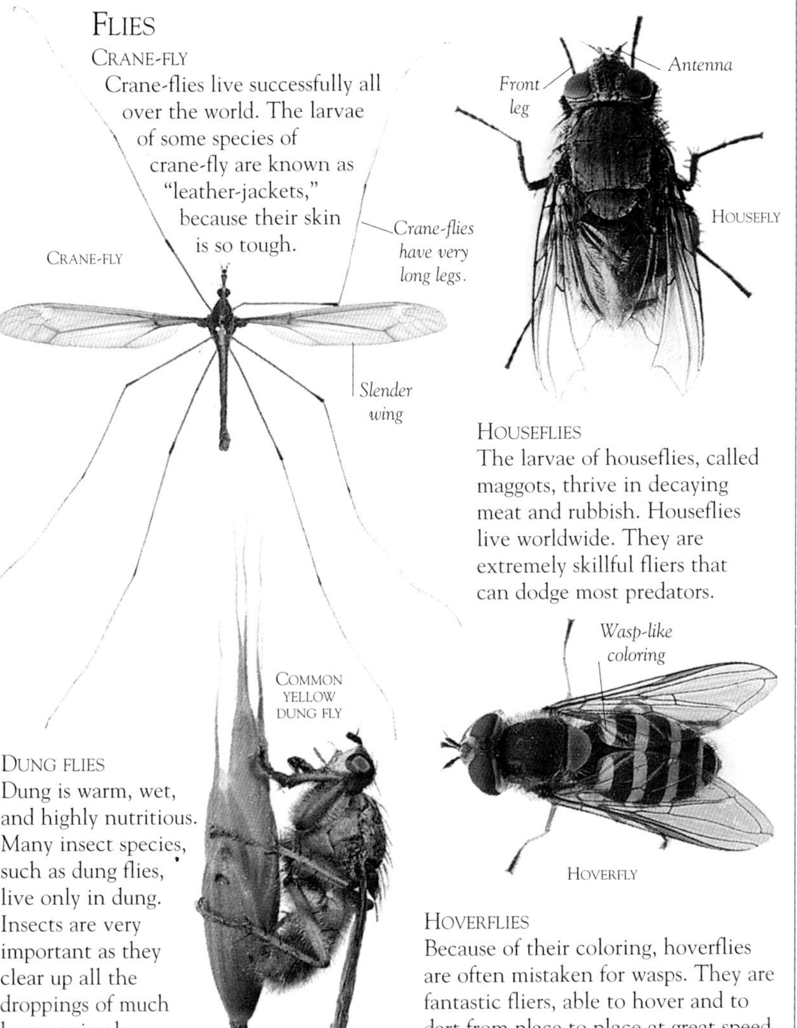

Houseflies

The larvae of houseflies, called maggots, thrive in decaying meat and rubbish. Houseflies live worldwide. They are extremely skillful fliers that can dodge most predators.

Dung flies

Dung is warm, wet, and highly nutritious. Many insect species, such as dung flies, live only in dung. Insects are very important as they clear up all the droppings of much larger animals.

Hoverflies

Because of their coloring, hoverflies are often mistaken for wasps. They are fantastic fliers, able to hover and to dart from place to place at great speed.

Bugs and other types

There are about 67,500 species of bug – they are the fifth-largest order of insects. Bugs have a feeding tube folded back between the legs, and most of them eat plant food. The many other orders of insects contain fewer species. Some of these orders are well known, such as fleas, cockroaches, dragonflies, and locusts.

Bugs

Feeding tubes

The mandibles (jaws) found in most insects are modified into needlelike tubes in bugs. The bug pierces food with the feeding tube and then sucks up juices.

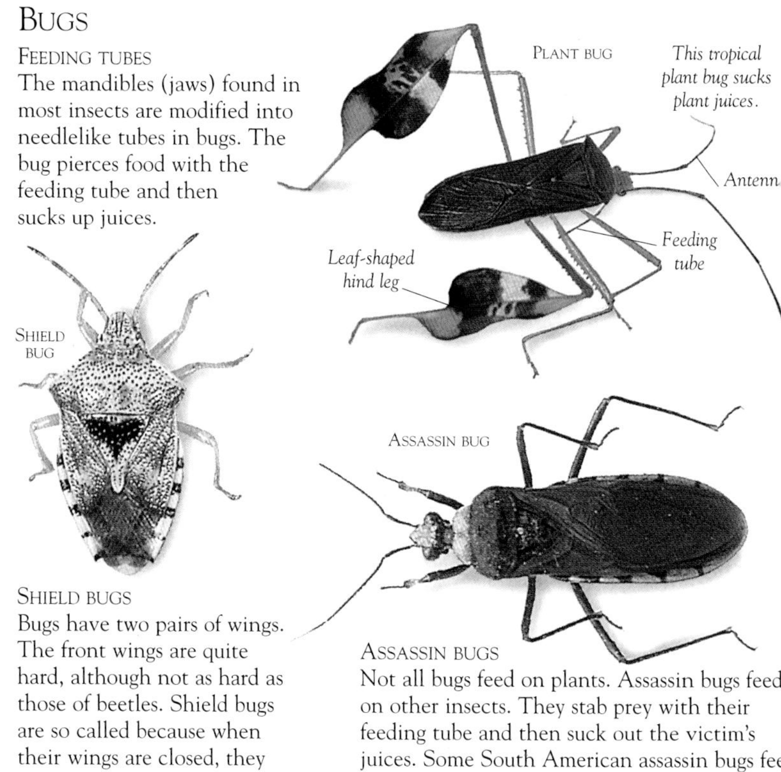

Shield bugs

Bugs have two pairs of wings. The front wings are quite hard, although not as hard as those of beetles. Shield bugs are so called because when their wings are closed, they look like colorful shields.

Assassin bugs

Not all bugs feed on plants. Assassin bugs feed on other insects. They stab prey with their feeding tube and then suck out the victim's juices. Some South American assassin bugs fee on the blood of humans and transmit diseases.

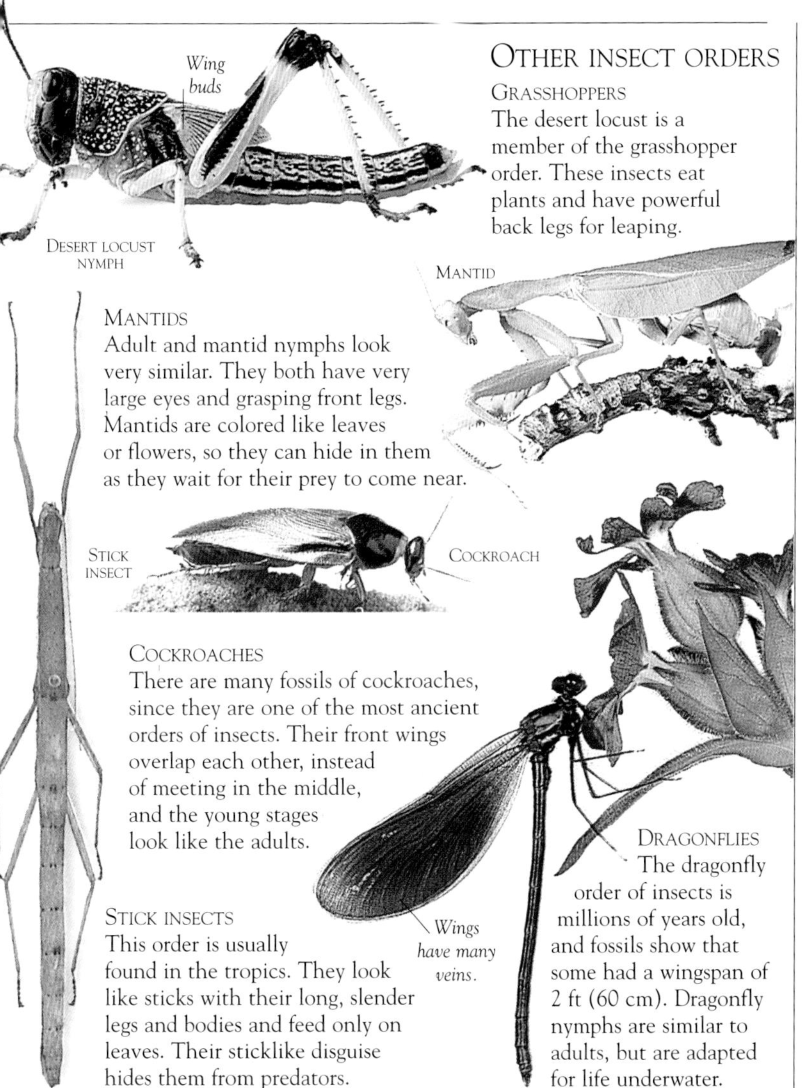

Other insect orders

Grasshoppers

The desert locust is a member of the grasshopper order. These insects eat plants and have powerful back legs for leaping.

Mantids

Adult and mantid nymphs look very similar. They both have very large eyes and grasping front legs. Mantids are colored like leaves or flowers, so they can hide in them as they wait for their prey to come near.

Cockroaches

There are many fossils of cockroaches, since they are one of the most ancient orders of insects. Their front wings overlap each other, instead of meeting in the middle, and the young stages look like the adults.

Stick insects

This order is usually found in the tropics. They look like sticks with their long, slender legs and bodies and feed only on leaves. Their sticklike disguise hides them from predators.

Dragonflies

The dragonfly order of insects is millions of years old, and fossils show that some had a wingspan of 2 ft (60 cm). Dragonfly nymphs are similar to adults, but are adapted for life underwater.

METAMORPHOSIS

INSECTS GO THROUGH several stages of growth before they become adults. This growing process is called metamorphosis. There are two types of metamorphosi incomplete and complete. Incomplete metamorphosis involves three main stages – egg, nymph, and adult. Complete metamorphosis has four main growth stage – egg, larva, pupa, and adult.

Incomplete metamorphosis

This growing process is a gradual transformation. The insects hatch from their eggs looking like miniature adults. These young insects are called nymphs. As they grow, they shed their skin several times before they reach the adult stage.

1 DAMSELFLY NYMPH
A damselfly nymph lives underwater. Paddle-like plates on its tail help it swim and breathe. It sheds its skin several times as it grows toward adulthood.

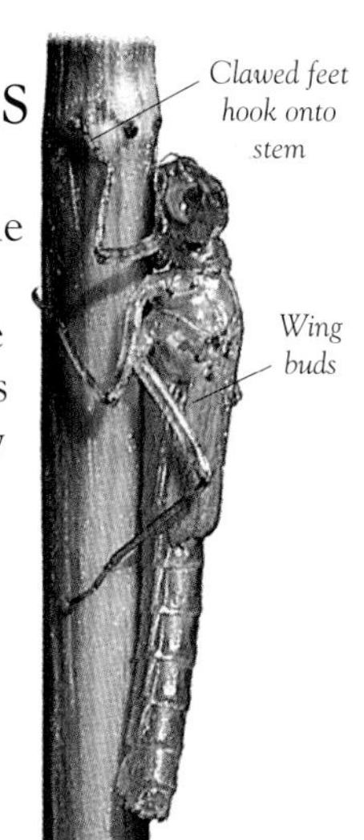

2 HOLDING ON
When the nymph is ready to change into an adult, it crawls out of the water up a plant stem.

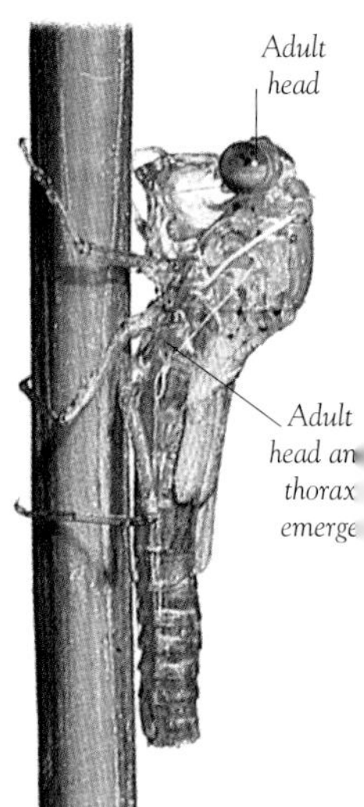

3 BREAKING OUT
The skin along the back splits open and the adult head and thorax start to emerge.

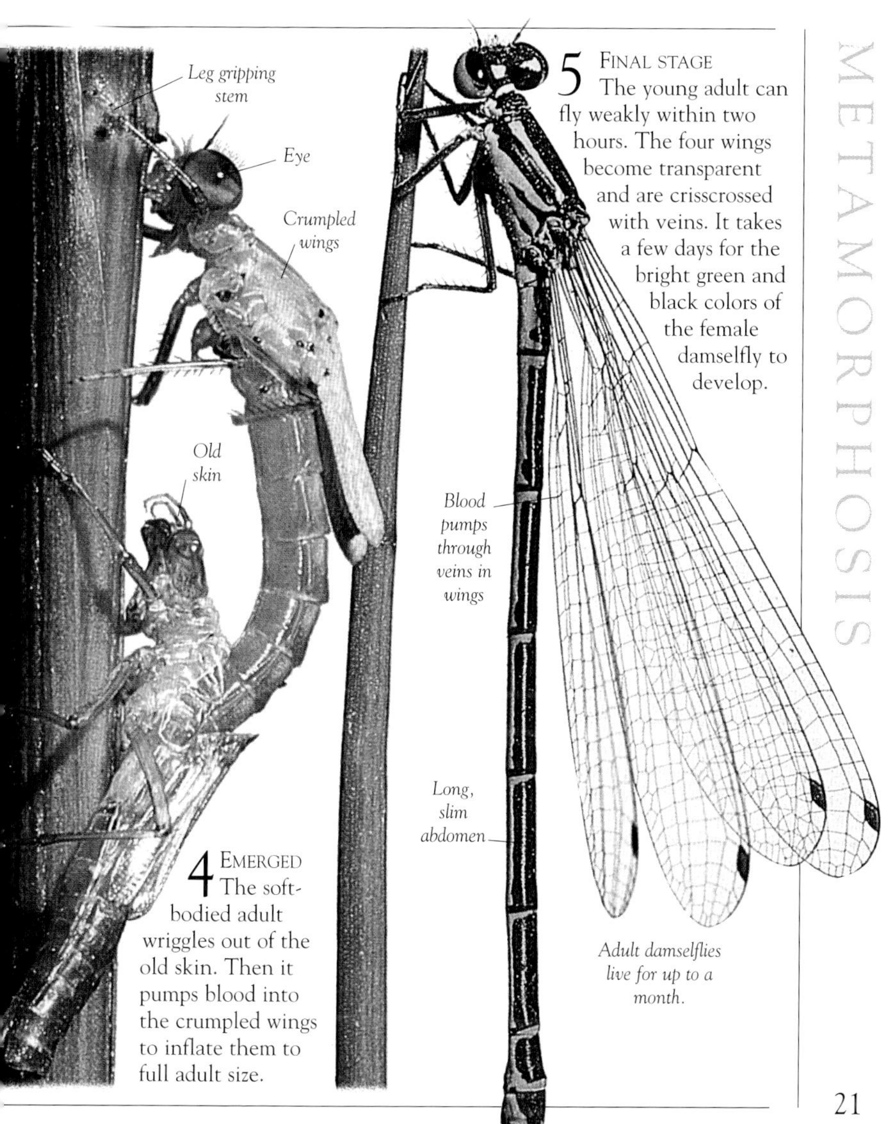

4 EMERGED
The soft-bodied adult wriggles out of the old skin. Then it pumps blood into the crumpled wings to inflate them to full adult size.

5 FINAL STAGE
The young adult can fly weakly within two hours. The four wings become transparent and are crisscrossed with veins. It takes a few days for the bright green and black colors of the female damselfly to develop.

Adult damselflies live for up to a month.

Complete metamorphosis

The four main growth stages in a complete metamorphosis are egg, larva, pupa, and adult. The larva bears no resemblance to the adult it will become. The pupal stage is when the larva makes the amazing transformation into an adult. Insects such as wasps, butterflies, beetles, and flies undergo complete metamorphosis.

1 LAYING EGGS
Butterflies lay eggs near leaves that caterpillars can eat when they hatch. Newly hatched caterpillars are too small to walk far to feed.

2 THE FIRST MEAL
When a caterpillar emerges, the first meal it eats is usually its own eggshell. The eggshell provides the caterpillar with valuable nutrients before it begins its diet of leaves.

Egg
Eggshell
Strong jaws slice food.

A caterpillar can increase its body weight by about 100 times in a few weeks.

3 GROWING
The caterpillar chews up hundreds of leaves and grows much bigger, shedding its skin several times. This growth prepares the caterpillar for the pupal stage of its life.

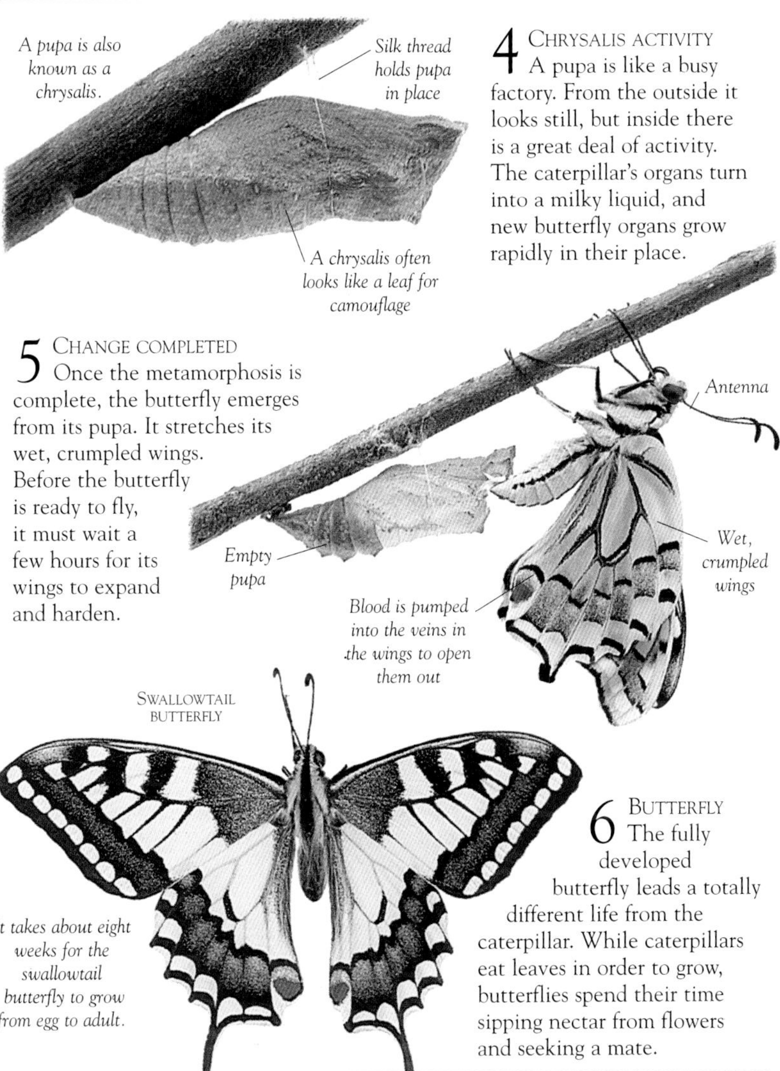
A pupa is also known as a chrysalis.
Silk thread holds pupa in place
A chrysalis often looks like a leaf for camouflage
Antenna
Empty pupa
Wet, crumpled wings
Blood is pumped into the veins in the wings to open them out
SWALLOWTAIL BUTTERFLY
t takes about eight weeks for the swallowtail butterfly to grow from egg to adult.

4 CHRYSALIS ACTIVITY

A pupa is like a busy factory. From the outside it looks still, but inside there is a great deal of activity. The caterpillar's organs turn into a milky liquid, and new butterfly organs grow rapidly in their place.

5 CHANGE COMPLETED

Once the metamorphosis is complete, the butterfly emerges from its pupa. It stretches its wet, crumpled wings. Before the butterfly is ready to fly, it must wait a few hours for its wings to expand and harden.

6 BUTTERFLY

The fully developed butterfly leads a totally different life from the caterpillar. While caterpillars eat leaves in order to grow, butterflies spend their time sipping nectar from flowers and seeking a mate.

How insects move

INSECTS MOVE using muscles that are attached to the inner surfaces of their hard outer skeleton. Many insects walk, but some larvae have no legs and have to crawl. Some insects swim, others jump, but most adult insects can fly and in this way they may travel long distances.

Legs

Insects use their legs for walking, running, jumping, and swimming. Many insects have legs modified for a number of other purposes. These include catching prey, holding a female when mating, producing songs, digging, fighting, and camouflage.

LEGS FOR SWIMMING
The water boatman has long, oar-shaped back legs, allowing the insect to "row" rapidly through water. The legs have flattened ends and a fringe of thick hairs. The front legs are short to grasp prey on the water surface.

LEGS FACTS

- Fairy flies, which live as parasites on the eggs of water insects, can "fly" underwater.
- Many butterflies walk on four legs; the front pair are used for tasting.
- The legless larvae of some parasitic wasps hitch a ride on a passing ant in order to enter an ant's nest.

1 PREPARING TO JUMP
The back legs of locusts are swollen and packed with strong muscles for jumping. Before leaping, a locust holds its back legs tightly under its body, near its center of gravity. This is the best position for the legs to propel the insect high into the air.

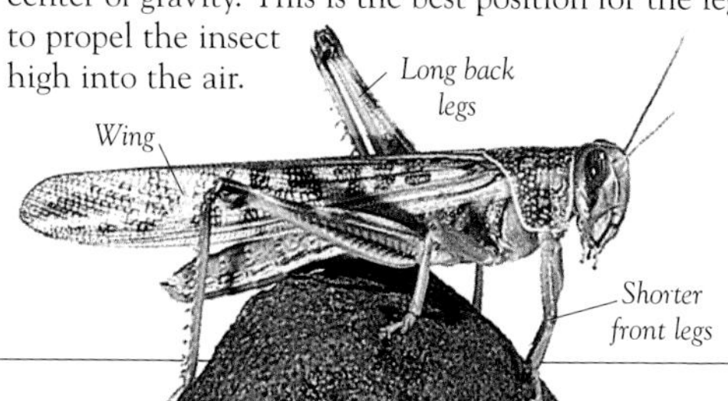

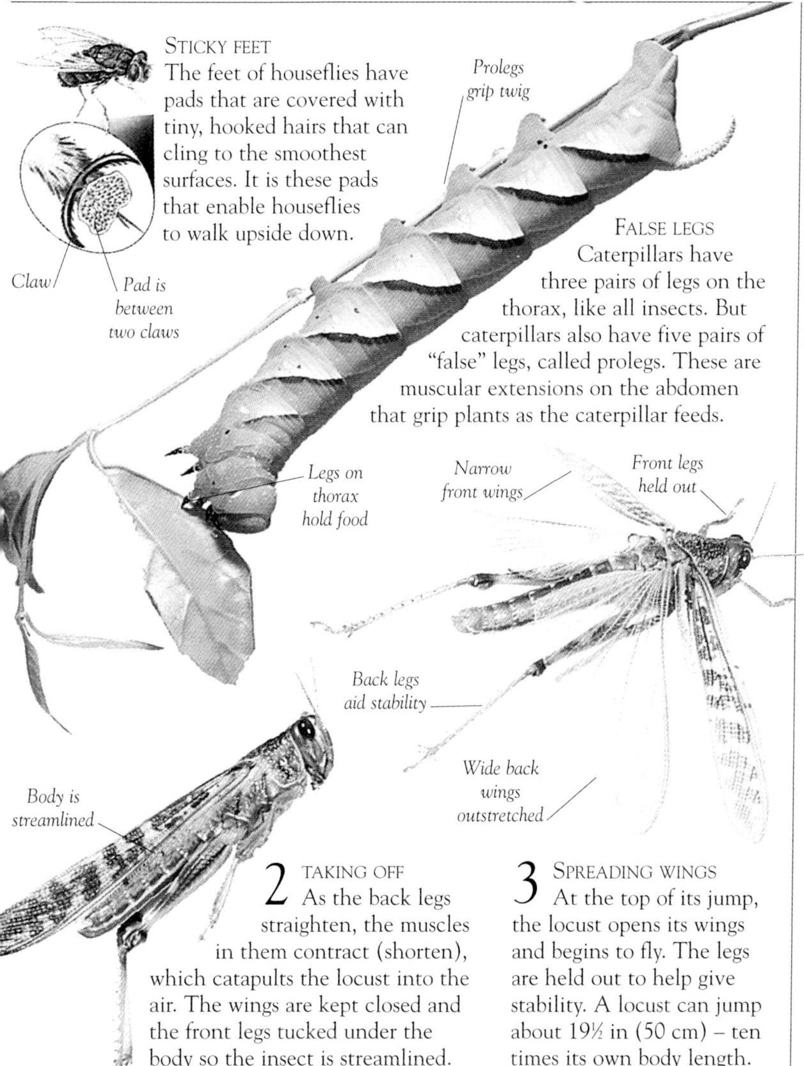

STICKY FEET
The feet of houseflies have pads that are covered with tiny, hooked hairs that can cling to the smoothest surfaces. It is these pads that enable houseflies to walk upside down.

FALSE LEGS
Caterpillars have three pairs of legs on the thorax, like all insects. But caterpillars also have five pairs of "false" legs, called prolegs. These are muscular extensions on the abdomen that grip plants as the caterpillar feeds.

2 TAKING OFF
As the back legs straighten, the muscles in them contract (shorten), which catapults the locust into the air. The wings are kept closed and the front legs tucked under the body so the insect is streamlined.

3 SPREADING WINGS
At the top of its jump, the locust opens its wings and begins to fly. The legs are held out to help give stability. A locust can jump about 19½ in (50 cm) – ten times its own body length.

Wings and scales

Insect wings are a wide variety of shapes and sizes. They are not used just for flying but also for attracting a mate or hiding from predators. Most insects have two pairs of wings, each with a network of veins to give strength. Flies have only one pair of wings – the second pair is modified into small balancing organs called halteres. Small insects have few wing veins since their wings are so tiny.

EXPERT FLIERS

Dragonflies are among the most accomplished fliers in the insect world. They can hover, fly fast or slow, change direction rapidly, and even fly backward. As they maneuver, their two pairs of wings beat independently of each other.

WING FACTS

- The scales of butterflies and moths contain waste products from the pupal stage.
- There is a hearing organ in one of the wing veins of green lacewings for hearing the shrieks of bats.
- Many species of island insects are wingless because of the risk of being blown out to sea.

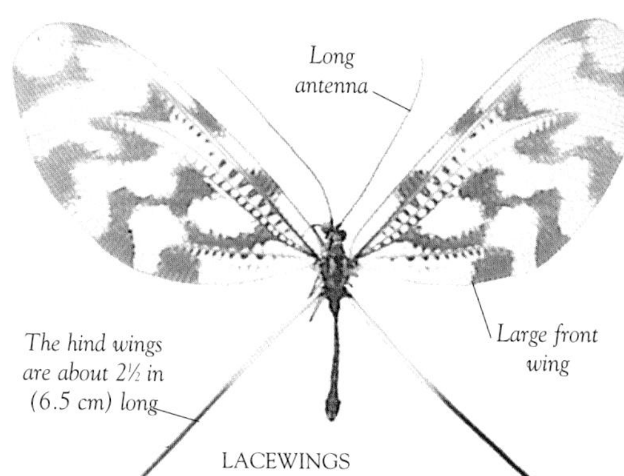
Long antenna
Large front wing
The hind wings are about 2½ in (6.5 cm) long

LACEWINGS

The hind wings of ribbon-tail lacewings are modified into long graceful streamers. Scientists are not sure what these are for, but they may act as stabilizers in flight, or even divert predators from attacking the lacewing's body. The lacewing's mottled patterns probably help to conceal it in the dry sandy places where it lives.

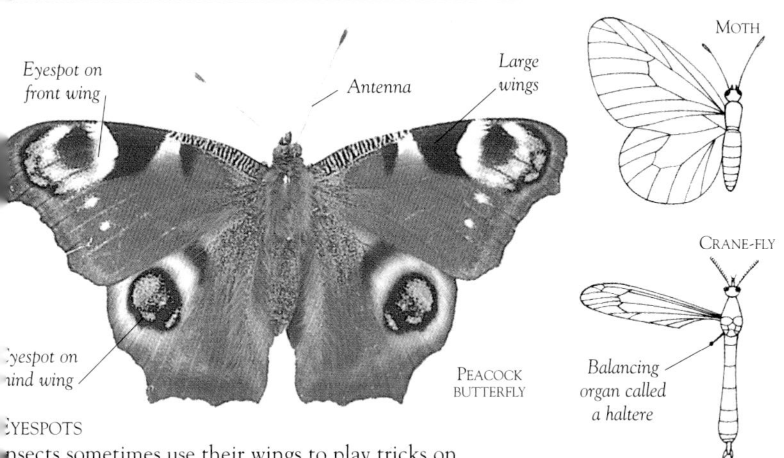

YESPOTS

nsects sometimes use their wings to play tricks on heir enemies. Many butterflies and moths have yespots on their wings. These are probably used to tartle predators when flashed suddenly. This gives he butterfly or moth a little more time to escape.

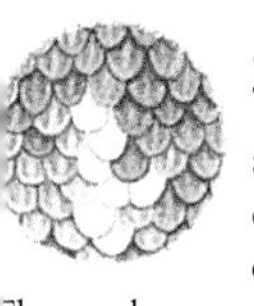

Scales

The wings of moths and butterflies are covered in over-lapping scales. he scales are formed from specially attened and ridged hairs.

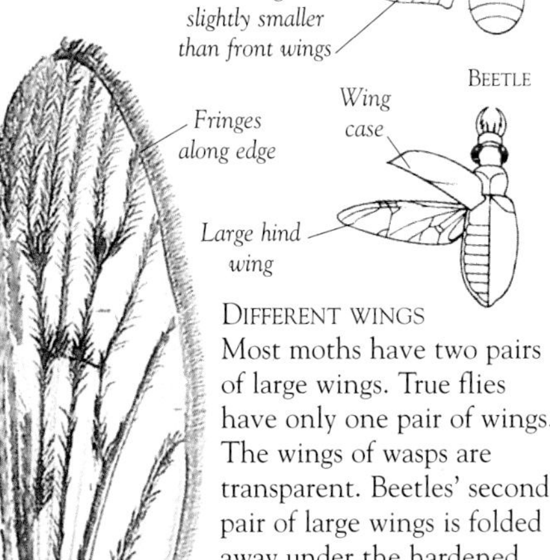

Fringed wings

Tiny insects have difficulty in flying, since air is very dense for them. To increase the size of their wings and so help improve lift, they often have fringes of hairs around the edges of the wings.

Different wings

Most moths have two pairs of large wings. True flies have only one pair of wings. The wings of wasps are transparent. Beetles' second pair of large wings is folded away under the hardened first pair, or wing cases.

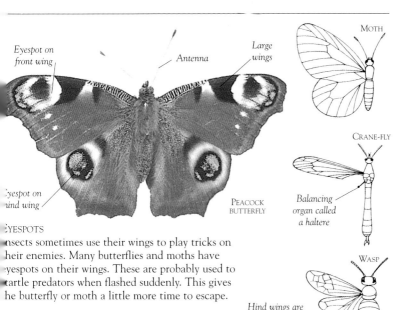

Flight

The ability to fly is one of the main reasons insects have survived for millions of years, and continue to flourish. Flight helps insects escape from danger. It also makes it easier to find food and new places to live. Sometimes insects fly thousands of miles to reach fresh food or warmer weather.

FLYING GROUPS

This African grasshopper has broad hind wings that allow it to glide for long distances. Locusts are a typ of grasshopper that fly in huge groups when they need new food. Sometimes as many as 100 million locusts fly together for hundreds of miles.

WARMING UP

An insect's flight muscles must be warm before the wings can be moved fast enough for flight. On cool mornings, insects like this shield bug shiver, vibrating their wings to warm themselves up.

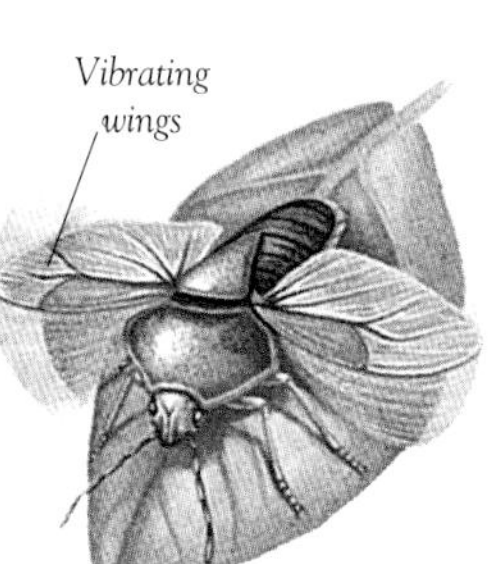

Elytra protect body

1 PREPARING TO FLY

This cockchafer beetle prepares for flight by climbing to the top of a plant and facing into the wind. It may open and shut its elytra (wing cases) several times while warming up.

2 OPENING THE WINGS

The hardened elytra, which protect the fragile hind wings, begin to open. The antennae are spread so tha the beetle can monitor the wind direction.

ACROBATS OF THE AIR
Hoverflies are capable of incredible acrobatics in the air. They can move like a helicopter – forward, backward, sideways, and directly upward or downward. They can also hover, a flight maneuver that very few insects are capable of.

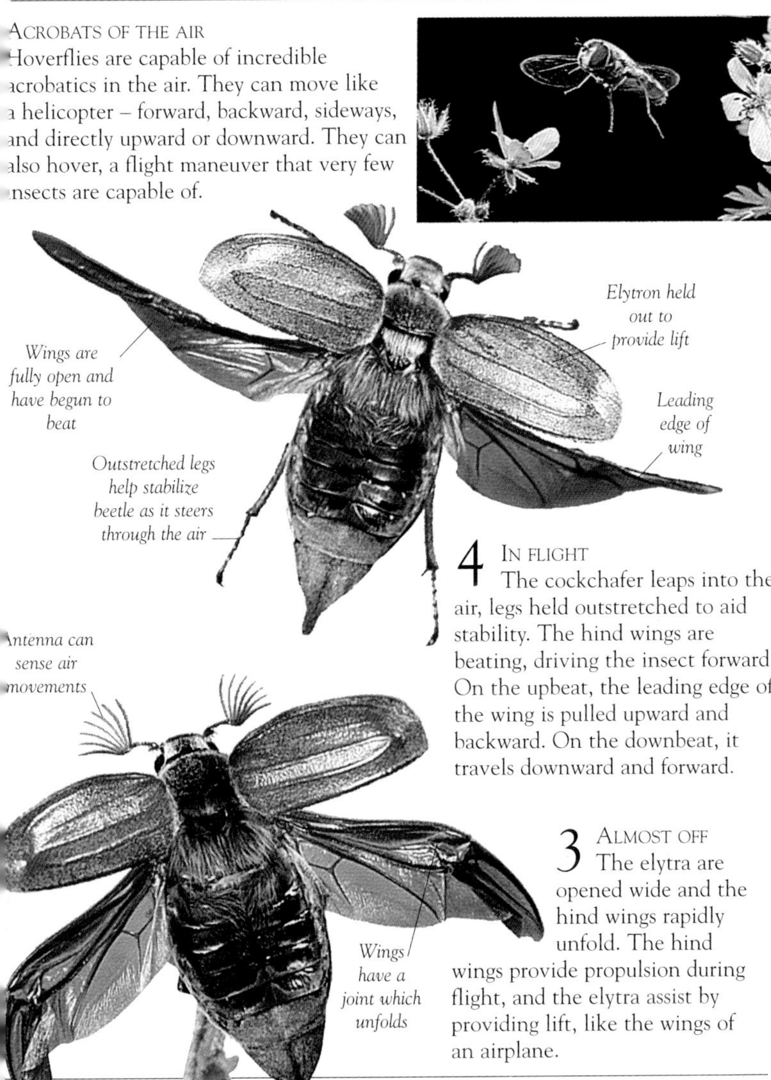
Elytron held out to provide lift
Wings are fully open and have begun to beat
Leading edge of wing
Outstretched legs help stabilize beetle as it steers through the air
Antenna can sense air movements
Wings have a joint which unfolds

4 IN FLIGHT
The cockchafer leaps into the air, legs held outstretched to aid stability. The hind wings are beating, driving the insect forward. On the upbeat, the leading edge of the wing is pulled upward and backward. On the downbeat, it travels downward and forward.

3 ALMOST OFF
The elytra are opened wide and the hind wings rapidly unfold. The hind wings provide propulsion during flight, and the elytra assist by providing lift, like the wings of an airplane.

INSECT SENSES

INSECTS NEED to be fully aware of the world around them in order to survive. Although insects are tiny, they have sharper senses than most larger animals. They can see colors and hear sounds that are undetectable to humans, as well as being able to detect smells from many miles away.

Sight

There are two types of insect eyes – simple and compound. Simple eyes can probably detect only light and shade. Compound eyes have hundreds of lenses, giving their owner excellent vision.

HEAD OF COMMON DARTER DRAGONFLY

SIMPLE EYES
Caterpillars never need to look far for their plant food – they are constantly surrounded by it. Because of this, they do not need sharp eyesight. They can manage perfectly well with a group of simple eyes.

Simple eyes

GOOD VISION
The eyes of dragonflies take up most of their head. This allows them to see what's in front, above, below, and behind them all at the same time. Dragonflies use their sight more than any other of their senses to catch prey.

COMMON DARTER DRAGONFLY

YE CONSTRUCTION
;ompound eyes are ıade up of many ıdividual facets, ılled ommatidia. ach ommatidium ıas a lens at the top, ith a second, conical-shaped ·ns underneath. The more mmatidia there are, the ıore sensitive is the eye.

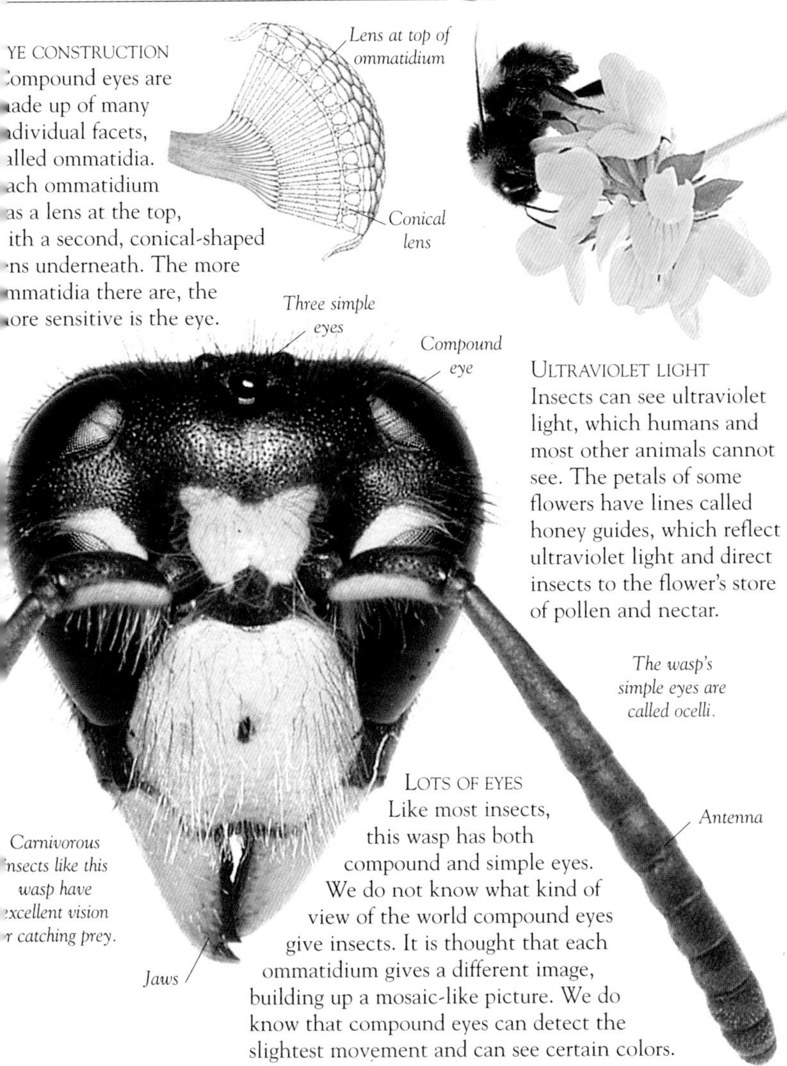

ULTRAVIOLET LIGHT
Insects can see ultraviolet light, which humans and most other animals cannot see. The petals of some flowers have lines called honey guides, which reflect ultraviolet light and direct insects to the flower's store of pollen and nectar.

The wasp's simple eyes are called ocelli.

Carnivorous ınsects like this wasp have ɛxcellent vision ɾ catching prey.

LOTS OF EYES
Like most insects, this wasp has both compound and simple eyes. We do not know what kind of view of the world compound eyes give insects. It is thought that each ommatidium gives a different image, building up a mosaic-like picture. We do know that compound eyes can detect the slightest movement and can see certain colors.

Smelling, hearing, and touching

The bodies of insects are covered in short hairs that are connected to the nervous system. These hairs can feel, or "hear," vibrations in the air due to sound or movement. Some hairs are modified to detect smells and flavors. Sensory hairs are often found on the antennae, but also occur on the feet and mouthpart

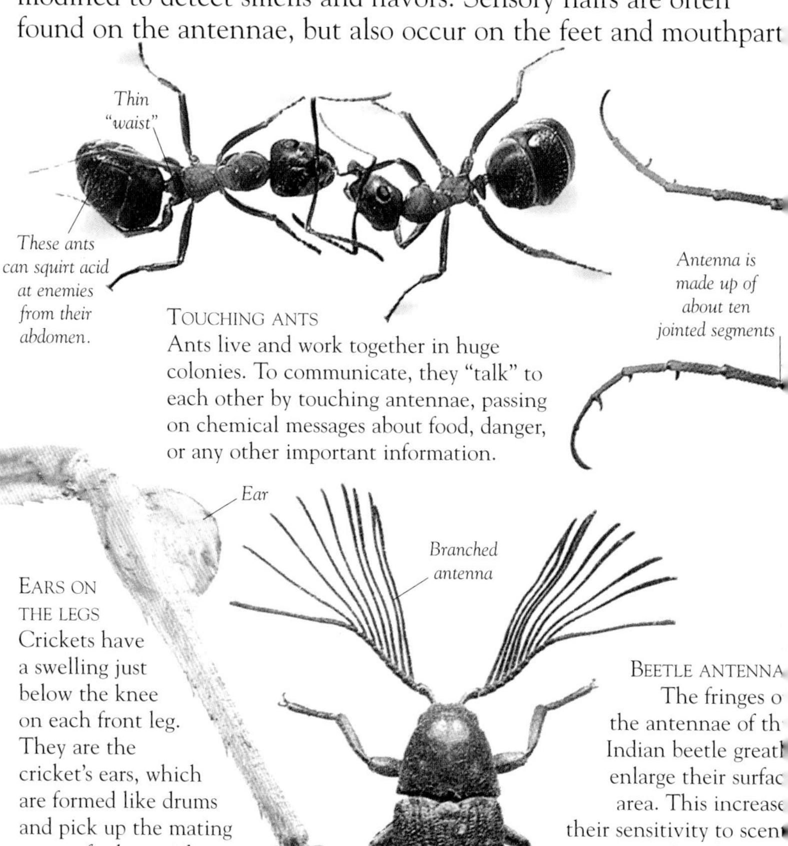

TOUCHING ANTS
Ants live and work together in huge colonies. To communicate, they "talk" to each other by touching antennae, passing on chemical messages about food, danger, or any other important information.

EARS ON THE LEGS
Crickets have a swelling just below the knee on each front leg. They are the cricket's ears, which are formed like drums and pick up the mating songs of other crickets.

BEETLE ANTENNA
The fringes o the antennae of th Indian beetle great enlarge their surfac area. This increase their sensitivity to scen carried in the win

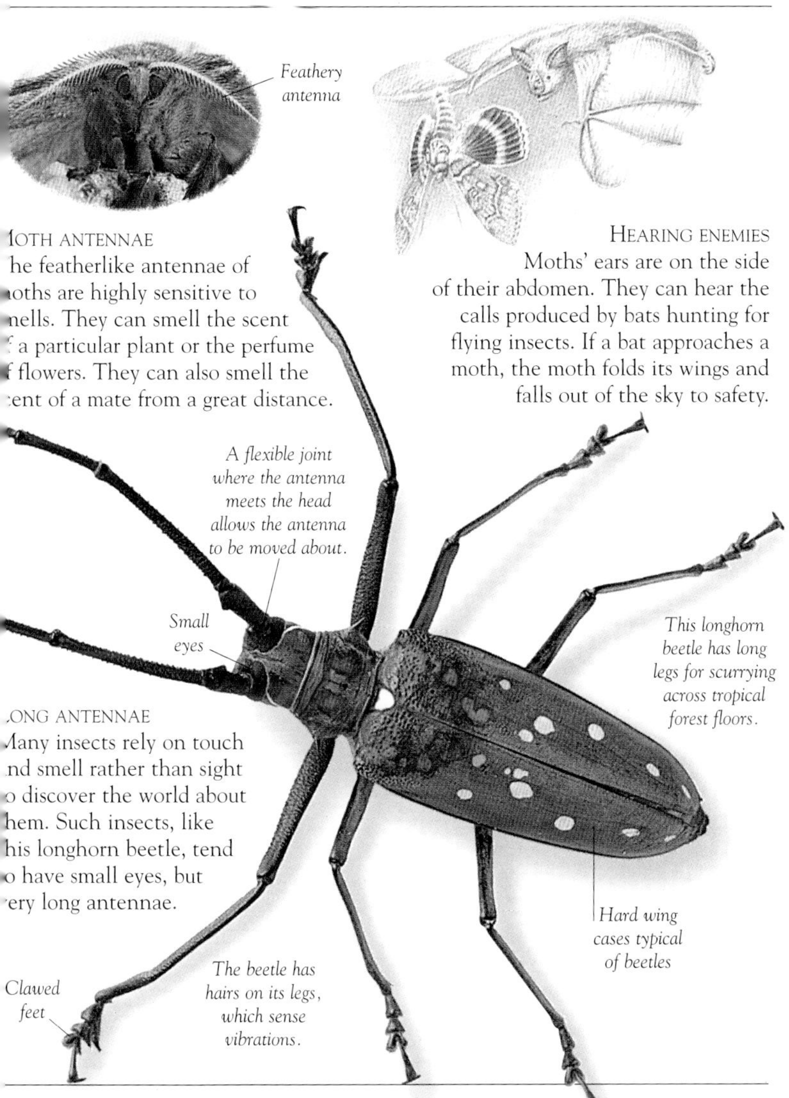
Feathery antenna
A flexible joint where the antenna meets the head allows the antenna to be moved about.
Small eyes
This longhorn beetle has long legs for scurrying across tropical forest floors.
Hard wing cases typical of beetles
The beetle has hairs on its legs, which sense vibrations.
Clawed feet

OTH ANTENNAE

he featherlike antennae of oths are highly sensitive to nells. They can smell the scent a particular plant or the perfume f flowers. They can also smell the ent of a mate from a great distance.

HEARING ENEMIES

Moths' ears are on the side of their abdomen. They can hear the calls produced by bats hunting for flying insects. If a bat approaches a moth, the moth folds its wings and falls out of the sky to safety.

ONG ANTENNAE

Many insects rely on touch nd smell rather than sight o discover the world about hem. Such insects, like his longhorn beetle, tend o have small eyes, but ery long antennae.

How insects feed

Insects have complex mouthparts. The insects that chew their food have a pair of strong jaws for chopping, a smaller pair of jaws for holding food, and two pairs of sensory organs, called palps, for tasting. Some insects drink only liquid food and have special tubular mouthparts like a straw.

Chewing

Predatory, chewing insects need sharp, pointed jaws for stabbing, holding, and chopping up their struggling prey. Insects that chew plants have blunter jaws for grinding their food.

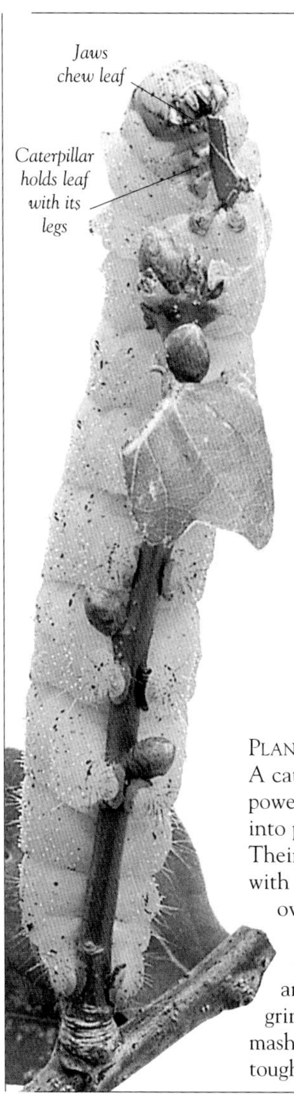

Plant chewer
A caterpillar needs powerful jaws to bite into plant material. Their jaws are armed with teeth that overlap when they close. Some caterpillars' jaws are modified into grinding plates for mashing up the toughest leaves.

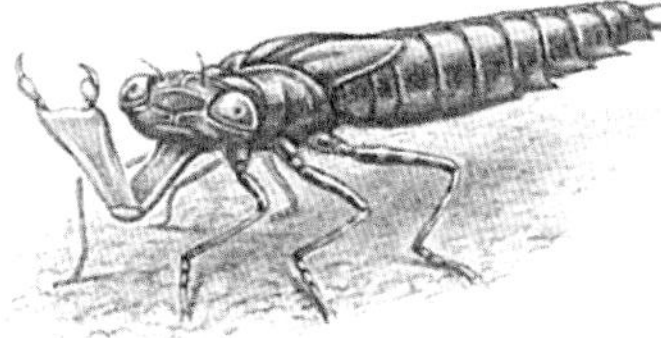

Thrusting jaws
Dragonfly larvae have pincers at the end of a hinged plate folded under the head. When catching prey, the plate unfolds, shoots forward, and the pincers grab the prey. Toothed jaws in the head reduce the victim to mincemeat.

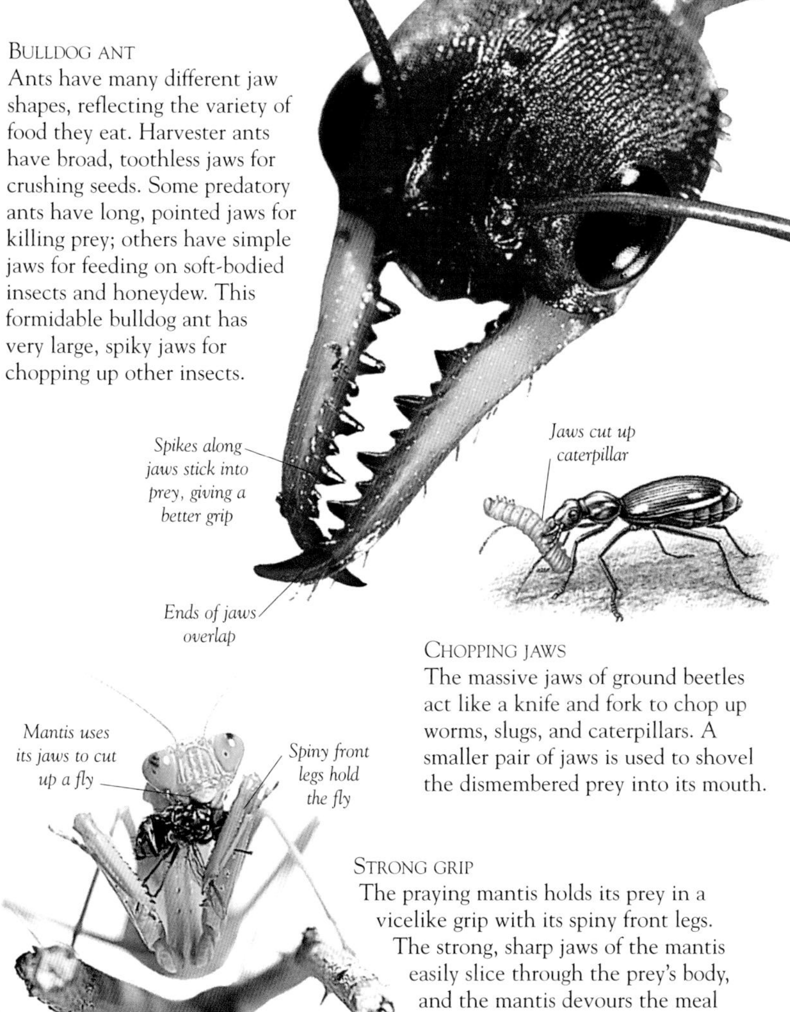

BULLDOG ANT

Ants have many different jaw shapes, reflecting the variety of food they eat. Harvester ants have broad, toothless jaws for crushing seeds. Some predatory ants have long, pointed jaws for killing prey; others have simple jaws for feeding on soft-bodied insects and honeydew. This formidable bulldog ant has very large, spiky jaws for chopping up other insects.

CHOPPING JAWS

The massive jaws of ground beetles act like a knife and fork to chop up worms, slugs, and caterpillars. A smaller pair of jaws is used to shovel the dismembered prey into its mouth.

STRONG GRIP

The praying mantis holds its prey in a vicelike grip with its spiny front legs. The strong, sharp jaws of the mantis easily slice through the prey's body, and the mantis devours the meal within a few minutes.

Drinking

For many insects, the main way of feeding is by drinking. The most nutritious foods to drink are nectar and blood. Nectar is rich in sugar, and blood is packed with proteins. Some insects drink by sucking through strawlike mouthparts. Others have spongelike mouthparts with which they mop up liquids.

HAWK-MOTH
Butterflies and moths have a long, tonguelike tube called a proboscis through which they drink. Darwin's hawk-moth has an extremely long proboscis for reaching the nectar in an extra-long flower.

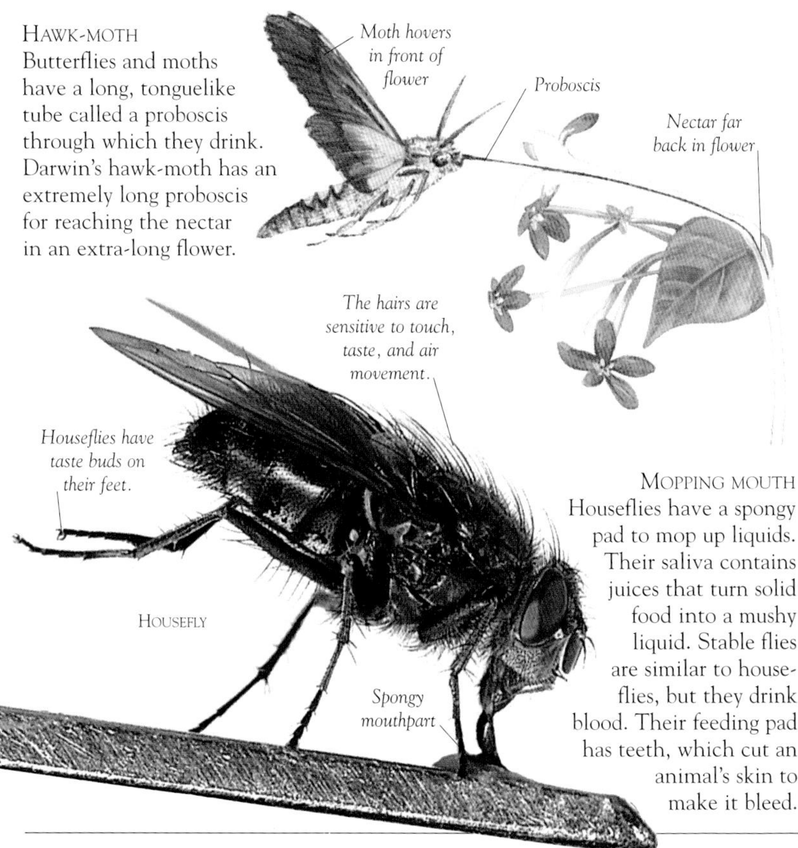
Moth hovers in front of flower
Proboscis
Nectar far back in flower
The hairs are sensitive to touch, taste, and air movement.
Houseflies have taste buds on their feet.
HOUSEFLY
Spongy mouthpart

MOPPING MOUTH
Houseflies have a spongy pad to mop up liquids. Their saliva contains juices that turn solid food into a mushy liquid. Stable flies are similar to houseflies, but they drink blood. Their feeding pad has teeth, which cut an animal's skin to make it bleed.

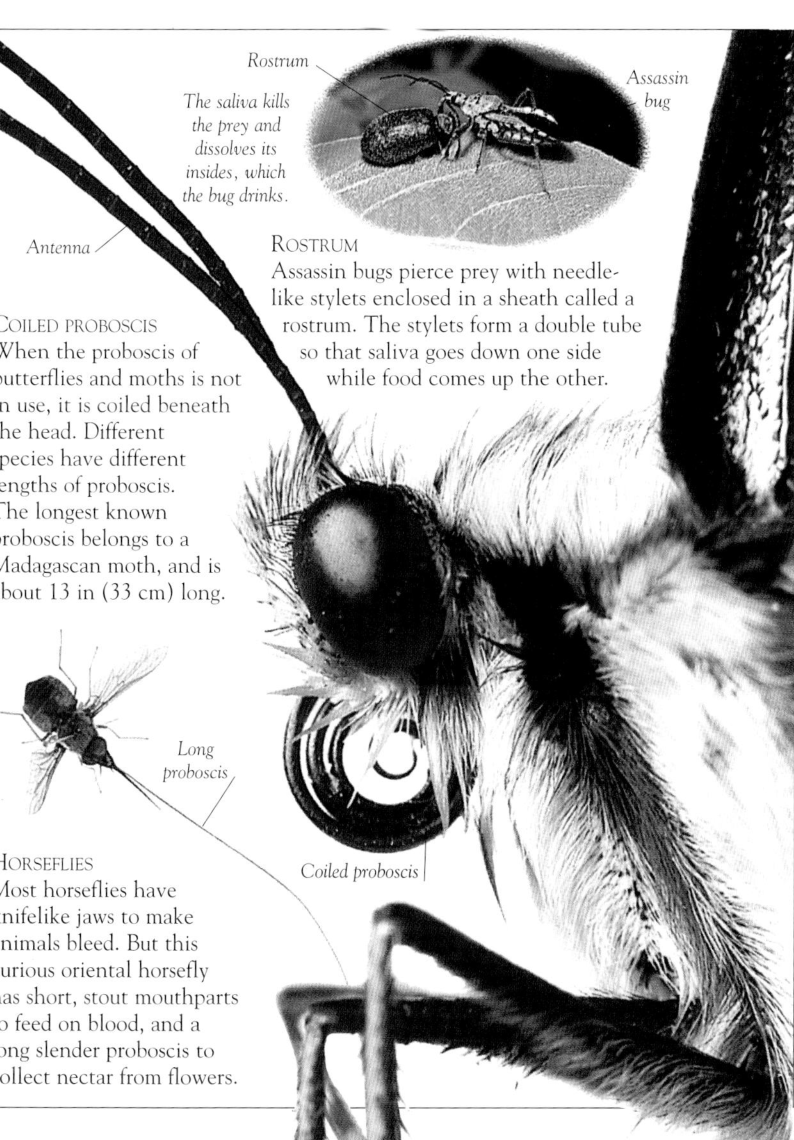

The saliva kills the prey and dissolves its insides, which the bug drinks.

ROSTRUM
Assassin bugs pierce prey with needle-like stylets enclosed in a sheath called a rostrum. The stylets form a double tube so that saliva goes down one side while food comes up the other.

COILED PROBOSCIS
When the proboscis of butterflies and moths is not in use, it is coiled beneath the head. Different species have different lengths of proboscis. The longest known proboscis belongs to a Madagascan moth, and is about 13 in (33 cm) long.

HORSEFLIES
Most horseflies have knifelike jaws to make animals bleed. But this curious oriental horsefly has short, stout mouthparts to feed on blood, and a long slender proboscis to collect nectar from flowers.

Courtship, birth, and growth

Reproduction is hazardous for insects. A female must first find and mate with a male of her own species, and lay eggs where the newly hatched young can feed. The larvae must shed their skin several times as they grow. All this time the insects must avoid being eaten.

The light is produced by a chemical reaction.

GUIDING LIGHT
Glowworms are the wingless females of certain beetle species. They attract males by producing a light near the tip of their abdomen. Some species flash a distinctive code to attract the correct males.

Courtship and mating

Males and females use special signals to ensure that their chosen mate is the right species. Courtship usually involves using scents, but may include color displays, dancing, caressing, and even gifts.

Butterflies find the scented chemicals, called pheromones, very attractive.

COURTSHIP FLIGHTS
Butterflies may recognize their own species by sight, but scent is more reliable. Butterfly courtship involves dancing flights with an exchange of scented chemical signals specific to each species.

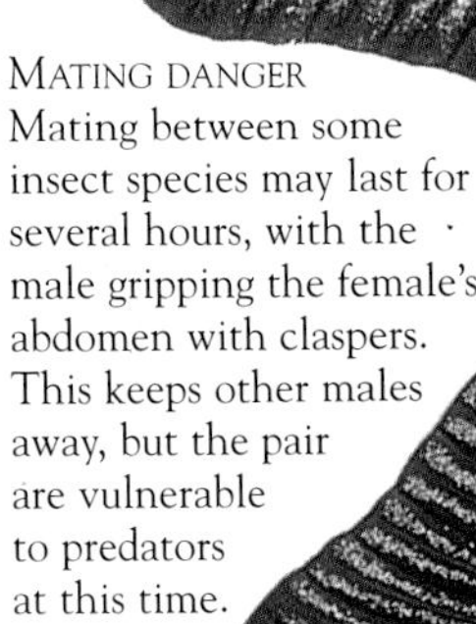

MATING DANGER
Mating between some insect species may last for several hours, with the male gripping the female's abdomen with claspers. This keeps other males away, but the pair are vulnerable to predators at this time.

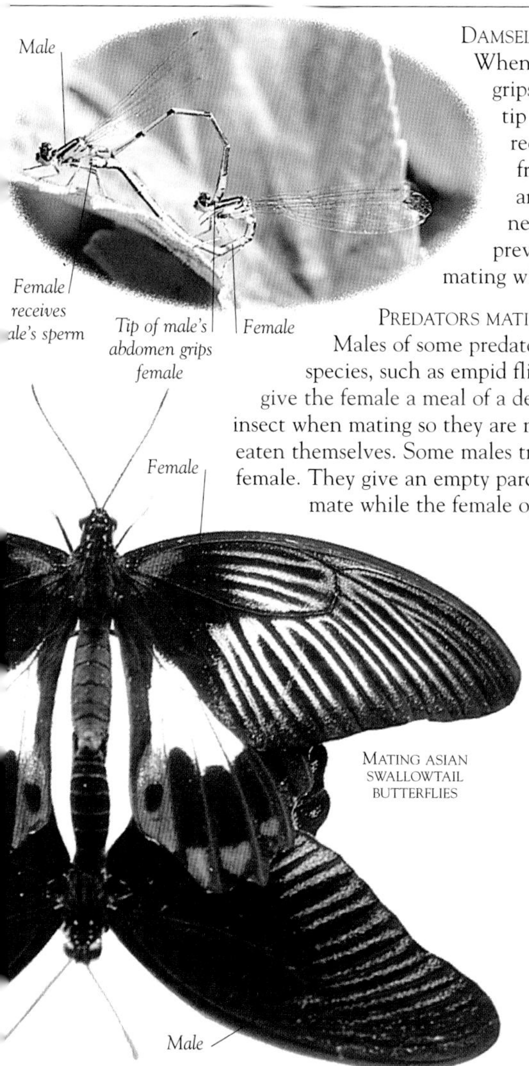

MATING ASIAN SWALLOWTAIL BUTTERFLIES

DAMSELFLIES

When mating, a male damselfly grips a female's neck with the tip of his abdomen. She receives a packet of sperm from a pouch near his legs, and he continues to hold her neck while she lays eggs. This prevents other males mating with her.

PREDATORS MATING

Males of some predatory species, such as empid flies, give the female a meal of a dead insect when mating so they are not eaten themselves. Some males trick the female. They give an empty parcel, and mate while the female opens it.

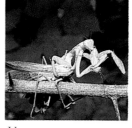

UNNATURAL BEHAVIOR

It is often said that a female mantis will eat a male while he is mating with her. But this probably only happens when the mantises are in captivity and their behavior is not natural.

Eggs and egg-laying

Insects use up a lot of energy producing eggs. To make sure this energy is not wasted, insects have many ways of protecting their eggs from predators. A few species of insect stay with their eggs to protect them until the larvae hatch. Some insects lay their eggs underground with a supply of food waiting for the newly hatched larvae. Most insects lay their eggs either in food, or near food, so the young larvae do not have to travel far to eat.

ICHNEUMON WAS[P]
The larvae of ichneumo[n] wasps are parasites, whic[h] means they feed on othe[r] living creatures. Whe[n] finding a host for its egg, a[n] adult ichneumon detects th[e] vibrations of a beetle gru[b] gnawing inside a tree trunk[.] The wasp drives its egg[-] laying tube into the trun[k] until it finds the grub. A[n] egg is laid on the grub, whic[h] then provides meat for th[e] wasp larva when it hatches[.]

The egg-laying tube, also known as an ovipositor, drills into the wood.

The ovipositor is longer than the ichneumon's body.

SUITABLE FOOD

Butterflies desert their eggs once they are laid. Different butterflies lay their eggs on different plants, depending on what the larvae eat. The Malay lacewing butterfly lays its eggs on vine tendrils.

CARING EARWIGS

A female earwig looks fter her eggs, licking them regularly to keep them clean. Vhen the nymphs hatch, she feeds them until they are big enough to leave the nest.

HUNTING WASPS

Most species of hunting wasp collect soft-bodied prey, such as caterpillars or spiders, for their grubs. But the weevil-hunting wasp collects adult beetles, which it stings in the throat, and then stores in a tunnel as food for its larvae.

DUNG BEETLES

The males and females of some dung beetle species work together to dig an underground tunnel with smaller tunnels branching off it. A female lays an egg in each of the smaller tunnels and fills them with animal dung, which the beetle grubs will feed on.

INSECT EGG FACTS

- Whitefly eggs have stalks that extract water from leaves.
- Tsetse flies develop their eggs internally and lay mature larvae.
- Green lacewing eggs have long stalks, making them difficult for predators to eat.

Birth and growth

As an insect grows from egg to adult, it sheds its skin several times to produce a larger exoskeleton. While this new skin hardens, the insect is soft and vulnerable. Insects show many life-cycle adaptations to protect their soft young stages.

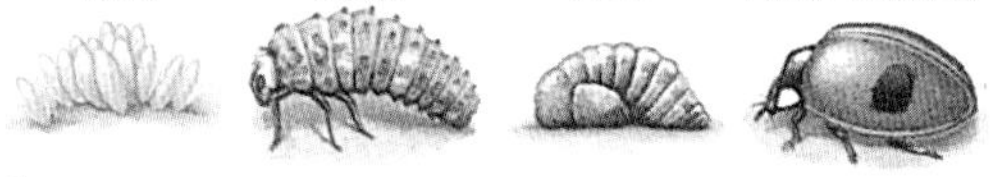

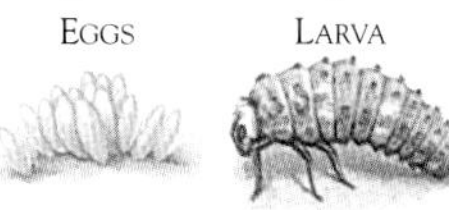

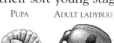

LADYBUG GROWTH
Ladybugs and all other beetles go through a complete metamorphosis. An adult ladybug lays its eggs on a plant where small insects called aphids feed. Ladybug larvae eat aphids and shed their skin three times as they grow. The colorful adult emerges from the dull resting stage, or pupa.

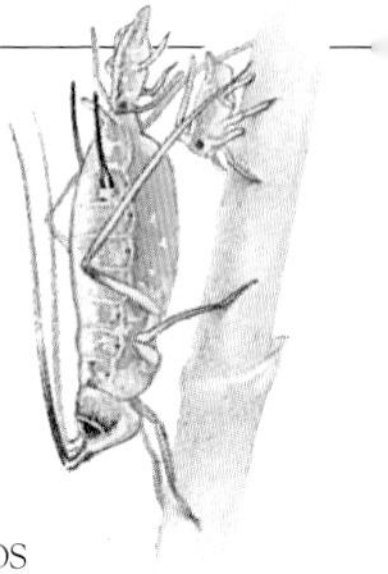

APHIDS
Female aphids can reproduce without mating. They give birth to live young rather than lay eggs and each female may have about 100 offspring. The newborn aphids can give birth after only a few days.

Frothy hideaway

FROTHY PROTECTION
Froghoppers are soft-bodied bugs like aphids. A froghopper nymph produces a frothy liquid from its anus. The froth protects the nymph from drying out, and also hides it from predators

PARENTAL CARE
The females of some species of shield bug stay with their eggs and young nymphs to protect them. If touched, the parent produces a powerful smell, giving these bugs the alternative name of stinkbugs.

SHIELD BUG NYMPHS WITH PARENT

ɪURROWING NYMPHS
ɩ female locust can xtend her abdomen to lmost twice its length ɾhen laying eggs. The eggs re placed deep in the soil ɔr protection. The ɩewborn nymphs, called oppers, must burrow to ɦe surface to feed.

FROGHOPPER NYMPH

LEAVING WATER
Unlike all other insects, mayflies have two adult stages. The first stage, the sub-adult, crawls out of the water where it lived as a nymph. It flies weakly and is dull colored. It soon molts to produce the true adult, which then mates.

Survival of the young

Predators eagerly hunt insect larvae since many are slow-moving, soft, and nutritious. To ensure survival, most insect species produ large numbers of young, which grow rapidly. Most insect larvae ar defenseless and have developed special ways of hiding from predators. But many insect larvae are fierce predators themselves, consuming other creatures for nourishment as they grow.

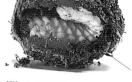

Grub in pupal cell

WELL HIDDEN
The larvae of chafer beetles live underground, safely hidden from most predators. The larvae, or grubs, may take many weeks to develop. They then produce a cell of hardened earth in which they will change into an adult.

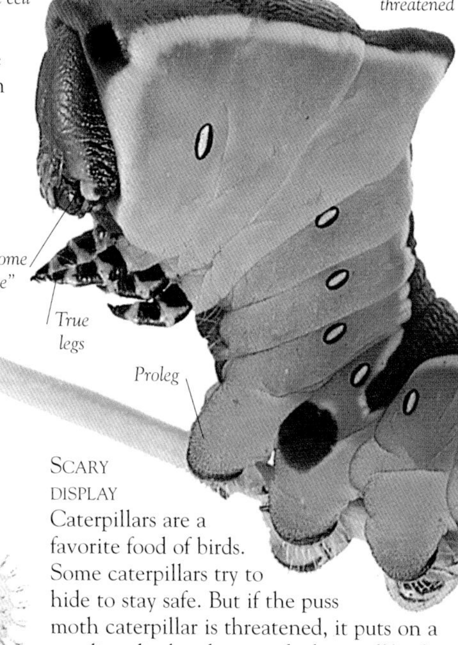

Caterpillar rears up when threatened

Fearsome "face"

True legs

Proleg

Sharp spines

SPINY LARVA
Mexican bean beetle larvae eat leaves and develop rapidly. They are covered with long, branched spines that may deter birds and other predators from attacking them.

SCARY DISPLAY
Caterpillars are a favorite food of birds. Some caterpillars try to hide to stay safe. But if the puss moth caterpillar is threatened, it puts on a startling display that can frighten off birds.

WATER LARVA
Stone-fly larvae live in cold water and grow slowly, spending about three years as a larva. They are slow-moving and hide from predators under rocks and among plants.

IGHT FEEDER
he mormon butterfly aterpillar feeds in the ark of night to avoid being en by predators. In fewer than ght hours, it will chew away a leaf at is more than twice its own ngth. During the day it rests as conspicuously as possible.

or a more frightening, display, the caterpillar aves these "tails" as if they were stings

SOFT BODIES
Young mantids are fierce predators. The body of some species resembles a flower. This disguise helps them to go unnoticed by prey, and also by predators such as birds.

Nests and societies

MOST INSECTS lead solitary lives, but some, particularly wasps, ants, bees, and termites, live in societies that are sometimes very ordered. There are queens, kings, workers, and soldiers. Each of these has particular jobs to do. Social insects live in nests that are often elaborate, where they protect each other and rear their young.

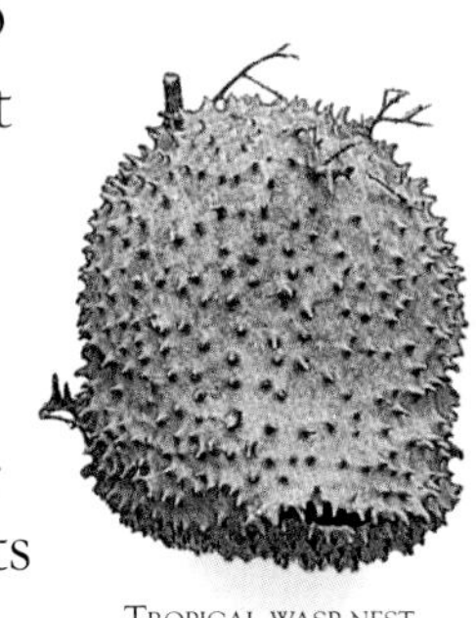

TROPICAL WASP NEST MADE OF CHEWED-UP PLANT FIBERS

Wasps, ants, and bees

The nest is cemented together with wasp saliva.

These insects produce a wide range of nests. Som are small with only a few dozen members, while larger nests may contain thousands c insects. Most have a single queen, and all the nest members are her offspring.

ANTS
A species of African tree ant builds its nest from fragments of plants and soil to produce a substance like dark cement. The ants live on a diet of honeydew, which they get from aphids. The aphids feed on the sap of leaves in the treetops and discharge the honeydew from their rear ends.

BEES
A bumblebee queen start her nest alone in spring i a hole in the ground. She makes cells for her eggs c of wax. She also makes a wax pot, which she fills with honey for food.

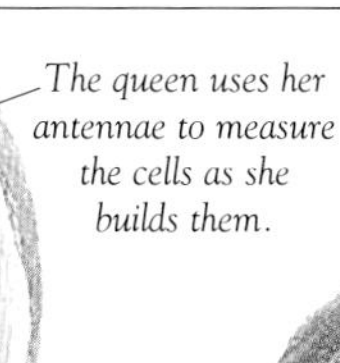

The queen uses her antennae to measure the cells as she builds them.

A NEW START
. European wasp colonies die out each 'inter. In spring, a queen begins a new nest of ›aper" made with chewed-up wood. She .akes a few cells for her eggs, building walls 'ound the cells to shield them.

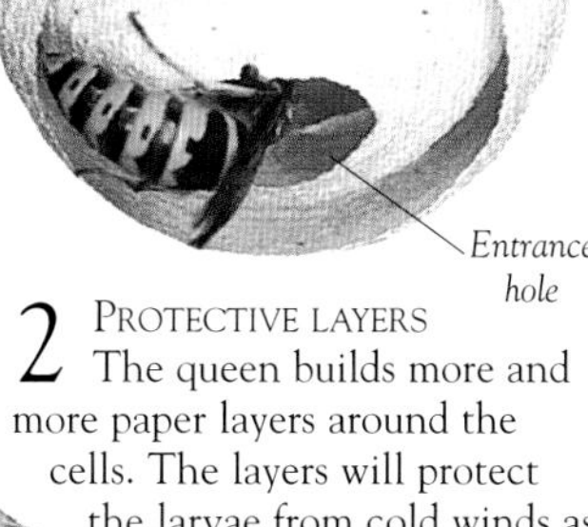

2 PROTECTIVE LAYERS
The queen builds more and more paper layers around the cells. The layers will protect the larvae from cold winds as well as from predators. The queen leaves an entrance hole at the bottom.

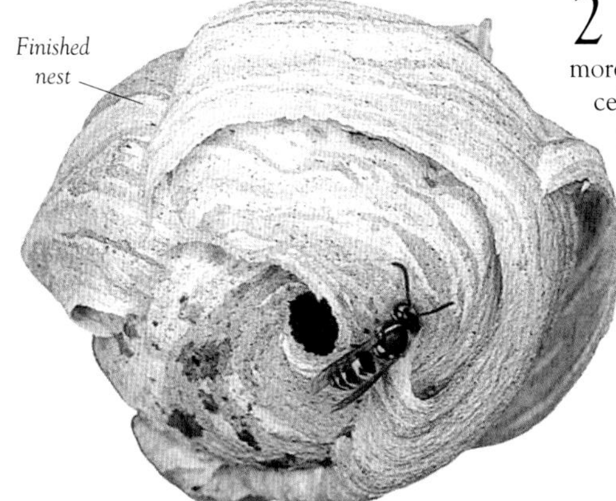

INSIDE THE NEST
The queen lays a single egg in each cell. When the larvae hatch, they stay in their cell and the queen feeds them with pieces of caterpillar.

3 HARD-WORKING FAMILY
The first brood the queen rears become workers, gathering food for more larvae and expanding the nest. By summer, a nest may have 500 wasps, all collecting caterpillars for the larvae. A large nest may be as much as 18 in (45 cm) in diameter.

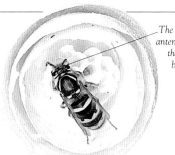

Termite nests

Termites have the most complex insect societies. Their elaborate nests, which may be in wood or underground, last for several years. Each nest has a single large queen and king, which are served by specialized small workers and large soldiers. Termites feed and protect each other, and one generation will help to raise the next generation of offspring.

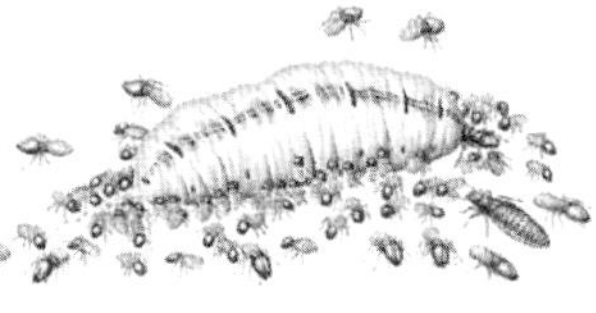

QUEEN TERMITE
In a termite society, the queen lays all the eggs. She is too fat to move, so the workers bring food to her. The queen lays 30,000 eggs each day and, as she lays them, the workers carry them off to special chambers for rearing.

NEST DEFENDERS
Termite soldiers fight enemies that attack the nest. Most termite species have soldiers with enlarged heads and powerful jaws. In some species, each soldier's head has a snout that squirts poison at invaders.

Layers of "umbrellas"

STRANGE NEST
The function of the "umbrellas" on this African nest is a mystery to scientists. The termite species that build this type of nest live underground. If an "umbrella" is damaged, it does not get repaired, but a new one may be built.

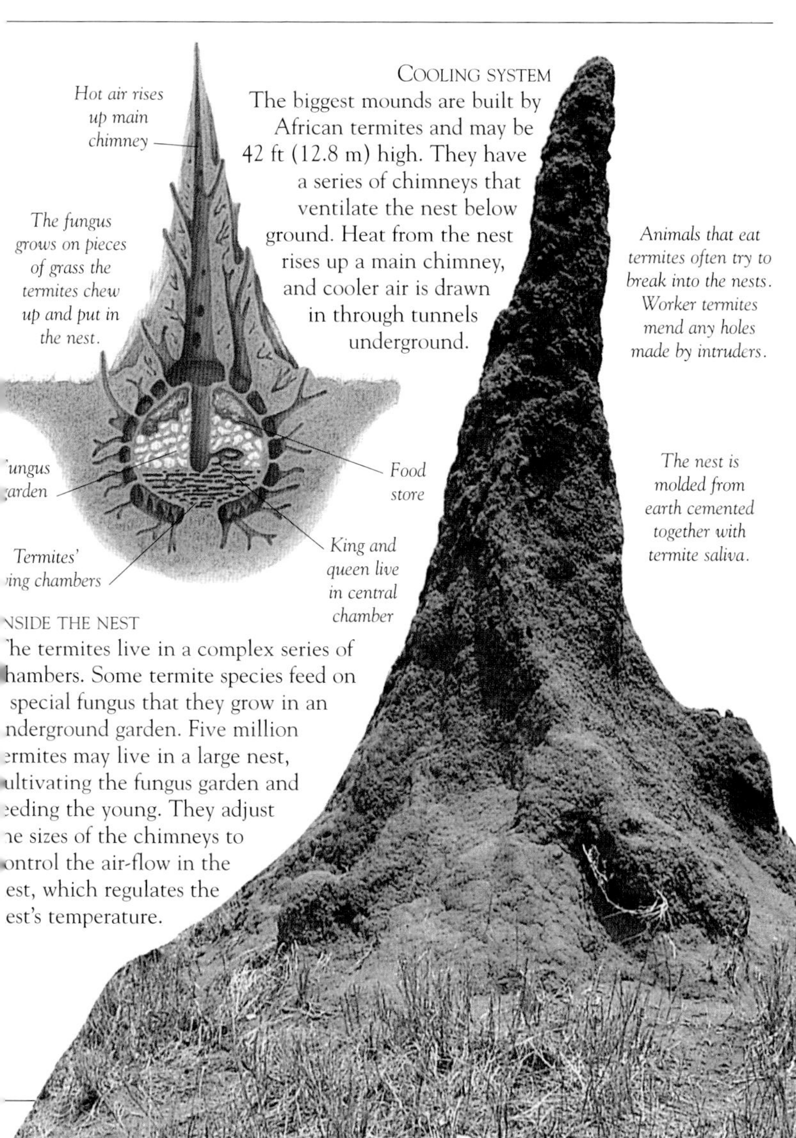

COOLING SYSTEM

The biggest mounds are built by African termites and may be 42 ft (12.8 m) high. They have a series of chimneys that ventilate the nest below ground. Heat from the nest rises up a main chimney, and cooler air is drawn in through tunnels underground.

NSIDE THE NEST

'he termites live in a complex series of hambers. Some termite species feed on special fungus that they grow in an nderground garden. Five million ermites may live in a large nest, ultivating the fungus garden and eeding the young. They adjust ne sizes of the chimneys to ontrol the air-flow in the est, which regulates the est's temperature.

Animals that eat termites often try to break into the nests. Worker termites mend any holes made by intruders.

The nest is molded from earth cemented together with termite saliva.

HUNTING AND HIDING

SOME INSECT SPECIES are deadly hunters, killing prey with poisonous stings and sharp jaws. Insects are also hunted by a huge number of animals. To hide from predators, many insects have developed special disguises and patterns of behavior.

Hunting insects

About one third of insect species are carnivorous (they eat meat). Some species eat decaying meat and dung, but most carnivorous insects hunt for their food.

KILLER BEETLE
Some insects are easily recognized as predators. The large jaws of this African ground beetle indicate that it is a hunter and its long legs show that it can run fast after its insect prey.

KILLER WASPS
There are many types of hunting wasp. Most adult hunting wasps are vegetarians – they hunt prey only as food for their larvae. Each hunting wasp species hunts a particular type of prey. The weevil-hunting wasp hunts only a type of beetle called a weevil.

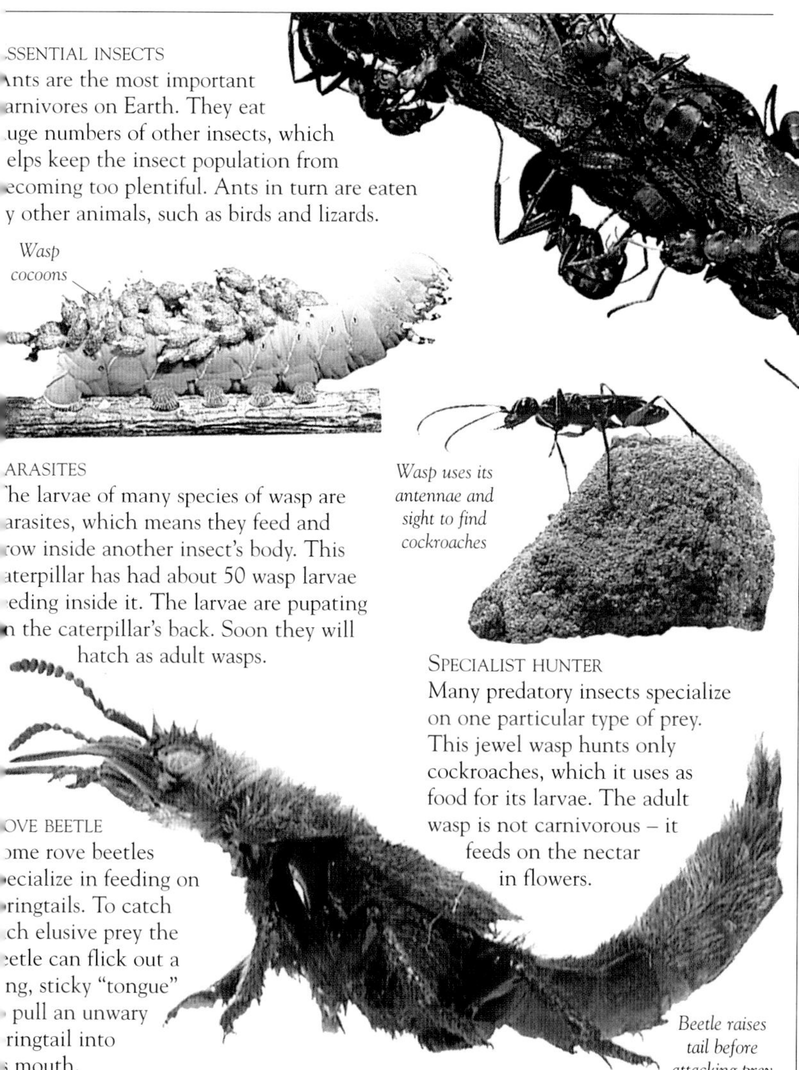

Wasp cocoons

Wasp uses its antennae and sight to find cockroaches

Beetle raises tail before attacking prey

.SSENTIAL INSECTS

ınts are the most important arnivores on Earth. They eat .uge numbers of other insects, which elps keep the insect population from ecoming too plentiful. Ants in turn are eaten y other animals, such as birds and lizards.

ARASITES

'he larvae of many species of wasp are arasites, which means they feed and row inside another insect's body. This aterpillar has had about 50 wasp larvae eding inside it. The larvae are pupating n the caterpillar's back. Soon they will hatch as adult wasps.

SPECIALIST HUNTER

Many predatory insects specialize on one particular type of prey. This jewel wasp hunts only cockroaches, which it uses as food for its larvae. The adult wasp is not carnivorous – it feeds on the nectar in flowers.

OVE BEETLE

ɔme rove beetles ecialize in feeding on ringtails. To catch .ch elusive prey the eetle can flick out a ng, sticky "tongue" pull an unwary ringtail into s mouth.

Camouflage

Insects whose body coloring matches their background are almost impossible to see. This method of hiding is known as camouflage. One of the first rules of successful camouflage is to keep still, as any movement can betray an insect to a sharp-eyed predator. Som insects use another type of camouflage called disruptive coloration. They disguise their body by breaking up its shape with stripes and blocks of color.

GRASSY DISGUISE
The stripe-winged grasshopper can be heard singing in meadow grasses, but its camouflaged body is very hard to spot.

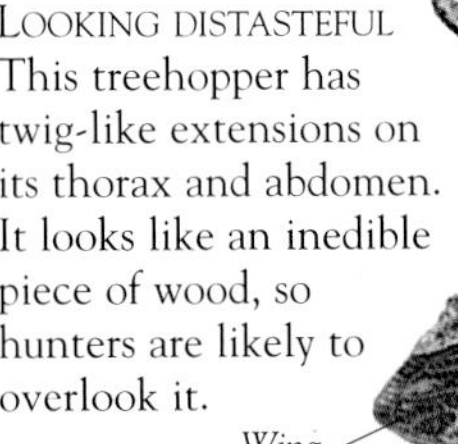

Grasshopper kicks any attackers with its back legs

DISRUPTIVE COLORATION
This tropical moth has disruptive coloration. The patterns on the wings break up their shape. A predator might notice the patterns, but not the whole moth.

LOOKING DISTASTEFUL
This treehopper has twig-like extensions on its thorax and abdomen. It looks like an inedible piece of wood, so hunters are likely to overlook it.

Still hunter

Insect predators use camouflage so their prey cannot see them. The brown coloring of this mantid perfectly matches the brown leaf on which it sits. It completely surprises any prey that comes within striking distance.

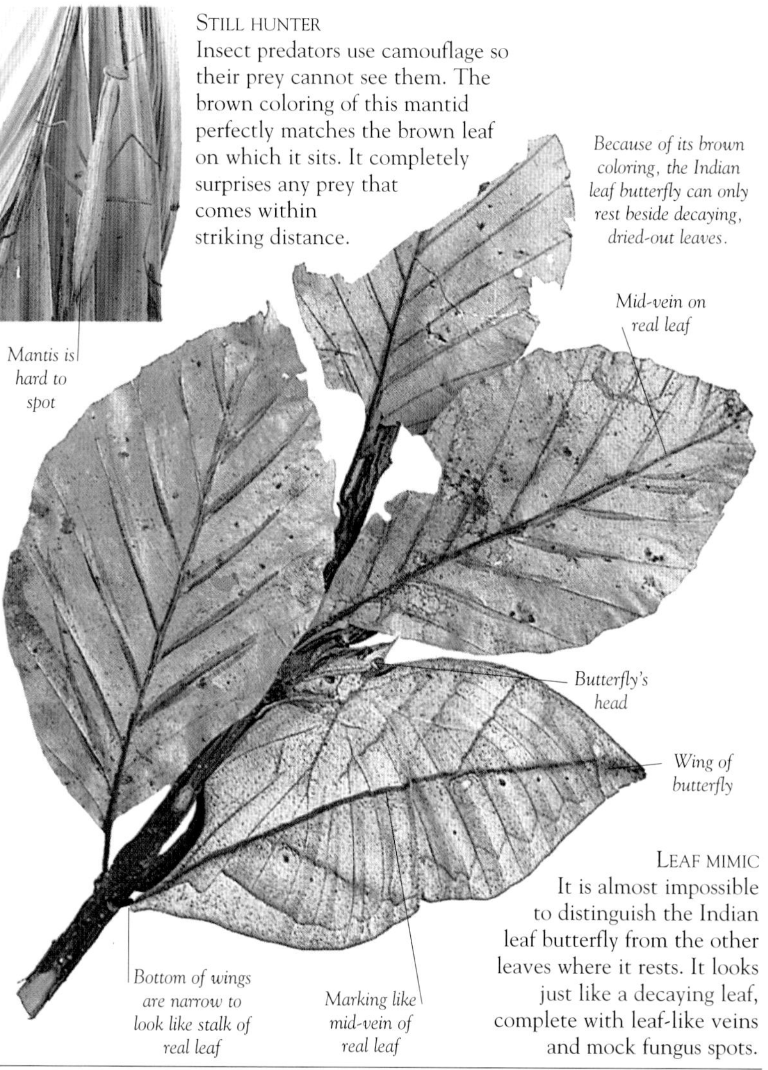

Mantis is hard to spot
Because of its brown coloring, the Indian leaf butterfly can only rest beside decaying, dried-out leaves.
Mid-vein on real leaf
Butterfly's head
Wing of butterfly
Bottom of wings are narrow to look like stalk of real leaf
Marking like mid-vein of real leaf

Leaf mimic

It is almost impossible to distinguish the Indian leaf butterfly from the other leaves where it rests. It looks just like a decaying leaf, complete with leaf-like veins and mock fungus spots.

Warning coloration

Birds, mammals, and other intelligent predators learn through experience that some insects are poisonous or harmful. Such insects do not camouflage themselves. Instead they have brightly colored bodies that warn predators that they have an unpleasant taste or a nasty sting. The most common warning colors are red, yellow, and black. Any insect with those colors is probably poisonous.

BASKER MOTH
Moths that fly by day are often brightly colored, particularly when they taste unpleasant. The red, yellow, and black coloring of this basker moth tells birds that it is not a tasty meal.

PAINFUL REMINDER
The saddle-back caterpillar is eye-catching with its vivid coloring and grotesque appearance. No young bird would ever forget the caterpillar if it tried a mouthful of the poisonous, stinging spines.

Poisonous spines

Vivid green coloring across back

Bright spot

WARNING SPOTS
This assassin bug is easily seen because of the two bright spots on its back. These bold markings warn predators that there is a reason for them to stay away. The bug's weapon is a needle-sharp beak that can give a very painful bite.

EYESPOTS

This silkmoth is camouflaged when its wings are closed. But when attacked by a predator, the moth flashes the eyespots on its hind wings. This startles the attacker briefly, and may give the moth time to escape.

POISONOUS BODY

This grasshopper tastes horrible. It gets its terrible flavor from eating poisonous plants and storing the poisons in its body. The yellow and black stripes advertise its unpleasantness to birds and other predators.

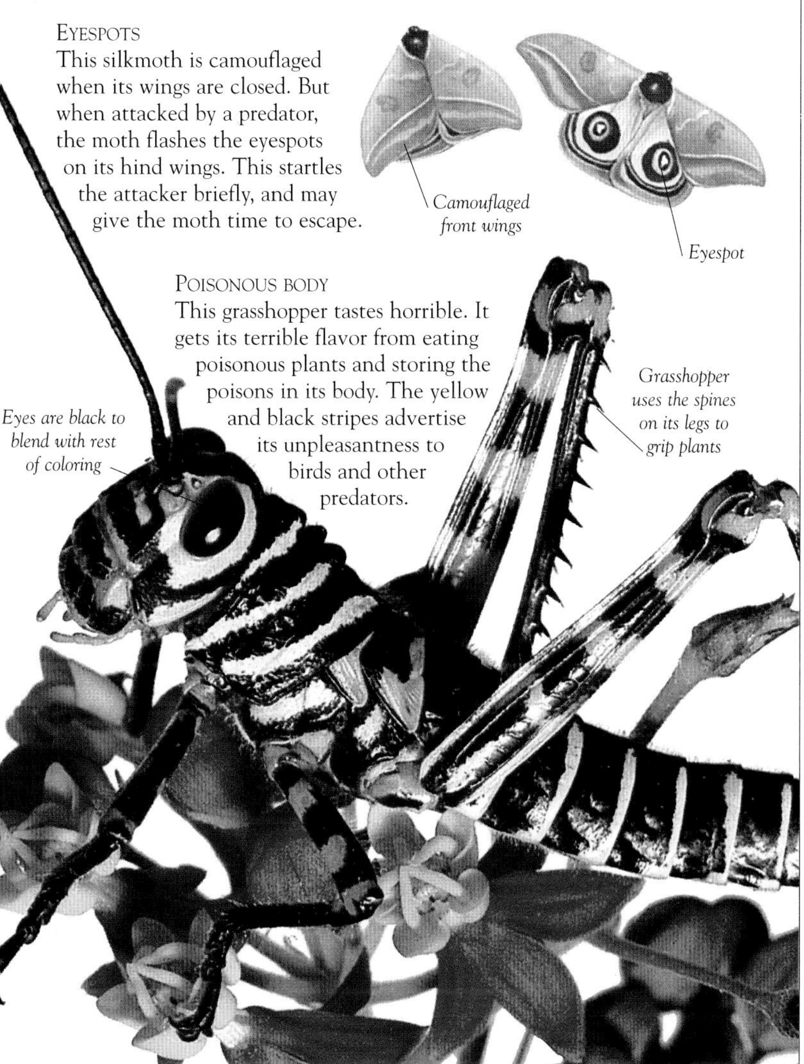

Mimicry

Predators usually avoid preying on dangerous animals. Many harmless insects take advantage of this by mimicking harmful creatures. Mimicking insects copy a dangerous animal's body shape and coloring. They also behave like the animal they're copying to make the disguise more convincing. Inedible objects, such as twigs and thorns, are also mimicked by insects.

The treehoppers only move when they need a fresh source of food.

Markings make head resemble alligator's head

Real eye of bug

ALLIGATOR MIMIC
Scientists can often only guess at the reasons for the strange look and behavior of some animals. It is not known why this tree-living bug looks like a tiny alligator. Perhaps its appearance briefly startles monkey predators, giving the bug time to fly off to safety.

HORNET MIMIC
The hornet moth looks ver like a large wasp called a hornet. When flying, the moth even behaves like a hornet. Many insects find protection by mimicking wasps – birds avoid them because they might sting.

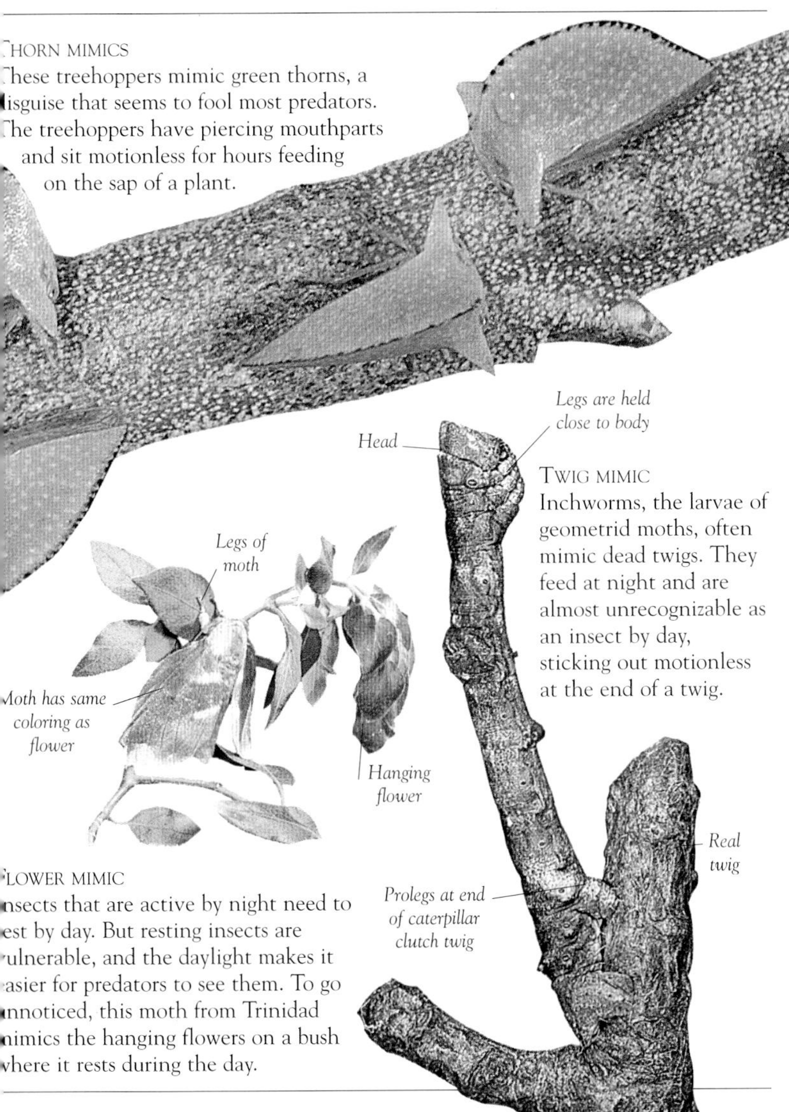

HORN MIMICS

hese treehoppers mimic green thorns, a isguise that seems to fool most predators. he treehoppers have piercing mouthparts and sit motionless for hours feeding on the sap of a plant.

TWIG MIMIC

Inchworms, the larvae of geometrid moths, often mimic dead twigs. They feed at night and are almost unrecognizable as an insect by day, sticking out motionless at the end of a twig.

LOWER MIMIC

nsects that are active by night need to est by day. But resting insects are ulnerable, and the daylight makes it asier for predators to see them. To go nnoticed, this moth from Trinidad nimics the hanging flowers on a bush vhere it rests during the day.

WHERE INSECTS LIVE

INSECTS LIVE everywhere there is warmth and moisture. Many of the five million or more species have specialized habitat requirements. They can live only in particular places, and easily become extinct when humans change or destroy their surroundings. Other species are able to adapt to changing conditions; these adaptable insects often become pests.

NORTH AMERICA

SOUTH AMERICA

TEMPERATE WOODLAND
The varied plant life and complex structure of temperate woodland provides insects with many different habitats. Trees, shrubs, and herbs all have flowers, fruits, and buds for insects to feed on, as well as stems and roots for insects to bore into.

GRASSLANDS AND HEATHLANDS
These habitats offer little shelter from bad weather. But they warm up quickly in the sun, and have a rich variety of flowering plants.

TOWNS AND GARDENS
Hundreds of insect species take advantage of human habitats. Insects find food and shelter in our roofs, cellars, food stores, kitchens, garbage cans, farms, and in our flower-filled gardens.

DESERTS, CAVES, AND SOIL
These are inhospitable habitats. Food and water are scarce in deserts. Caves are dark and cold. And it is hard for insects to move and communicate in dense soil.

TROPICAL FORESTS
This is the richest habitat for insect species. Thousands of species of plants provide countless niches for insects to live in, from treetop fruits to dead leaves and twigs on the ground.

LAKES AND RIVERS
Freshwater insects are highly specialized. They have had to modify their bodies to be able to swim and breathe underwater.

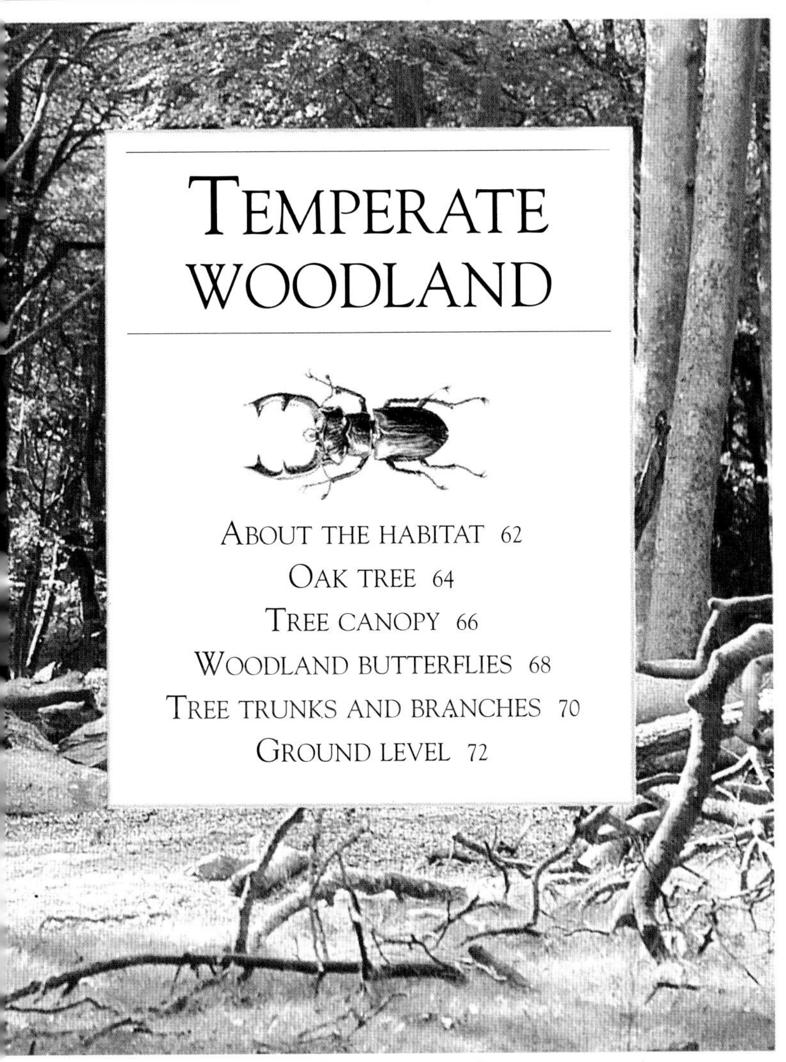

TEMPERATE WOODLAND

ABOUT THE HABITAT

TEMPERATE WOODLANDS are often dominated by one tree species, such as oak, which is deciduous (the trees lose their leaves in winter). The types of insect found, and their numbers, will vary with the seasons, as well as with the types of tree species in the woodlands.

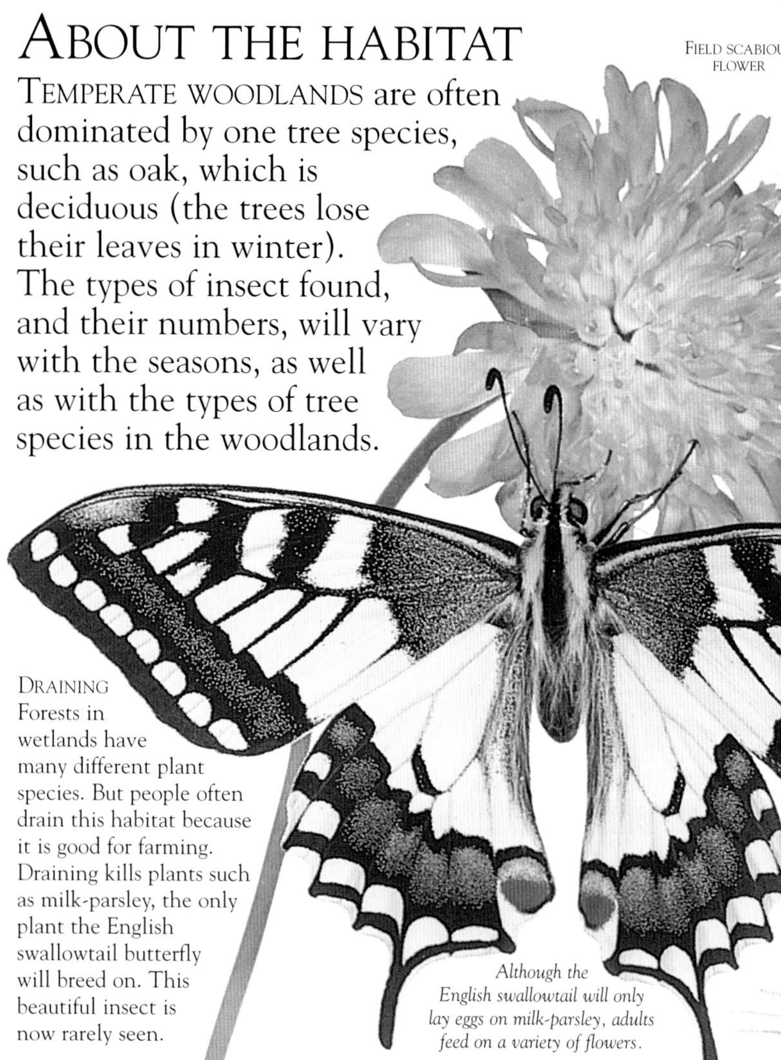

FIELD SCABIOU FLOWER

DRAINING
Forests in wetlands have many different plant species. But people often drain this habitat because it is good for farming. Draining kills plants such as milk-parsley, the only plant the English swallowtail butterfly will breed on. This beautiful insect is now rarely seen.

Although the English swallowtail will only lay eggs on milk-parsley, adults feed on a variety of flowers.

WOODLAND FACTS

- The woodland edge supports the greatest number of insect species.
- Each pair of blue tit birds needs about 5,000 caterpillars to feed to its chicks.
- In Britain, over 280 species of insect live on native oak trees.
- Temperate rain forests in the northwestern United States are disappearing faster than tropical rain forests.

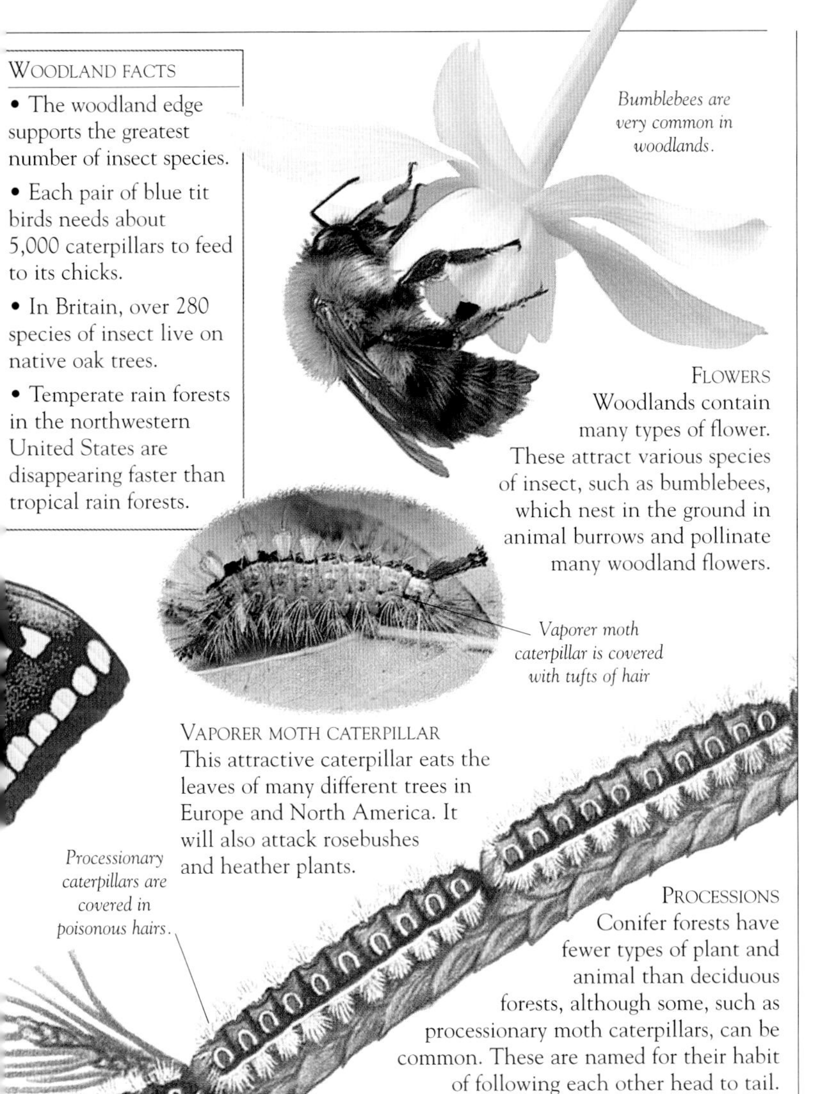

Bumblebees are very common in woodlands.

FLOWERS

Woodlands contain many types of flower. These attract various species of insect, such as bumblebees, which nest in the ground in animal burrows and pollinate many woodland flowers.

Vaporer moth caterpillar is covered with tufts of hair

VAPORER MOTH CATERPILLAR

This attractive caterpillar eats the leaves of many different trees in Europe and North America. It will also attack rosebushes and heather plants.

Processionary caterpillars are covered in poisonous hairs.

PROCESSIONS

Conifer forests have fewer types of plant and animal than deciduous forests, although some, such as processionary moth caterpillars, can be common. These are named for their habit of following each other head to tail.

OAK TREE

IN EUROPE AND North America, oak trees support a rich variety of insects. There are insects living on every part of the oak tree – the leaves, buds, flowers, fruits, wood, bark, and on decaying leaves and branches. All these insects provide food for the many birds and other animals found in oak woodland.

OAK TREE

GREEN OAK TORTRIX MOTH ON LEAF

GREEN OAK TORTRIX CATERPILLAR

GREEN OAK TORTRIX MOTH
The green wings of the green oak tortrix moth camouflage it on leaves. Green oak tortrix caterpillars are extremely common on oak trees. The caterpillars hide from predators by rolling themselves up in a leaf.

Leaf rolle around gre oak tortri caterpilla

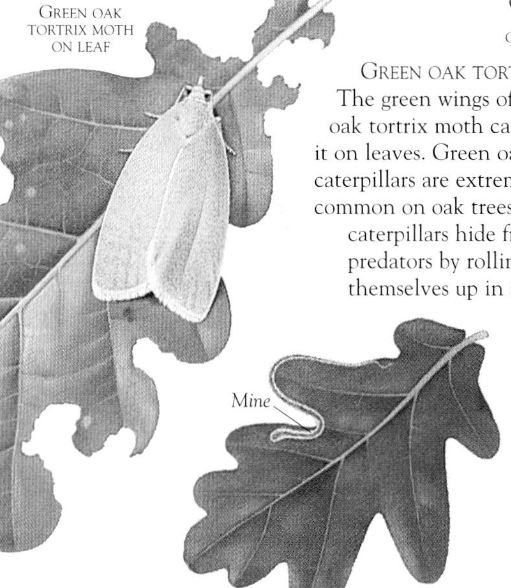

MAKING A TUNNEL
The caterpillars of some sma moths tunnel between the upper and lower surfaces of a leaf. They eat the green tissu between these surfaces as th tunnel, and leave a see-through trail called a mine.

Galls

Oak trees have many tiny growths called galls. Galls are grown by the tree around eggs laid by gall wasps. When the eggs hatch, each gall provides food and shelter for up to 30 wasp larvae. Parasitic wasps called chalcid wasps sometimes burrow inside galls and lay their eggs beside the gall wasp eggs. When the chalcid larvae hatch, they eat the gall wasp larvae.

Nut weevils

Acorns are used as food by nut weevils. They drill a hole in an acorn with their long, thin snout, and then lay their eggs inside. The larvae feed inside the acorn, which turns the acorn black.

TREE CANOPY

THE UPPER BRANCHES and leaves of a tree are called the canopy. Like a living green umbrella, the canopy forms a protective covering over the lower plants. Countless insects find their food in the canopy, and they, in turn, are food for many different birds.

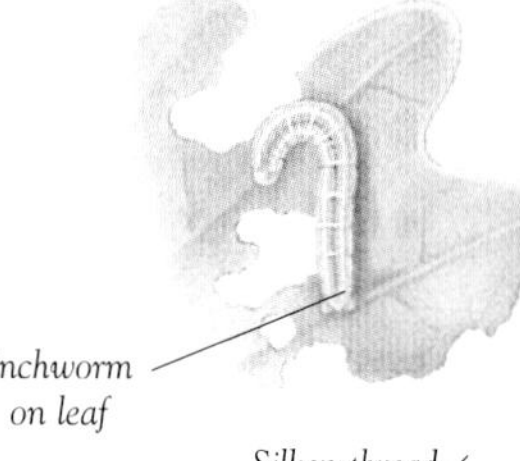

Inchworm on leaf

Silken thread suspends inchworm

INCHWORMS
Some young birds like to feed on inchworms, the caterpillars of geometrid moths. When in danger, inchworms can drop from a leaf and hang below by a silken thread.

Very long antennae help cricket find its way in the dark and alert it to the approach of enemies

Compound eye

OAK BUSH CRICKETS
At night, male oak bush crickets drum on leaves with their feet so that a female oak bush cricket, like this one, knows where to find a mate. The cricket's green body blends in well with its leafy surroundings.

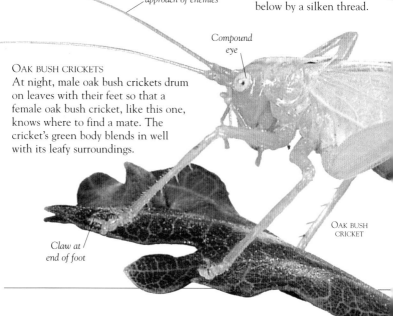

Claw at end of foot

OAK BUSH CRICKET

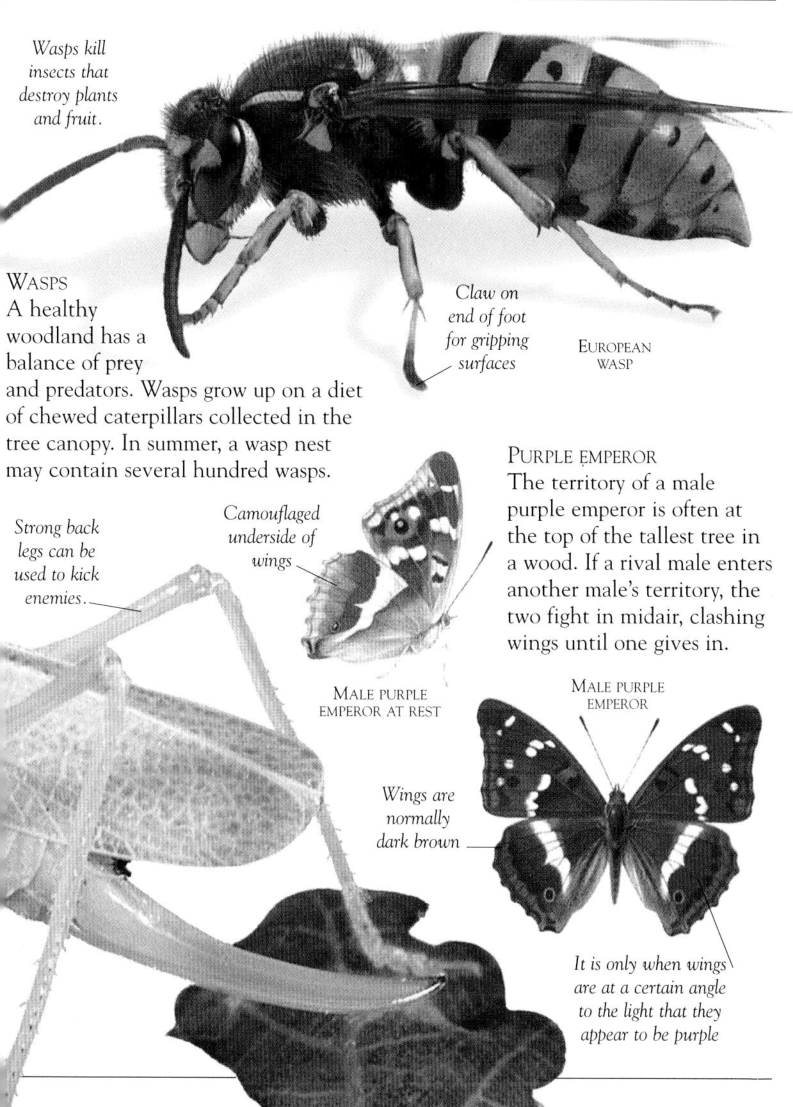
Wasps kill insects that destroy plants and fruit.
Claw on end of foot for gripping surfaces
EUROPEAN WASP
Camouflaged underside of wings
Strong back legs can be used to kick enemies.
MALE PURPLE EMPEROR AT REST
MALE PURPLE EMPEROR
Wings are normally dark brown
It is only when wings are at a certain angle to the light that they appear to be purple

WASPS

A healthy woodland has a balance of prey and predators. Wasps grow up on a diet of chewed caterpillars collected in the tree canopy. In summer, a wasp nest may contain several hundred wasps.

PURPLE EMPEROR

The territory of a male purple emperor is often at the top of the tallest tree in a wood. If a rival male enters another male's territory, the two fight in midair, clashing wings until one gives in.

WOODLAND BUTTERFLIES

THE RICH VARIETY of habitats in woodland supports many butterfly species. Some live in the canopy, others feed on low shrubs. But most butterflies need sunshine and can be found on flowers in sunny clearings.

SILVER-WASHED FRITILLARY
This butterfly lays its eggs in cracks in the bark of mossy tree trunks, close to where violets are growing. The caterpillars feed on the leaves of these plants.

Brown upperside

Green underside

GREEN HAIRSTREAK
Whether it is sitting on a branch or resting on a leaf, the green hairstreak butterfly is well camouflaged. Its upperside is a woody brown, while its underside is a leafy green.

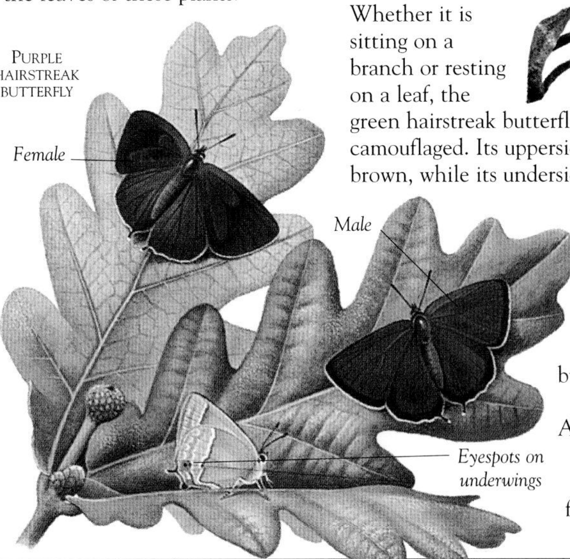

PURPLE HAIRSTREAK
High in the canopy of oak trees, the caterpillars of the purple hairstreak butterfly feed on flowers and young leaves. Adult purple hairstreaks spend most of their lives in the treetops feeding and sunbathing with their wings open.

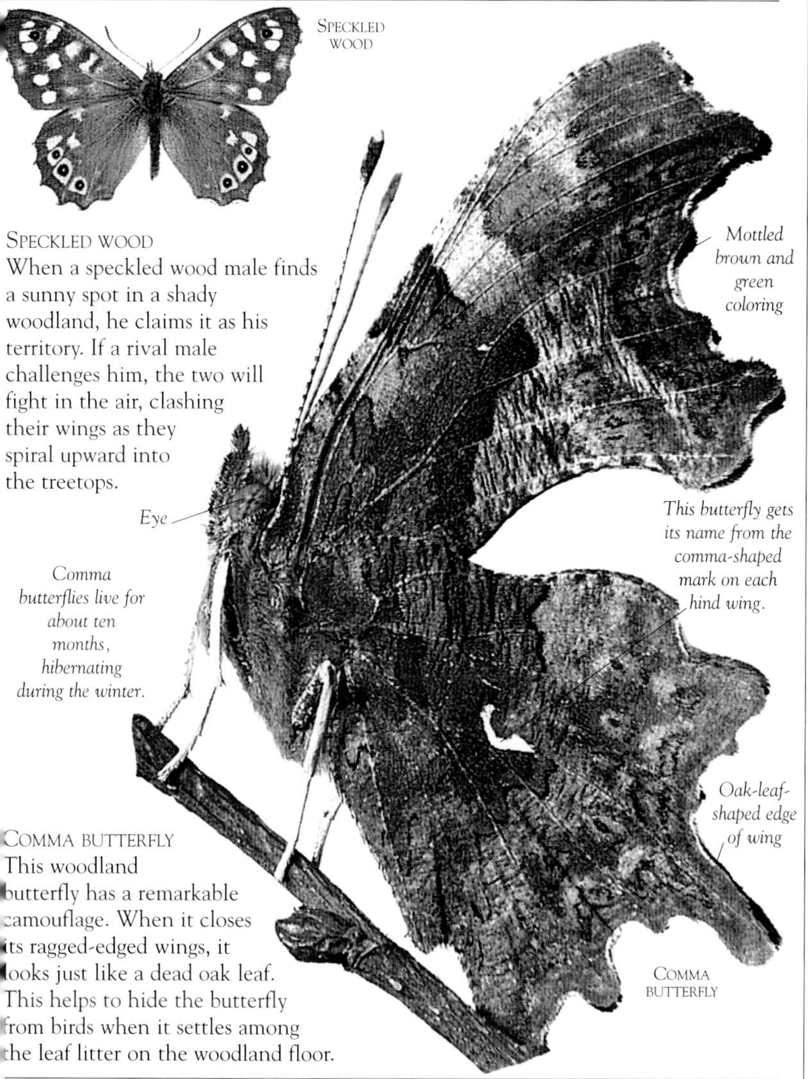

SPECKLED WOOD
When a speckled wood male finds a sunny spot in a shady woodland, he claims it as his territory. If a rival male challenges him, the two will fight in the air, clashing their wings as they spiral upward into the treetops.

Comma butterflies live for about ten months, hibernating during the winter.

COMMA BUTTERFLY
This woodland butterfly has a remarkable camouflage. When it closes its ragged-edged wings, it looks just like a dead oak leaf. This helps to hide the butterfly from birds when it settles among the leaf litter on the woodland floor.

TREE TRUNKS AND BRANCHES

CRACKS IN THE bark of trees provide a hiding place for many species of insect. Some burrow into the wood and live completely concealed from predators. Many insects also live and feed among the different plant life that grows on tree trunks and branches.

BARK INSECTS
Insects that live on bark are usually camouflaged, such as barklice, which feed on tiny fungi and algae. Another bark insect, the snakefly, is a predator. When it hunts, it looks like a tiny snake about to strike, holding its head high looking for prey.

WOOD WASP
This female giant wood wasp has a long, stout egg-laying tube, or ovipositor, which looks like a fearsome sting. It lays eggs deep inside the soft wood of dead or dying trees.

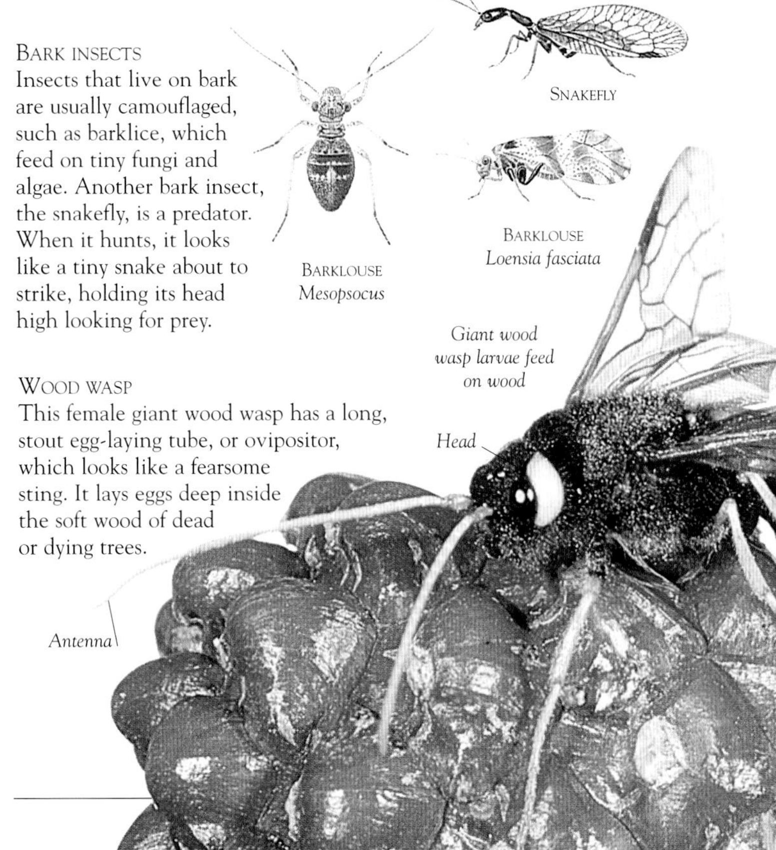
Giant wood wasp larvae feed on wood
Head
Antenna

SNAKEFLY

BARKLOUSE *Mesopsocus*

BARKLOUSE *Loensia fasciata*

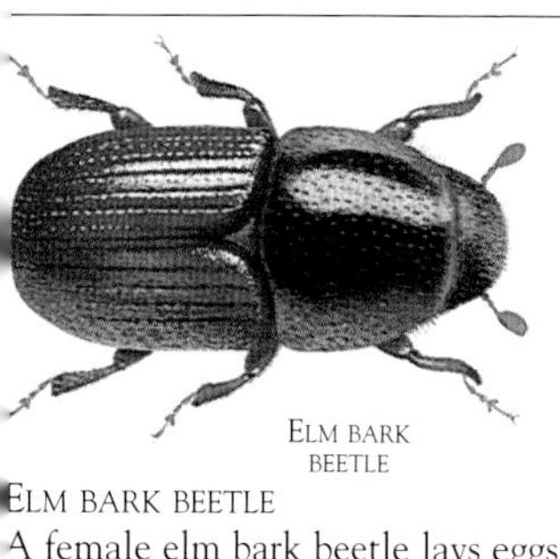

ELM BARK BEETLE

ELM BARK BEETLE

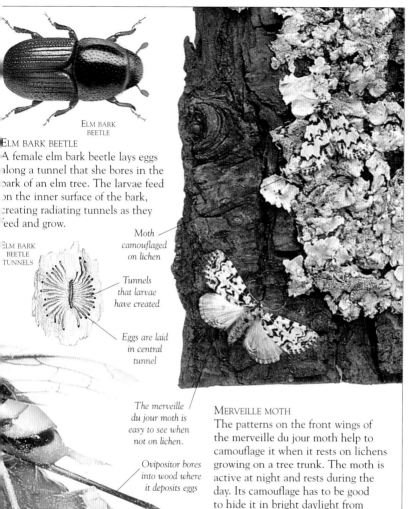

A female elm bark beetle lays eggs along a tunnel that she bores in the bark of an elm tree. The larvae feed on the inner surface of the bark, creating radiating tunnels as they feed and grow.

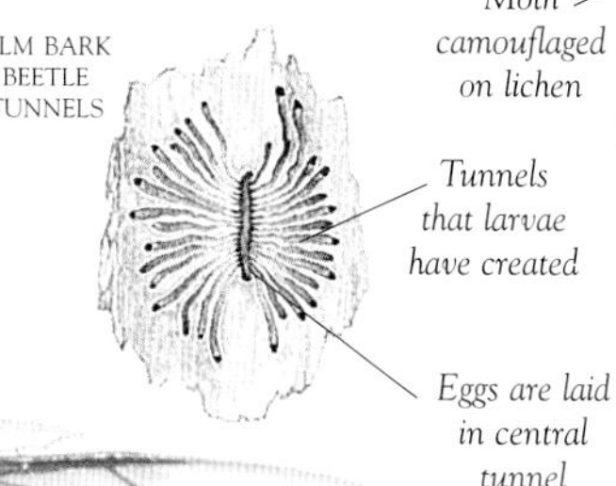

Moth camouflaged on lichen

The merveille du jour moth is easy to see when not on lichen.

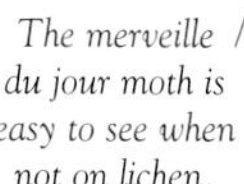

Ovipositor bores into wood where it deposits eggs

MERVEILLE MOTH

The patterns on the front wings of the merveille du jour moth help to camouflage it when it rests on lichens growing on a tree trunk. The moth is active at night and rests during the day. Its camouflage has to be good to hide it in bright daylight from predators such as birds and lizards.

GROUND LEVEL

THE WOODLAND floor does not get much sunlight, so few plants grow there. Most insects at ground level feed on plant and animal debris falling from the canopy, or, if they are carnivorous, eat other insects.

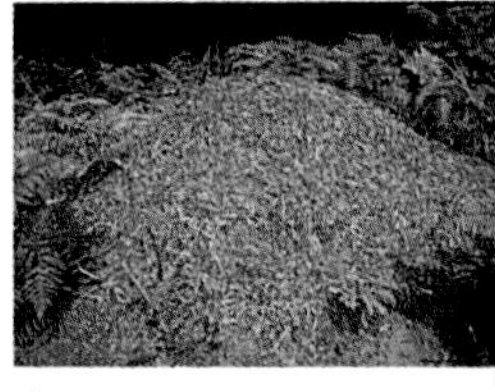

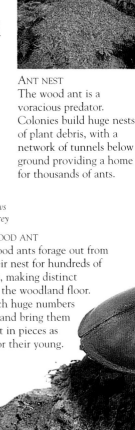

ANT NEST
The wood ant is a voracious predator. Colonies build huge nests of plant debris, with a network of tunnels below ground providing a home for thousands of ants.

WOOD CRICKET
Most crickets are nocturnal (active at night). But the wood cricket is active on sunny days when it can be heard chirping loudly. It is unable to fly because of its short wings.

Strong jaws bite into prey

Ant can squirt poison from abdomen

WOOD ANT
Wood ants forage out from their nest for hundreds of yards, making distinct paths on the woodland floor. They catch huge numbers of insects and bring them to the nest in pieces as food for their young.

WHITE ADMIRALS
On sunny days, white admiral butterflies can be spotted near the ground feeding on the nectar of bramble flowers. They can often be seen in the morning sipping water from puddles. They spend much of their time in the tree canopy, basking in the sunshine.

VIOLET GROUND BEETLE
This beetle can run fast on its long legs, catching other insects among the leaf litter. It grips its prey with powerful jaws, and hunts mainly at night.

STAG BEETLE
The larvae of stag beetles spend about three years feeding on rotting wood inside a dead tree. These handsome beetles are now becoming rare because dead wood is often cleared away and burned.

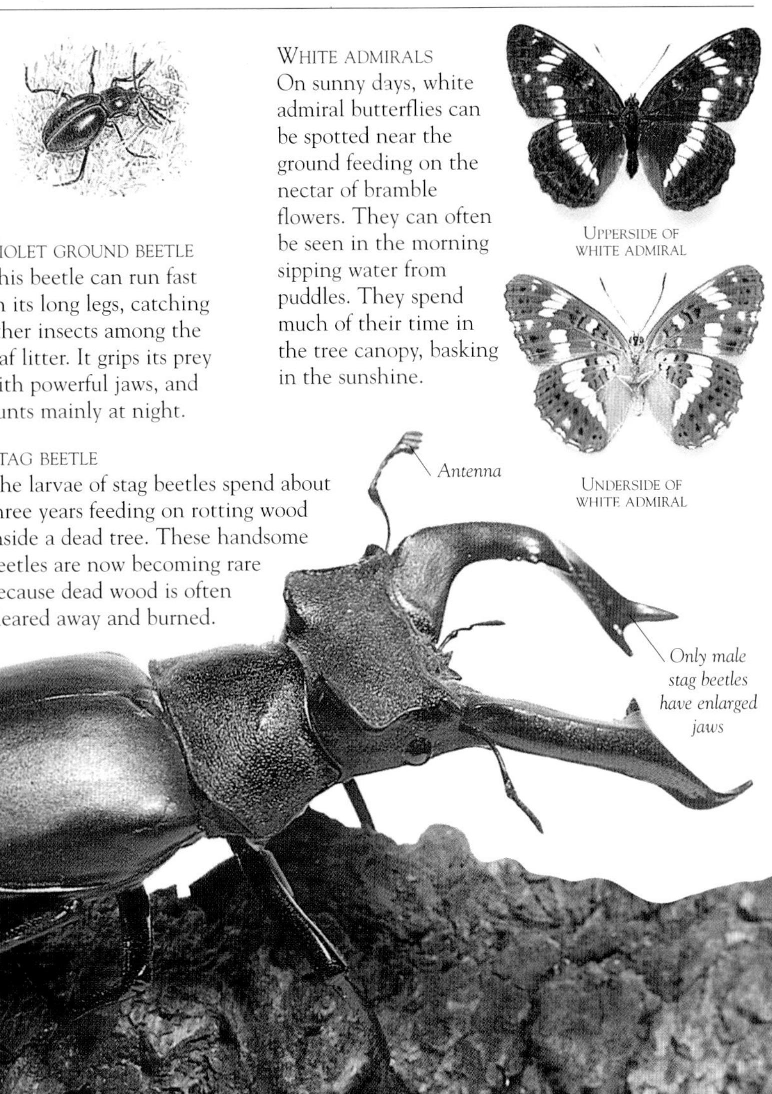
Antenna
Only male stag beetles have enlarged jaws

UPPERSIDE OF WHITE ADMIRAL

UNDERSIDE OF WHITE ADMIRAL

GRASSLANDS AND HEATHLANDS

ABOUT THE HABITAT

GRASSLANDS AND HEATHLANDS have no protective tree canopy, which means they change quickly with the weather – from hot and dry, to windy, cold, or wet. These habitats are less complex than forest or woodland. They provide fewer dwelling places for insects, since there is little wood to burrow into, and hardly any leaf litter to live underneath.

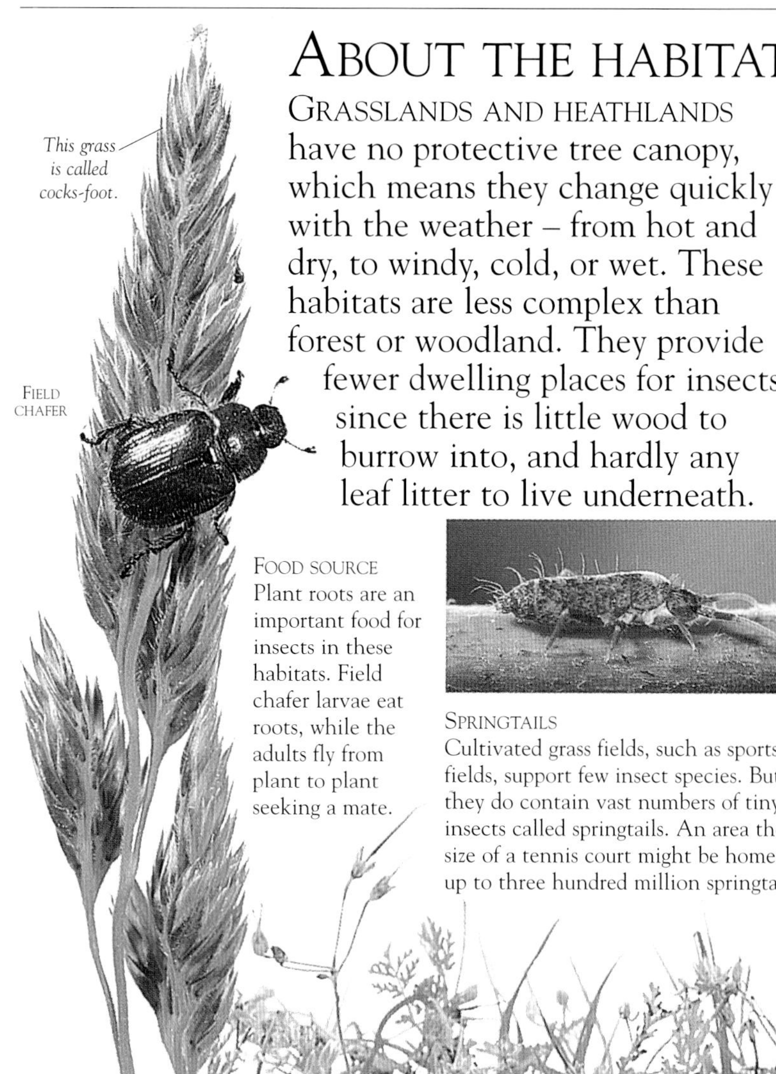

This grass is called cocks-foot.

FIELD CHAFER

FOOD SOURCE
Plant roots are an important food for insects in these habitats. Field chafer larvae eat roots, while the adults fly from plant to plant seeking a mate.

SPRINGTAILS
Cultivated grass fields, such as sports fields, support few insect species. But they do contain vast numbers of tiny insects called springtails. An area the size of a tennis court might be home up to three hundred million springtai

xFORD RAGWORT
weed called the xford ragwort is a mmon invader of glected pasture in rope. The cinnabar oth lays its eggs on is weed, and its terpillars eat e leaves.

The moth has arning coloration because it tastes unpleasant.

An Oxford ragwort is often stripped of its leaves by feeding caterpillars

CH IN PLANT LIFE
atural grassland and athland have a huge riety of grasses d flowering ants. These rich bitats buzz with sect life the mmer onths.

GRASSLAND AND HEATHLAND FACTS

- The grasslands of Argentina are called Pampas, or "plains" in the language of the native people.
- Prairies of the US have long grasses
- Steppes (prairielike land) of Siberia have short grasses.

RARE BUTTERFLY
The English large copper butterfly was once common in fenland but is now extinct. This is a result of intensive land development for agriculture, which destroyed the butterfly's special food plant.

GRASSLAND INSECTS

MOST INSECT species cannot survive in cultivated gra[ss]lands, such as garden lawns, since they usually contai[n] only one type of grass. Also, fertilizers and other chemicals harm many insects. But natural grasslands, with their variety of plants, support thousands of inse[ct] species that have adapted to this open, windy habitat

DUNG BEETLES
These beetles are common in grasslands where cattle graze. Dung beetles lay their eggs in animal dung, which their larvae feed on when they hatch. The adults collect the dung by molding it into balls and rolling it to their underground burrows.

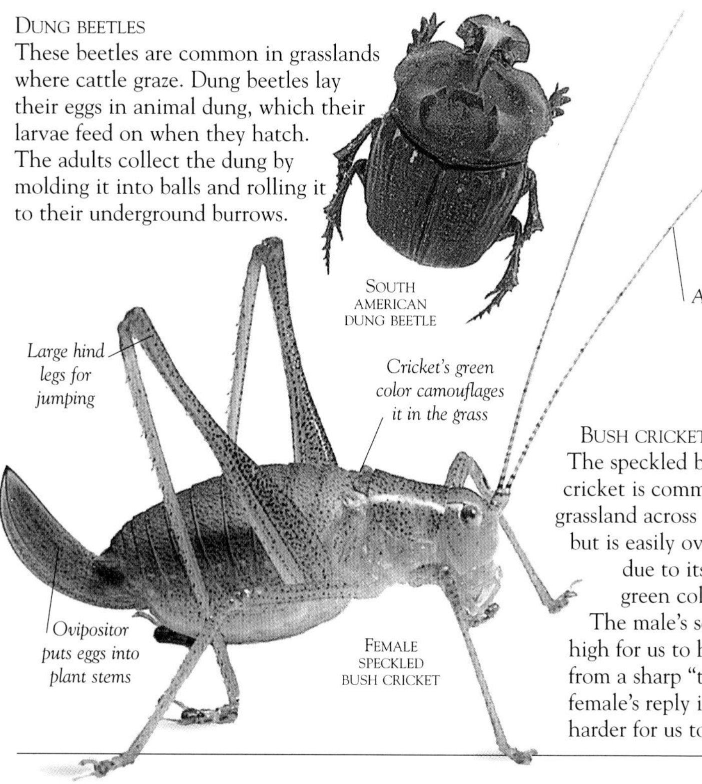
Antenna
Large hind legs for jumping
Cricket's green color camouflages it in the grass
Ovipositor puts eggs into plant stems

SOUTH AMERICAN DUNG BEETLE

FEMALE SPECKLED BUSH CRICKET

BUSH CRICKET
The speckled bush cricket is common in grassland across Europe, but is easily overlooked due to its grass-green coloring. The male's song is to[o] high for us to hear, apa[rt] from a sharp "tick." The female's reply is even harder for us to hear.

ANTEATER

ıNTEATER

'here are so many ants in ıe grasslands of South ımerica and Africa ıat specialized nt-eating ıammals have volved. They ave powerful claws to break pen ant nests and long sticky ɔngues to collect the ants.

LARGE BLUE BUTTERFLY

This butterfly lays its eggs on the wild thyme plant, and the newly hatched caterpillars feed on thyme flowers. The caterpillars attract red ants with a special milk. The ants are deceived into carrying the caterpillars into their nest, where the caterpillars eat the ant eggs and larva.

ΛARBLED WHITE BUTTERFLY

'his butterfly can be found in a 'ariety of grassland habitats, including rassy areas inside a wood. Marbled vhites often gather in groups to ɔask in the early morning and arly evening sunshine.

OLDIER BEETLES

ome insects feed on one particular ower, while others, such as ɔldier beetles, eat pollen from arious flowers. These feeding tes are also good places for ısects to find a mate.

Heathland insects

MANY BURROWING insects live in heathland since the soil is loose and easy to dig into. Heathland occurs in parts of the world with a climate of rainy winters and warm, dry summers. It has a rich mixture of plants, and the soil, which is often sandy, warms up quickly in the sunshine.

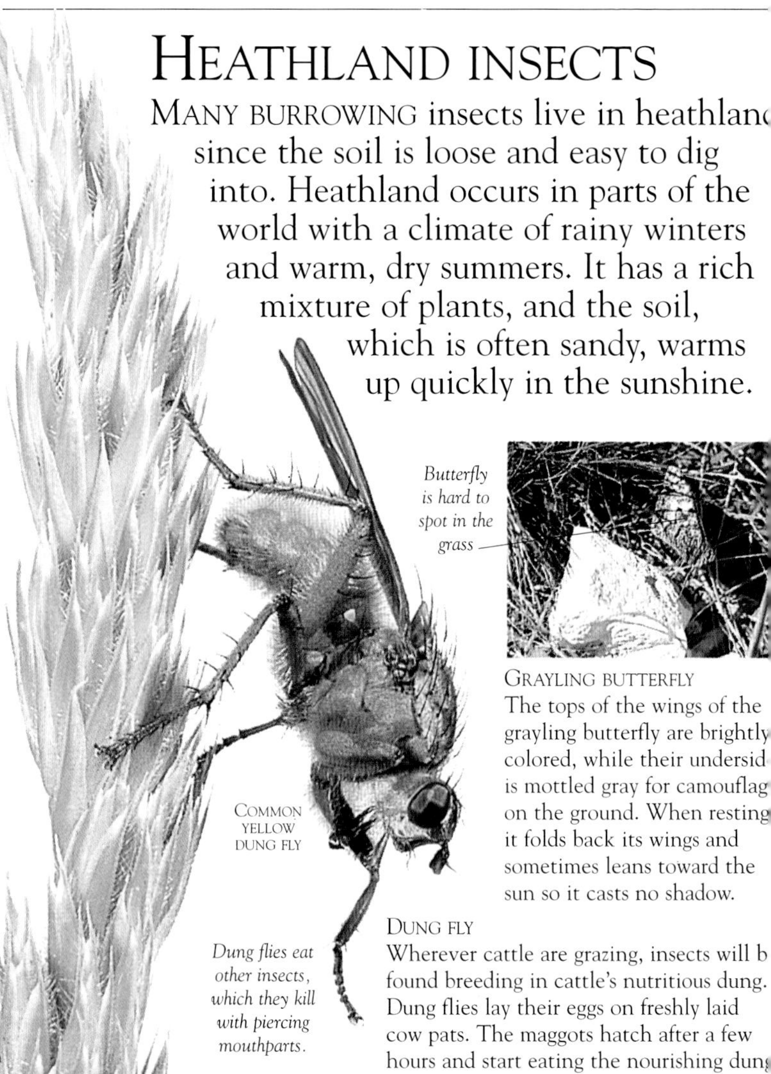

Butterfly is hard to spot in the grass

GRAYLING BUTTERFLY

The tops of the wings of the grayling butterfly are brightly colored, while their underside is mottled gray for camouflage on the ground. When resting it folds back its wings and sometimes leans toward the sun so it casts no shadow.

COMMON YELLOW DUNG FLY

Dung flies eat other insects, which they kill with piercing mouthparts.

DUNG FLY

Wherever cattle are grazing, insects will be found breeding in cattle's nutritious dung. Dung flies lay their eggs on freshly laid cow pats. The maggots hatch after a few hours and start eating the nourishing dung

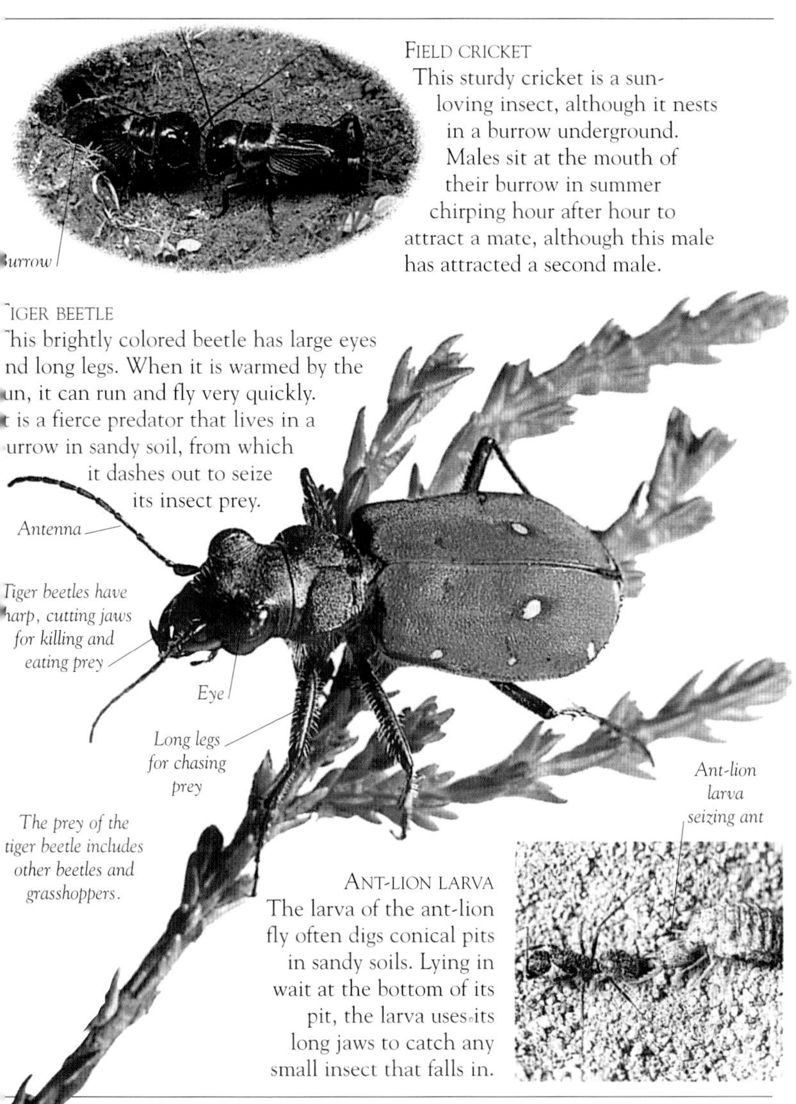

FIELD CRICKET
This sturdy cricket is a sun-loving insect, although it nests in a burrow underground. Males sit at the mouth of their burrow in summer chirping hour after hour to attract a mate, although this male has attracted a second male.

IGER BEETLE
his brightly colored beetle has large eyes nd long legs. When it is warmed by the un, it can run and fly very quickly. t is a fierce predator that lives in a urrow in sandy soil, from which it dashes out to seize its insect prey.

The prey of the tiger beetle includes other beetles and grasshoppers.

ANT-LION LARVA
The larva of the ant-lion fly often digs conical pits in sandy soils. Lying in wait at the bottom of its pit, the larva uses its long jaws to catch any small insect that falls in.

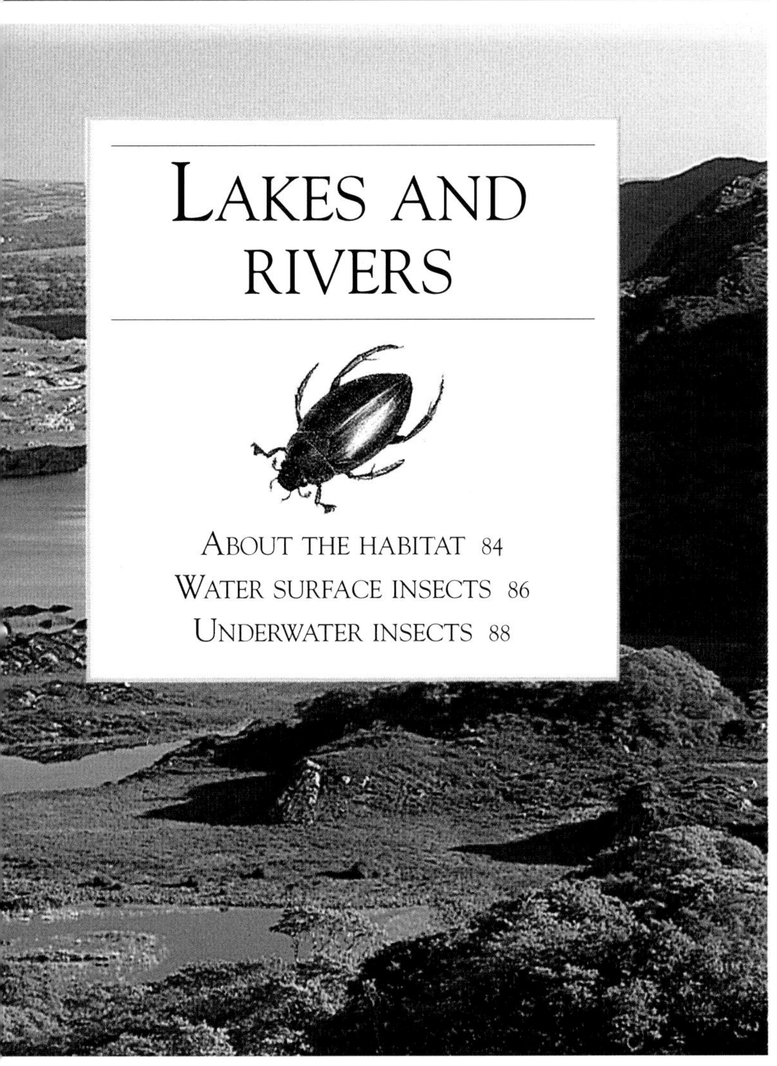

LAKES AND RIVERS

ABOUT THE HABITAT

INSECTS CAN be found in all sorts of freshwater habitats: lakes, fast-flowing streams, ponds, puddles, damp moss, and wet leaf litter. These insects have many adaptations for surviving in their watery homes.

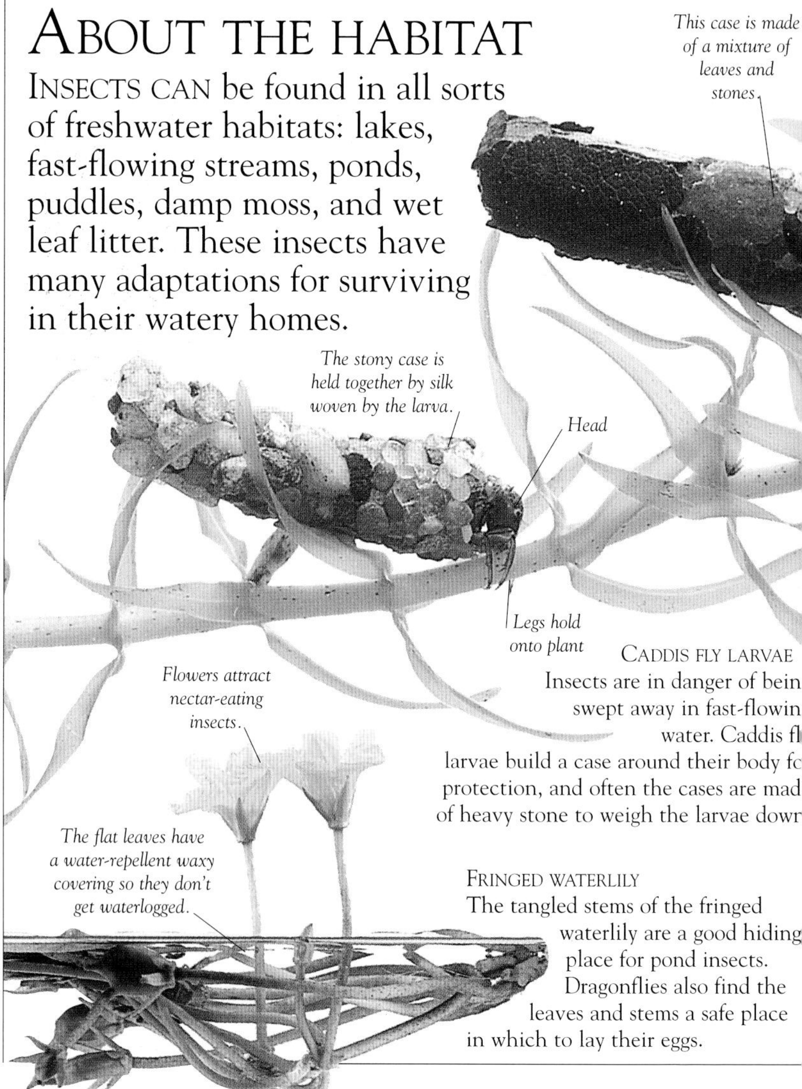

This case is made of a mixture of leaves and stones.
The stony case is held together by silk woven by the larva.
Head
Legs hold onto plant
Flowers attract nectar-eating insects.
The flat leaves have a water-repellent waxy covering so they don't get waterlogged.

CADDIS FLY LARVAE
Insects are in danger of bein swept away in fast-flowin water. Caddis fl larvae build a case around their body fc protection, and often the cases are mad of heavy stone to weigh the larvae dowr

FRINGED WATERLILY
The tangled stems of the fringed waterlily are a good hiding place for pond insects. Dragonflies also find the leaves and stems a safe place in which to lay their eggs.

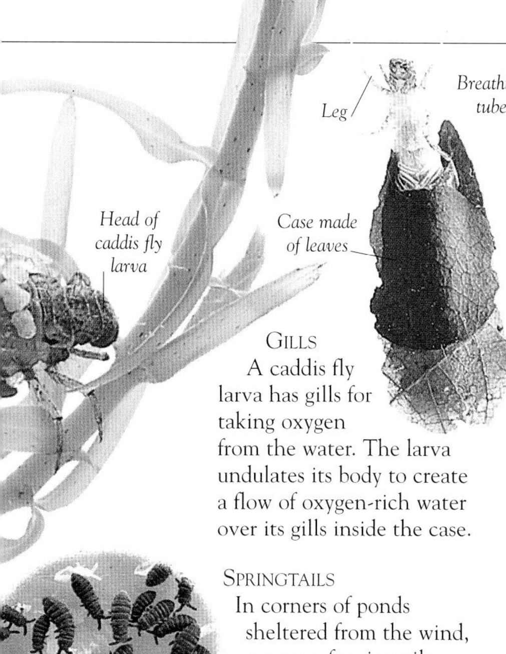

GILLS

A caddis fly larva has gills for taking oxygen from the water. The larva undulates its body to create a flow of oxygen-rich water over its gills inside the case.

WATER SCORPION

The water scorpion has a breathing tube on its rear end so that it can breathe the outside air while it is underwater. Insects with breathing tubes can survive in warm ponds or polluted waters that are low in oxygen.

SPRINGTAILS

In corners of ponds sheltered from the wind, swarms of springtails sometimes gather on the surface of the water. They feed on organic debris that has blown into the pond.

FAST STREAMS

Insects that live in fast-flowing streams have streamlined bodies and strong claws to help them cling to stones. The water that passes over their gills is always rich in oxygen, but cool temperatures mean that larvae develop more slowly than they would in a shallow, sun-warmed pond.

LAKES AND RIVERS FACTS

- Fish populations depend on plenty of insects as food.
- Dragonfly larvae are considered a delicacy in New Guinea.
- Swarms of nonbiting midges are sometimes so dense in African lakes that anglers have been suffocated.

WATER SURFACE INSECTS

A WATER SURFACE behaves like a skin due to a force called surface tension. This force enables certain insects to walk on the "skin" and others to hang beneath it. Many of these insects are predators, and much of their food comes from the constant supply of flying insects that have fallen into the water.

WHIRLIGIG

The whirligig beetle swims around and around very fast on the water surface. It hunts insects trapped on the surface tension. The whirligig's eyes are divided into two halves, allowing it to see both above and below the water surface at the same time.

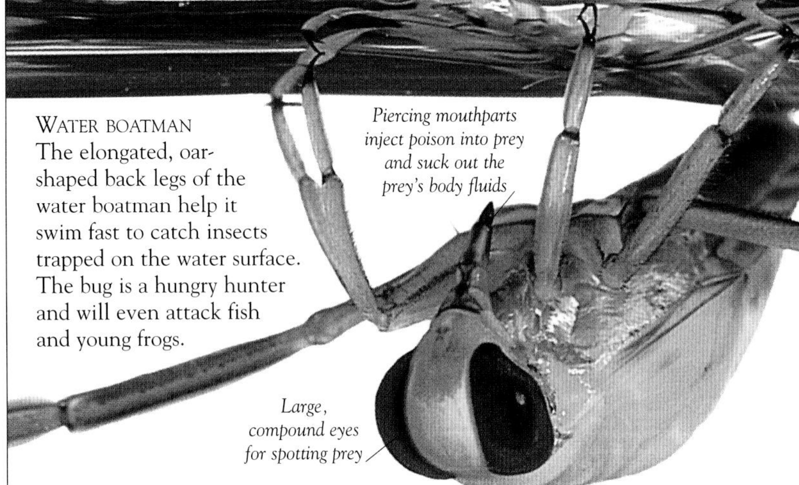
Piercing mouthparts inject poison into prey and suck out the prey's body fluids
Large, compound eyes for spotting prey

WATER BOATMAN

The elongated, oar-shaped back legs of the water boatman help it swim fast to catch insects trapped on the water surface. The bug is a hungry hunter and will even attack fish and young frogs.

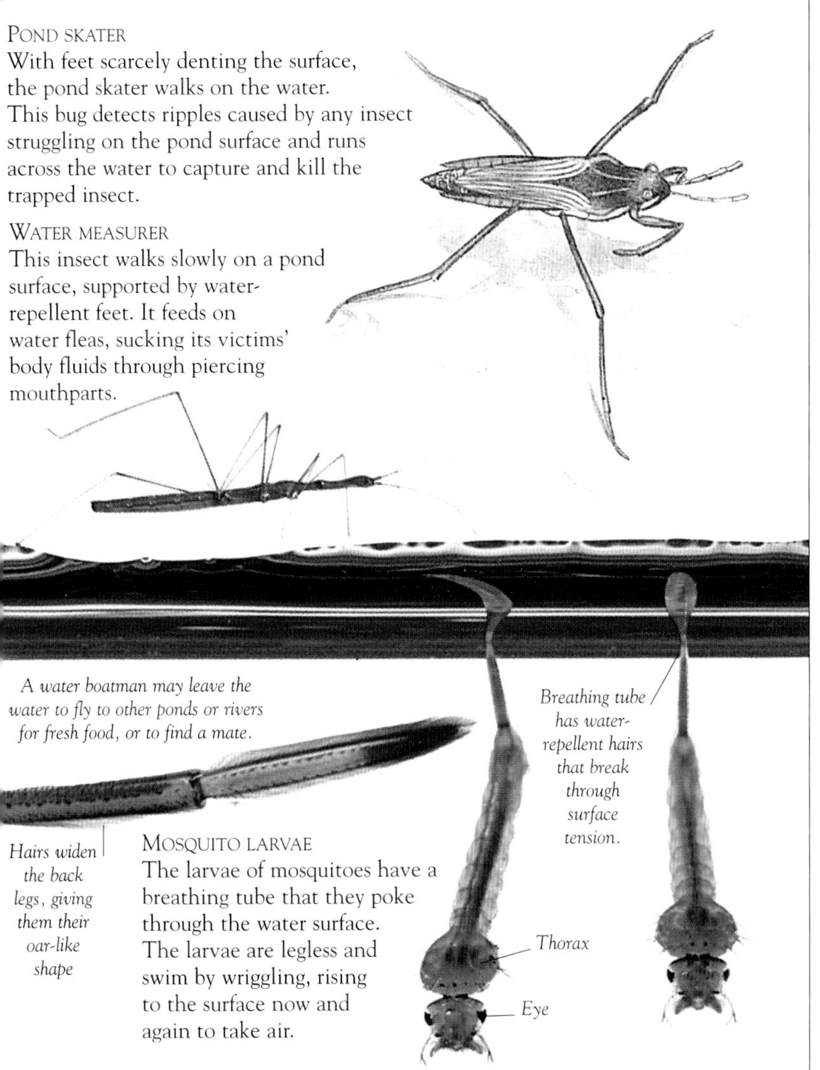
Breathing tube has water-repellent hairs that break through surface tension.
Thorax
Eye
Hairs widen the back legs, giving them their oar-like shape

Pond skater

With feet scarcely denting the surface, the pond skater walks on the water. This bug detects ripples caused by any insect struggling on the pond surface and runs across the water to capture and kill the trapped insect.

Water measurer

This insect walks slowly on a pond surface, supported by water-repellent feet. It feeds on water fleas, sucking its victims' body fluids through piercing mouthparts.

A water boatman may leave the water to fly to other ponds or rivers for fresh food, or to find a mate.

Mosquito larvae

The larvae of mosquitoes have a breathing tube that they poke through the water surface. The larvae are legless and swim by wriggling, rising to the surface now and again to take air.

UNDERWATER INSECTS

MANY OF THE insects that live underwater are carnivorous, either hunting their prey or scavenging. Some of these insects are fierce, sometimes killing prey larger than themselves.

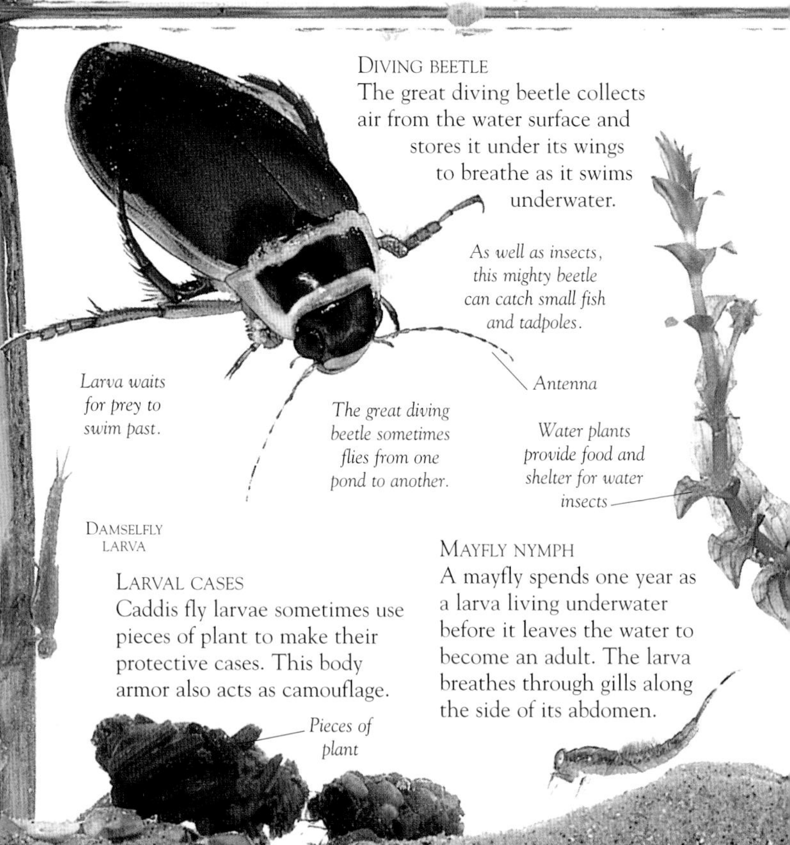

DIVING BEETLE
The great diving beetle collects air from the water surface and stores it under its wings to breathe as it swims underwater.

As well as insects, this mighty beetle can catch small fish and tadpoles.

Larva waits for prey to swim past.

The great diving beetle sometimes flies from one pond to another.

Water plants provide food and shelter for water insects

DAMSELFLY LARVA

LARVAL CASES
Caddis fly larvae sometimes use pieces of plant to make their protective cases. This body armor also acts as camouflage.

MAYFLY NYMPH
A mayfly spends one year as a larva living underwater before it leaves the water to become an adult. The larva breathes through gills along the side of its abdomen.

Jelly holds
eggs in place

ADULT DRAGONFLY

Male darter dragonflies perch on plants that emerge from the water. They fiercely attack and drive away any rival males of the same species, but attempt to mate with any female darter dragonfly that flies past.

DRAGONFLY EGGS

Darter dragonflies scatter their eggs in the water. The eggs are surrounded by a sticky, jellylike substance, and hatch after a few days.

BEETLE LARVA

The larva of the great diving beetle injects juices into prey with its jaws. The juices turn the prey's insides into liquid for the larva to suck out.

DRAGONFLY NYMPH

Dragonfly larvae breathe by pumping water in and out of their rear end, where they have complex gills.

TROPICAL FOREST

ABOUT THE HABITAT

INSECTS THRIVE in the humid heat and flourishing plant life of tropical forests. These forests have a complex structure that provides many habitats for insects. Trees vary in shape and size; vines and dead branches are everywhere, and thick leaf litter covers the ground.

ORCHID

ORCHIDS

Tropical forests contain a spectacular variety of plants – there are about 25,000 species of orchid alone. It is quite dark near the forest floor, and orchids are strongly scented to help insects find them.

EPIPHYTES

Many plants grow on the trunks and branches of trees where birds have wiped seeds from their beaks. These tree-dwelling plants, called epiphytes, provide extra habitats for insects.

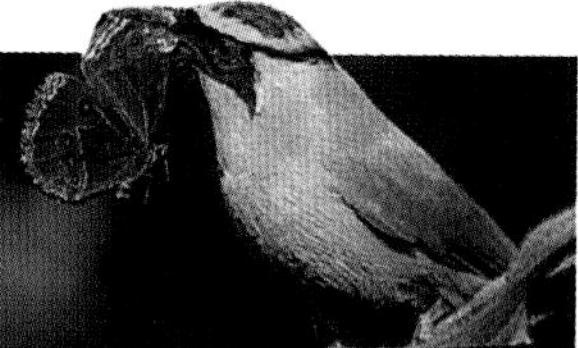

INSECT PREDATORS

A tropical forest is a rich habitat for birds as well as insects. Tropical birds feed on countless insects each day. This high rate of predation is a major reason for the evolution of camouflage and mimicry in tropical insects.

FRUITY NOURISHMENT

Some tropical butterflies live for several months. An important source of fuel for their continued activity is rotting fruit and dung on the forest floor. This gives them not only sugars for energy, but also amino acids and vitamins to stay healthy.

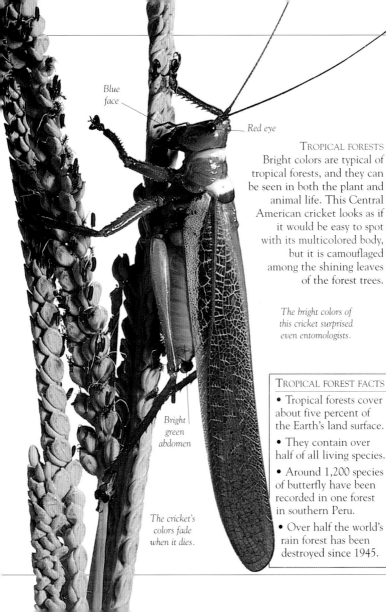

Tropical forests

Bright colors are typical of tropical forests, and they can be seen in both the plant and animal life. This Central American cricket looks as if it would be easy to spot with its multicolored body, but it is camouflaged among the shining leaves of the forest trees.

The bright colors of this cricket surprised even entomologists.

The cricket's colors fade when it dies.

Tropical forest facts

- Tropical forests cover about five percent of the Earth's land surface.
- They contain over half of all living species.
- Around 1,200 species of butterfly have been recorded in one forest in southern Peru.
- Over half the world's rain forest has been destroyed since 1945.

IN THE CANOPY

THERE IS WARMTH, light, and plenty of food to eat in the canopy of tropical trees. The canopy provides living space for thousands of insect species. In one day, 3,000 different species were collected from a single tree in a forest in Borneo.

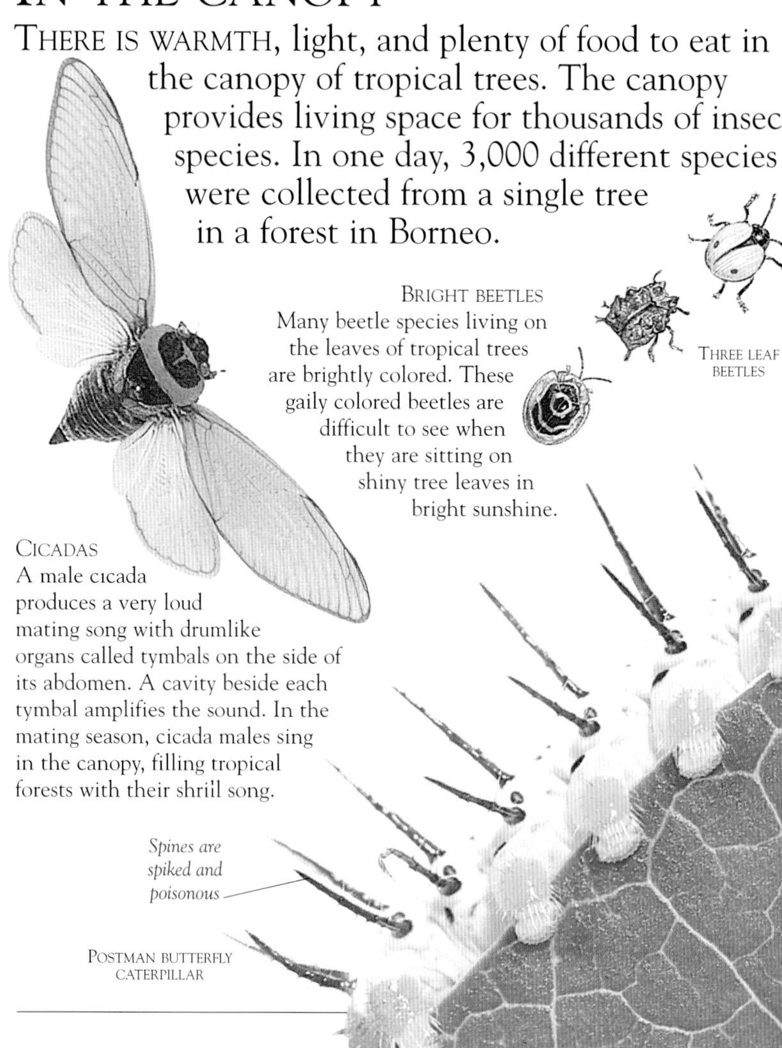
Spines are spiked and poisonous

BRIGHT BEETLES
Many beetle species living on the leaves of tropical trees are brightly colored. These gaily colored beetles are difficult to see when they are sitting on shiny tree leaves in bright sunshine.

THREE LEAF BEETLES

CICADAS
A male cicada produces a very loud mating song with drumlike organs called tymbals on the side of its abdomen. A cavity beside each tymbal amplifies the sound. In the mating season, cicada males sing in the canopy, filling tropical forests with their shrill song.

POSTMAN BUTTERFLY CATERPILLAR

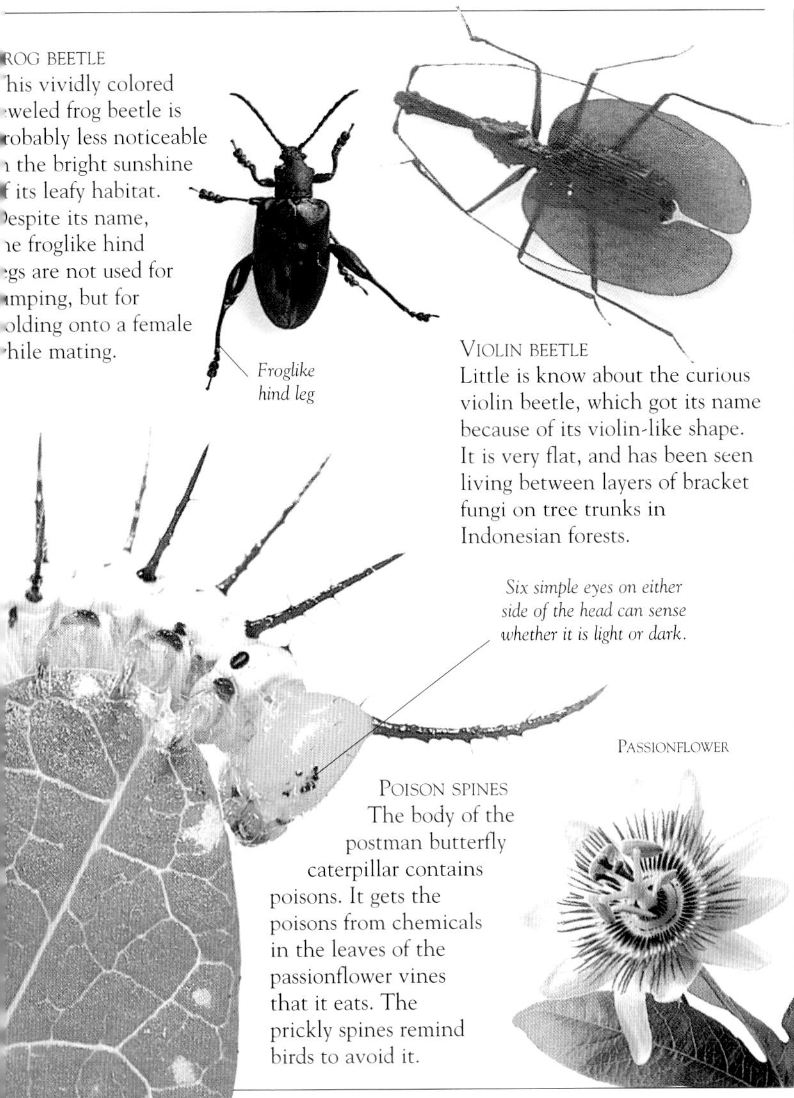
Froglike hind leg
Six simple eyes on either side of the head can sense whether it is light or dark.

ROG BEETLE
'his vividly colored :weled frog beetle is robably less noticeable ı the bright sunshine f its leafy habitat.)espite its name, ıe froglike hind :gs are not used for ımping, but for olding onto a female 'hile mating.

VIOLIN BEETLE
Little is know about the curious violin beetle, which got its name because of its violin-like shape. It is very flat, and has been seen living between layers of bracket fungi on tree trunks in Indonesian forests.

PASSIONFLOWER

POISON SPINES
The body of the postman butterfly caterpillar contains poisons. It gets the poisons from chemicals in the leaves of the passionflower vines that it eats. The prickly spines remind birds to avoid it.

NESTS IN THE CANOPY

WITH SO MANY insects feeding in the forest canopy, it is not surprising that the insect-eating ants and wasps build their nests there. But these ants and wasps are in turn hunted by mammals and lizards, so their nests must give protection.

Nest is m
of paper-l
materia

GREEN WEAVER ANTS

Each green weaver ant colony has several nests made of leaves. To make a nest, the ants join forces to pull leaves together and sew the edges. They sew using silk that the larvae produce when they are squeezed by the adult ants. These carnivorous ants hunt through the tree canopy, catching other insects and carrying the prey in pieces back to the ants' nests.

WASP NESTS

Each wasp species makes a different type of nest. This ne
from South America has beer
cut in half to reveal the "floor
that house the larvae. There i
one small opening at the bott
where the wasps defend the n
from invading ants.

Ants pulling leaves together

This nest hangs from a branch of a tree

There may be half a million ants in one weaver ant colony.

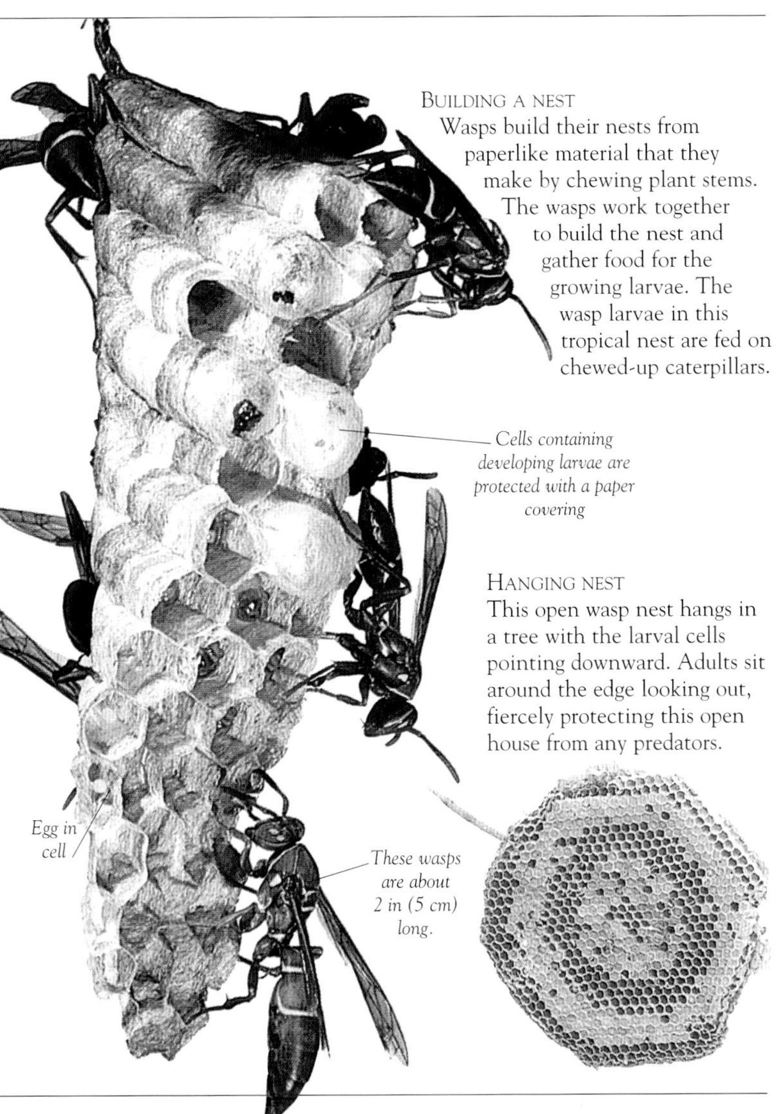
Cells containing developing larvae are protected with a paper covering
Egg in cell
These wasps are about 2 in (5 cm) long.

BUILDING A NEST

Wasps build their nests from paperlike material that they make by chewing plant stems. The wasps work together to build the nest and gather food for the growing larvae. The wasp larvae in this tropical nest are fed on chewed-up caterpillars.

HANGING NEST

This open wasp nest hangs in a tree with the larval cells pointing downward. Adults sit around the edge looking out, fiercely protecting this open house from any predators.

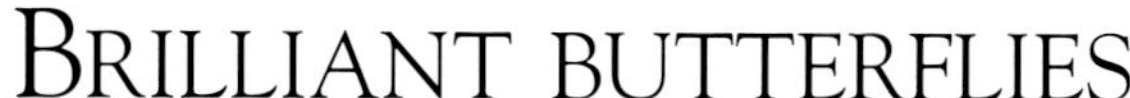

BRILLIANT BUTTERFLIES

MANY TROPICAL butterflies are large and brilliantly colored, which ought to make it easy for predators to catch them. But they fly rapidly and erratically, flash their bright colors in the sun, and then seem to disappear, darting into the deep shade of the forest.

BLUE MORPHO

The iridescent blue of South American morpho butterflies is so vivid it can be seen from a great distance. But its underwings are a muddy brown for camouflage when feeding on the ground.

SOUTHEAST ASIAN MOTH

The vivid colors of this Southeast Asian moth show that some day-flying moths can be as colorful as butterflies. The bright colors warn predators that this moth is poisonous.

NERO BUTTERFLY

The bright yellow Nero butterfly drinks from streams and puddles near mammal dung. This habit is common in butterflies of tropical forests. It supplies them with nutrients that are not available in flowers.

Tops of
wings are
bright and
colorful

POSTMAN BUTTERFLY
Brightly colored and slow-flying, the postman butterfly is poisonous. Birds quickly learn to avoid it. At night, groups of postman butterflies often sleep together on branches.

BIRDWING BUTTERFLIES
The males of Southeast Asian birdwing butterflies differ in size, color, and behaviour from the females. The brightly colored males sometimes fly near the ground, but the larger brownish females remain in the treetops.

FEMALE BIRDWING

MALE BIRDWING

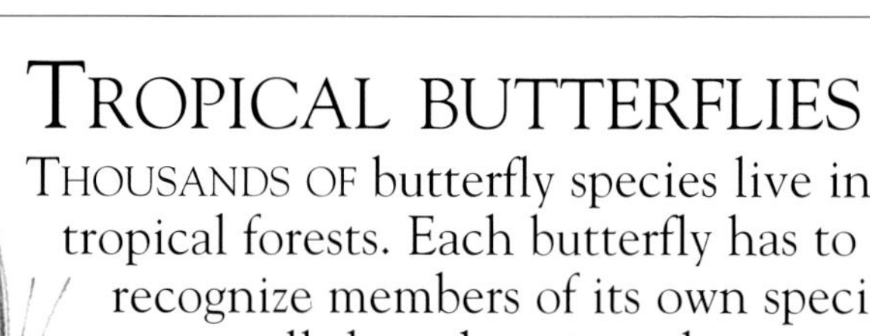

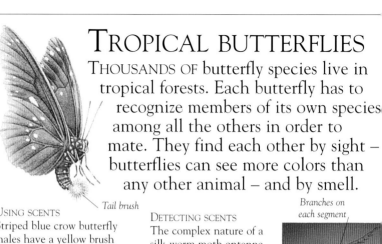

TROPICAL BUTTERFLIES

THOUSANDS OF butterfly species live in tropical forests. Each butterfly has to recognize members of its own species among all the others in order to mate. They find each other by sight – butterflies can see more colors than any other animal – and by smell.

Tail brush

USING SCENTS

Striped blue crow butterfly males have a yellow brush at the end of their abdomen. When a male has found a female, he uses his brush to dust scented scales on her. The arousing scent encourages the female to mate with him.

DETECTING SCENTS

The complex nature of a silk-worm moth antenna can be seen when viewed at high magnification. It is divided into segments, and each bears two branches. The branches increase the antenna's surface area making it more sensitive.

Branches on each segment

Scent chemicals stimulate nerves in the silkmoth's antennae.

SITTING TOGETHER

At sunny spots in the forest, butterflies gather at muddy puddles to drink water and salts. Butterflies of the same species usually sit together, so that white-colored species form one group, blue another, and so on.

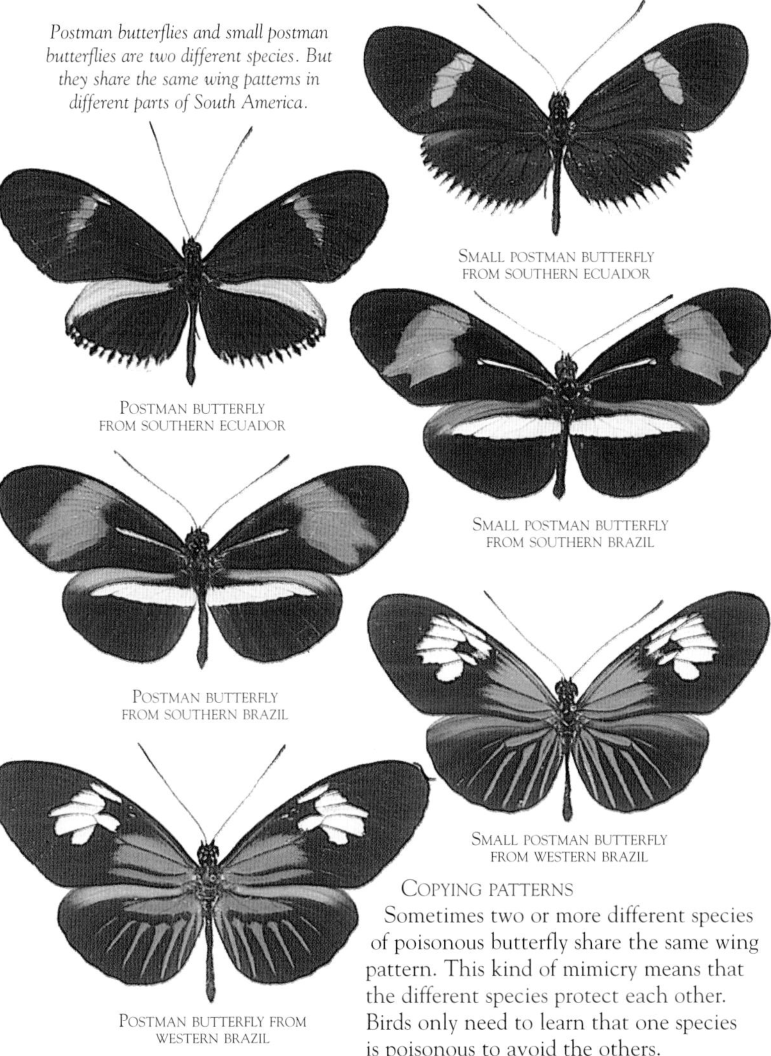

Postman butterflies and small postman butterflies are two different species. But they share the same wing patterns in different parts of South America.

SMALL POSTMAN BUTTERFLY FROM SOUTHERN ECUADOR

POSTMAN BUTTERFLY FROM SOUTHERN ECUADOR

SMALL POSTMAN BUTTERFLY FROM SOUTHERN BRAZIL

POSTMAN BUTTERFLY FROM SOUTHERN BRAZIL

SMALL POSTMAN BUTTERFLY FROM WESTERN BRAZIL

POSTMAN BUTTERFLY FROM WESTERN BRAZIL

COPYING PATTERNS

Sometimes two or more different species of poisonous butterfly share the same wing pattern. This kind of mimicry means that the different species protect each other. Birds only need to learn that one species is poisonous to avoid the others.

HORNED BEETLES

WITH SO MANY millions of insects in tropical forests, individuals must sometimes compete for the best living space in which to mate and lay eggs. Horned beetles have horns that they use as weapons in battle. A male may lock horns with other males to claim a good territory, and then attract females to him.

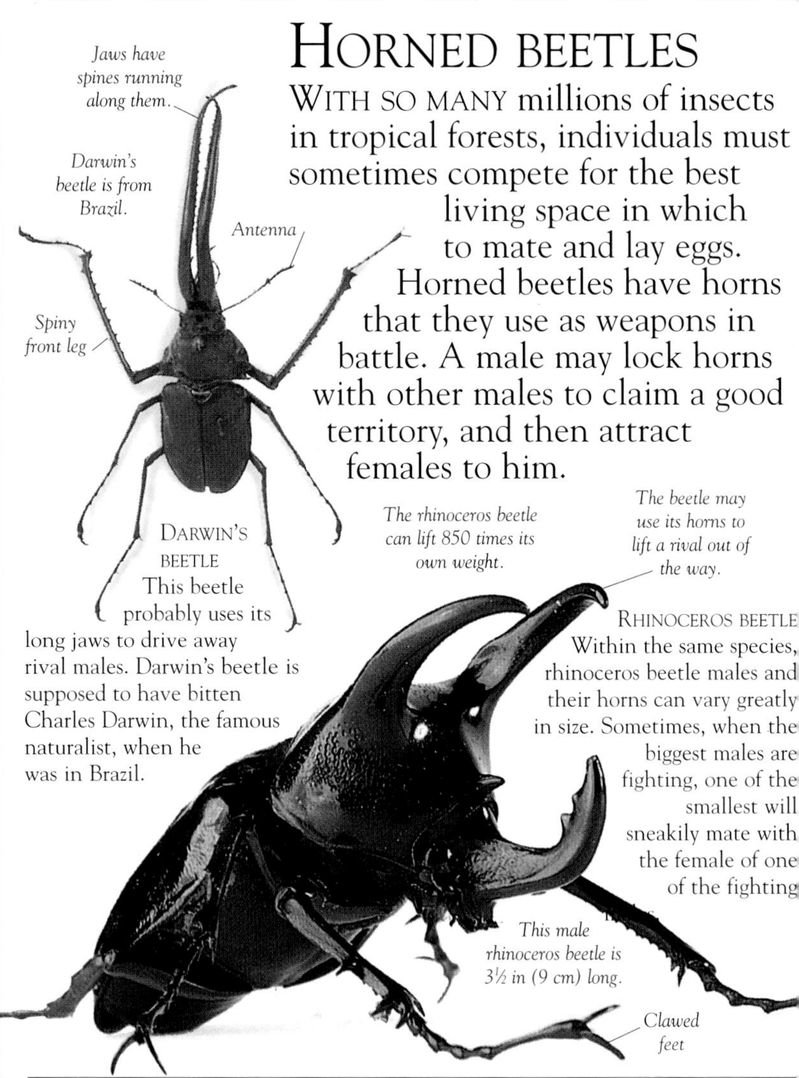
Jaws have spines running along them.
Darwin's beetle is from Brazil.
Antenna
Spiny front leg
The rhinoceros beetle can lift 850 times its own weight.
The beetle may use its horns to lift a rival out of the way.
This male rhinoceros beetle is 3½ in (9 cm) long.
Clawed feet

DARWIN'S BEETLE
This beetle probably uses its long jaws to drive away rival males. Darwin's beetle is supposed to have bitten Charles Darwin, the famous naturalist, when he was in Brazil.

RHINOCEROS BEETLE
Within the same species, rhinoceros beetle males and their horns can vary greatly in size. Sometimes, when the biggest males are fighting, one of the smallest will sneakily mate with the female of one of the fighting

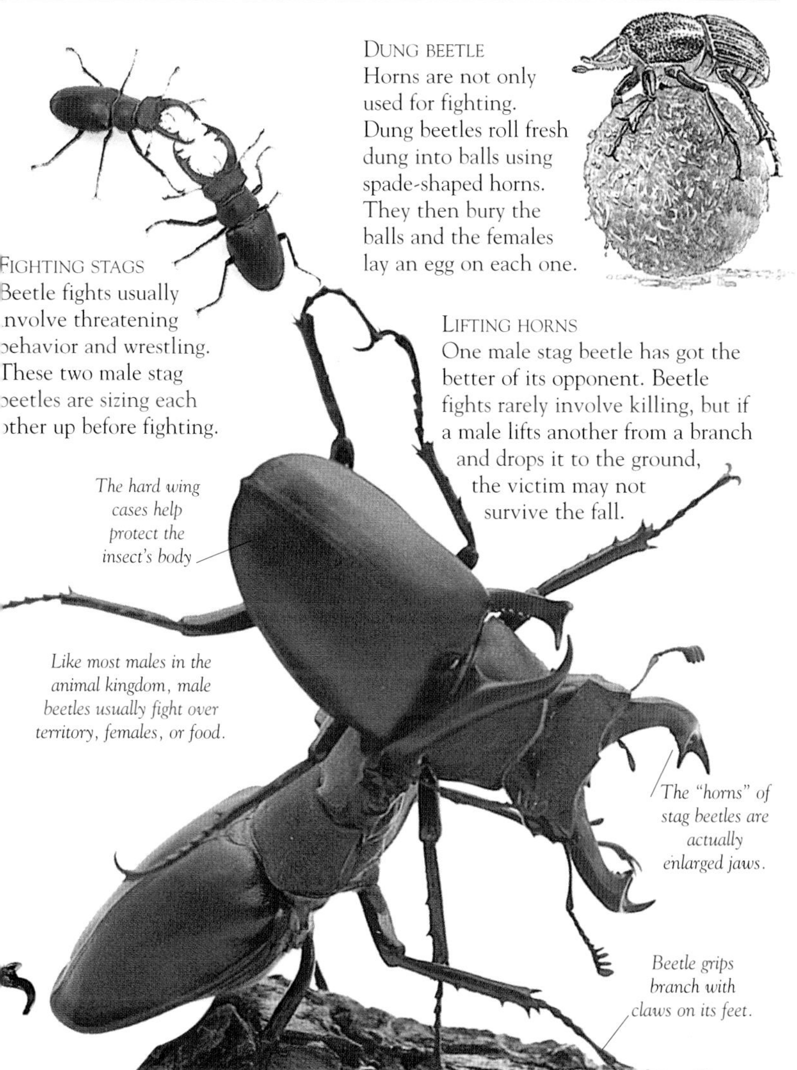

Dung beetle

Horns are not only used for fighting. Dung beetles roll fresh dung into balls using spade-shaped horns. They then bury the balls and the females lay an egg on each one.

Fighting stags

Beetle fights usually involve threatening behavior and wrestling. These two male stag beetles are sizing each other up before fighting.

Lifting horns

One male stag beetle has got the better of its opponent. Beetle fights rarely involve killing, but if a male lifts another from a branch and drops it to the ground, the victim may not survive the fall.

The hard wing cases help protect the insect's body

Like most males in the animal kingdom, male beetles usually fight over territory, females, or food.

The "horns" of stag beetles are actually enlarged jaws.

Beetle grips branch with claws on its feet.

THE LARGEST INSECTS

SOME OF THE largest insects live in tropical forests, where the warm temperatures and abundance of food allow them to grow quickly. But insects cannot grow very large, since their simple breathing system could not get oxygen around a large body. Big insects would also be easy prey for birds and mammals.

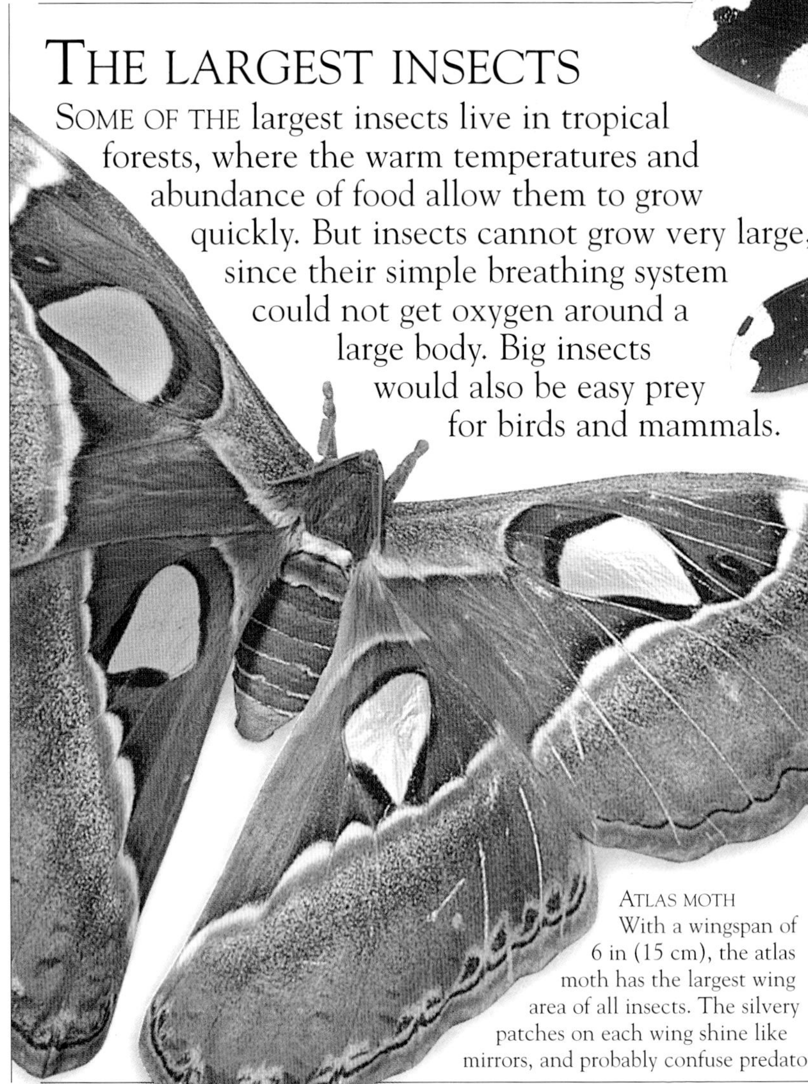

ATLAS MOTH
With a wingspan of 6 in (15 cm), the atlas moth has the largest wing area of all insects. The silvery patches on each wing shine like mirrors, and probably confuse predator

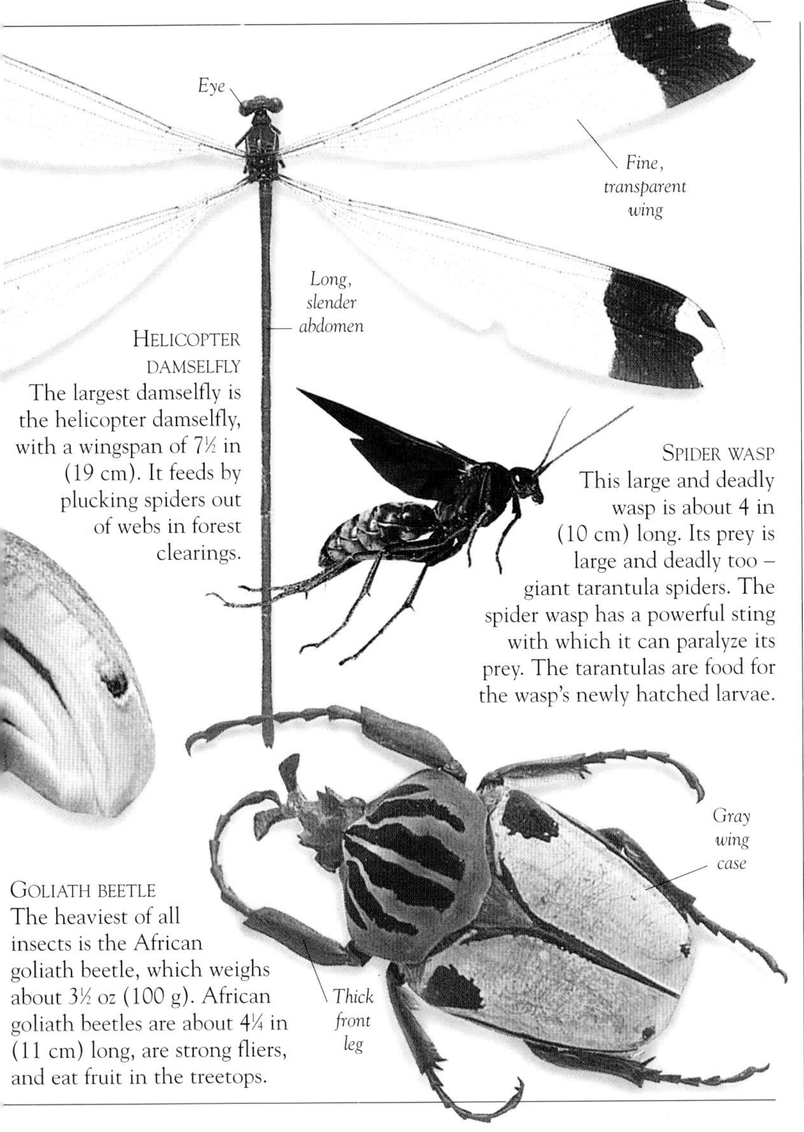

HELICOPTER DAMSELFLY
The largest damselfly is the helicopter damselfly, with a wingspan of 7½ in (19 cm). It feeds by plucking spiders out of webs in forest clearings.

SPIDER WASP
This large and deadly wasp is about 4 in (10 cm) long. Its prey is large and deadly too – giant tarantula spiders. The spider wasp has a powerful sting with which it can paralyze its prey. The tarantulas are food for the wasp's newly hatched larvae.

GOLIATH BEETLE
The heaviest of all insects is the African goliath beetle, which weighs about 3½ oz (100 g). African goliath beetles are about 4¼ in (11 cm) long, are strong fliers, and eat fruit in the treetops.

STICK AND LEAF INSECTS

A TROPICAL FOREST is alive with animals, most of which eat insects. To survive, insects adopt many strategies. Stick and leaf insects hide from predators by keeping still and resembling their background of leaves and sticks.

STICK INSECTS
Some stick insects are slender, brown, or green, just like the twigs and leaf stalks they sit on. Other species are shorter and fatter, with spines and other projections. These often look like curled dead leaves.

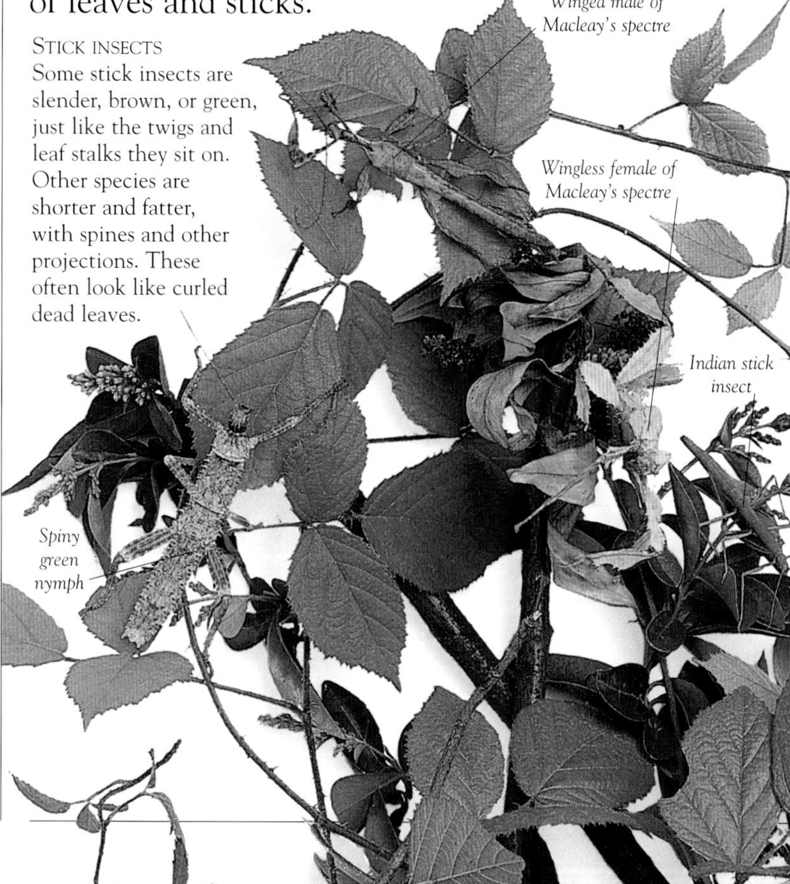

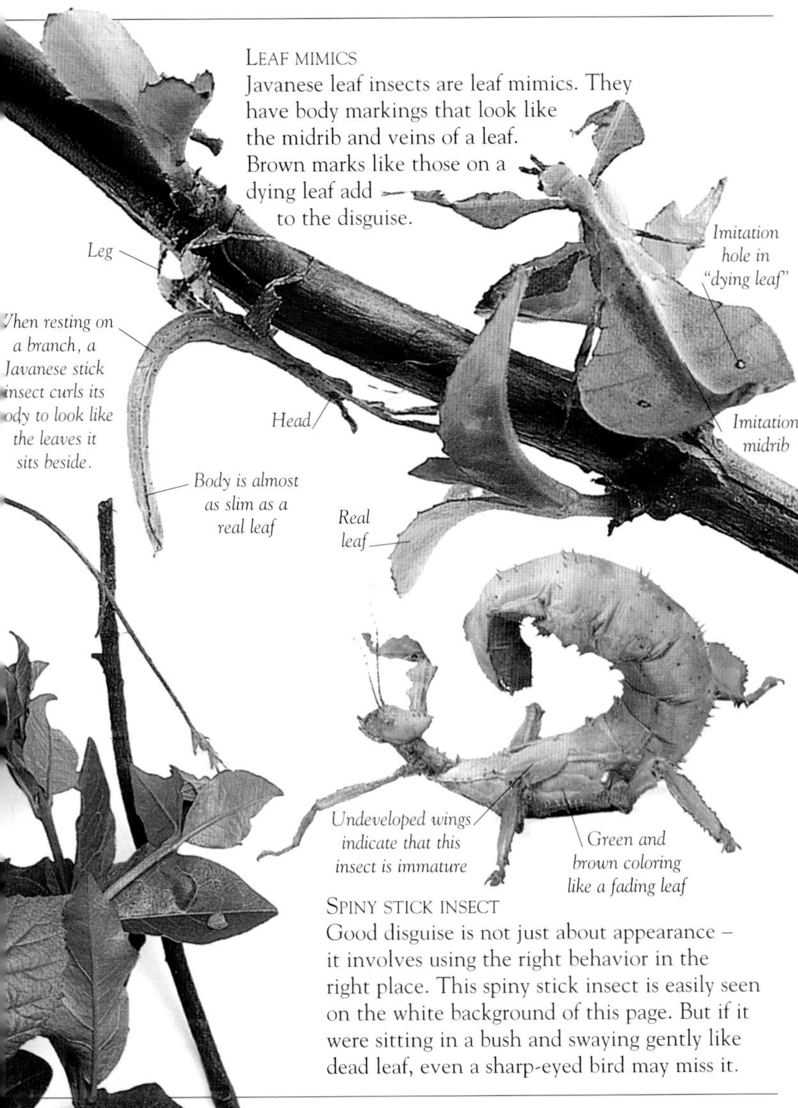
Leg
When resting on a branch, a Javanese stick insect curls its body to look like the leaves it sits beside.
Head
Body is almost as slim as a real leaf
Real leaf
Imitation hole in "dying leaf"
Imitation midrib
Undeveloped wings indicate that this insect is immature
Green and brown coloring like a fading leaf

LEAF MIMICS

Javanese leaf insects are leaf mimics. They have body markings that look like the midrib and veins of a leaf. Brown marks like those on a dying leaf add to the disguise.

SPINY STICK INSECT

Good disguise is not just about appearance – it involves using the right behavior in the right place. This spiny stick insect is easily seen on the white background of this page. But if it were sitting in a bush and swaying gently like dead leaf, even a sharp-eyed bird may miss it.

ARMIES ON THE GROUND

ANTS ARE THE dominant creatures of tropical forests. They live in colonies made up of any number from 20 individuals to many thousands. Ants are mostly carnivorous. Some species make slaves of other ant species by invading their nest and killing their queen.

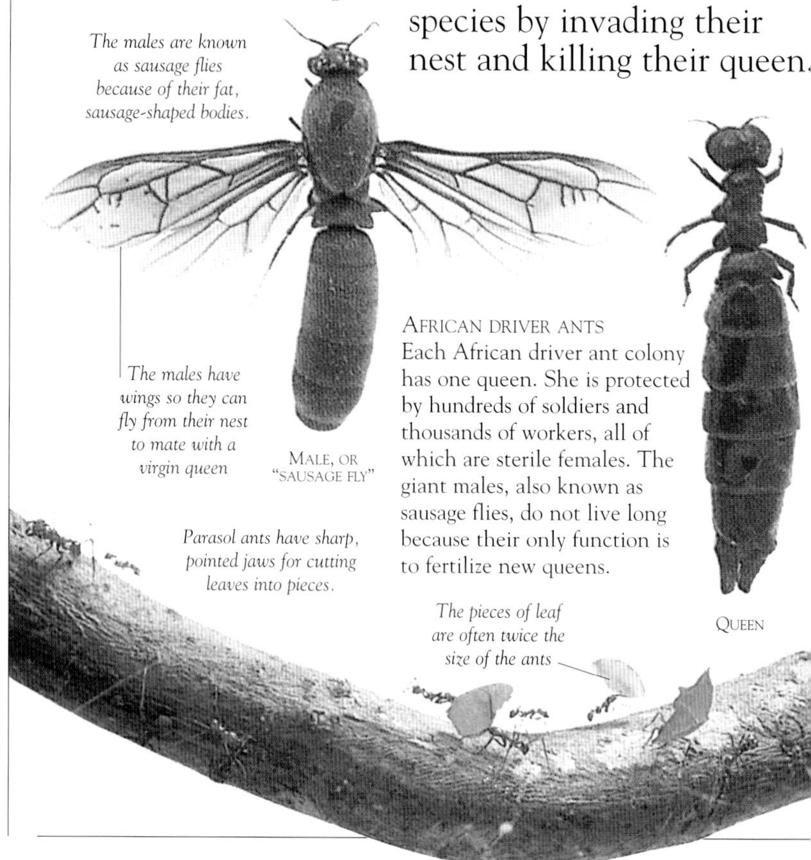

The males are known as sausage flies because of their fat, sausage-shaped bodies.

The males have wings so they can fly from their nest to mate with a virgin queen

MALE, OR "SAUSAGE FLY"

Parasol ants have sharp, pointed jaws for cutting leaves into pieces.

AFRICAN DRIVER ANTS
Each African driver ant colony has one queen. She is protected by hundreds of soldiers and thousands of workers, all of which are sterile females. The giant males, also known as sausage flies, do not live long because their only function is to fertilize new queens.

The pieces of leaf are often twice the size of the ants

QUEEN

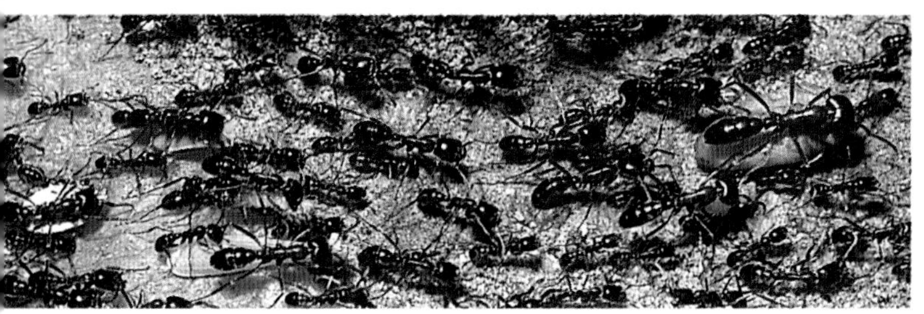

DRIVER ANTS MARCHING
These ants get their name from the way a colony sweeps through an area, catching all the insects it can find. They move their nests from place to place regularly, unlike most ants, which have a permanent nest and territory.

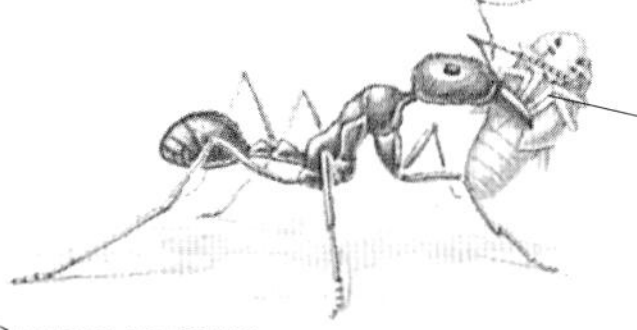

Beetle pupae are among the prey of driver ants

CARRYING PREY
Ants in a column collaborate to cut large insects they have caught into smaller pieces. This is so that they can carry their food back to the nest. Smaller prey can be carried whole.

ATTENTIVE SOLDIER
Driver ant soldiers have very large jaws. Often they can be seen standing beside a marching column of ants with their jaws wide open, waiting to attack intruders, such as parasitic flies.

Ant returning for more leaves

PARASOL ANTS
These South American ants are not carnivorous. They feed on fungus that they cultivate in huge underground nests. The fungus is grown on pieces of leaf that the ants bring to the nest.

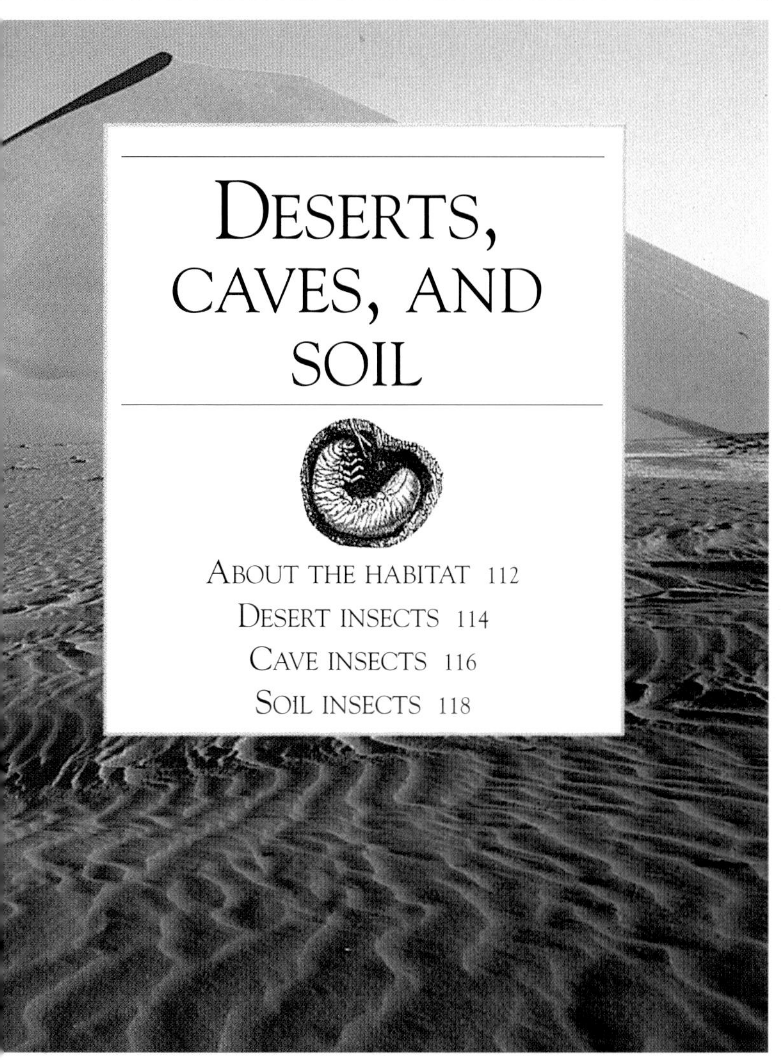

DESERTS, CAVES, AND SOIL

ABOUT THE HABITAT

SOME INSECTS flourish in habitats where it is difficult for living things to survive. Desert habitats, for example, lack water and have very high temperatures. Caves are dark and lack plant life for food. Life in soil makes communication, both by scent and sight, difficult for insects.

Tiger beetle larva has hooks on body to help it climb upward.

HIDING IN SOIL
Life in the soil is only a passing phase for some insect species. This tiger beetle larva hides underground by day. At night it waits in its vertical tunnel with its jaws projecting at the ground surface, and snatches passing insects to devour in its burrow.

CAVE DWELLER
This cockroach lives all its life in the dark. Like other cave creatures, it feeds on debris from the outside world. Bat dung, dead animals, and pieces of plants washed into the cave provide the cockroach with its nourishment.

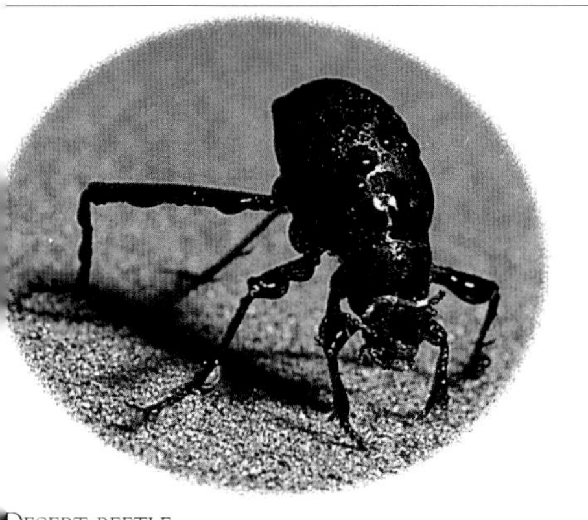

DESERT BEETLE
The lack of water in deserts means that insects have to find devious ways to obtain moisture. This darkling beetle lives in the Namib Desert where sea winds bring mists each night. The beetle holds its abdomen high to catch the moisture, which then runs down into its mouth.

DESERT HEAT
The hot and dry days in deserts can lead to rapid water loss and death for animals. Most living creatures hide under stones or in the sand to avoid drying out. These animals are active at night when it is much cooler.

DESERT FACTS

- The Sahara Desert spreads at a rate of 3 miles (5 km) per year.
- In deserts, the temperature may range from 90°F (30°C) in the day to below 32°F (0°C) at night.
- Caves are a nearly constant temperature throughout the year.
- 20% of the Earth's land surface is desert.

CACTUS FLOWER

DESERT PLANTS
Rain may not fall in a desert for months, or even years. Most desert plants store water so they can survive, and some desert animals rely on these plants for food. But many animals, including some insects, migrate in search of rain and the plant growth it produces.

DESERT INSECTS

HOT, DRY DESERTS are dangerous places in which to live. Animals often die from sunstroke and dehydrati (drying out). To prevent this, insects avoid the sun b staying in the shade or burrowing in the sand. Some insects have special methods of collecting water. Mar feed only at night because the surface of the sand is t hot for them to walk on during the day.

NAMIB DESERT BEETLE
Long legs keep the body of the Namib desert beetle off the hot sand. The larvae live in the sand, scavenging on detritus (organic debris), and complete their development in about six months. The adults live for several years.

DESERT LOCUSTS
Adult desert locusts fly in swarms to find fresh food. When there is enough food, they breed rapidly, and huge groups of wingless nymphs hop across the desert sand.

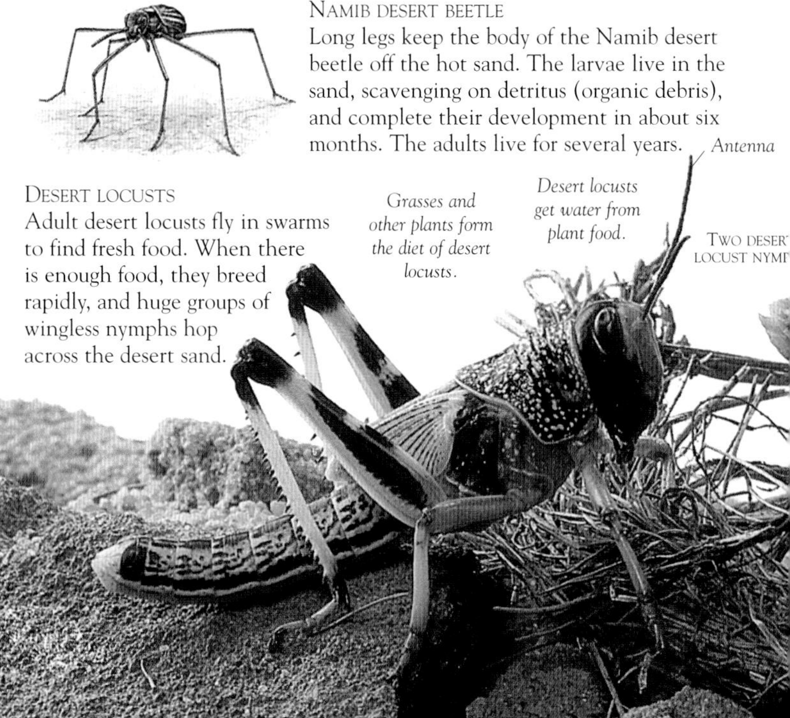
Antenna
Grasses and other plants form the diet of desert locusts.
Desert locusts get water from plant food.
TWO DESER
LOCUST NYMP

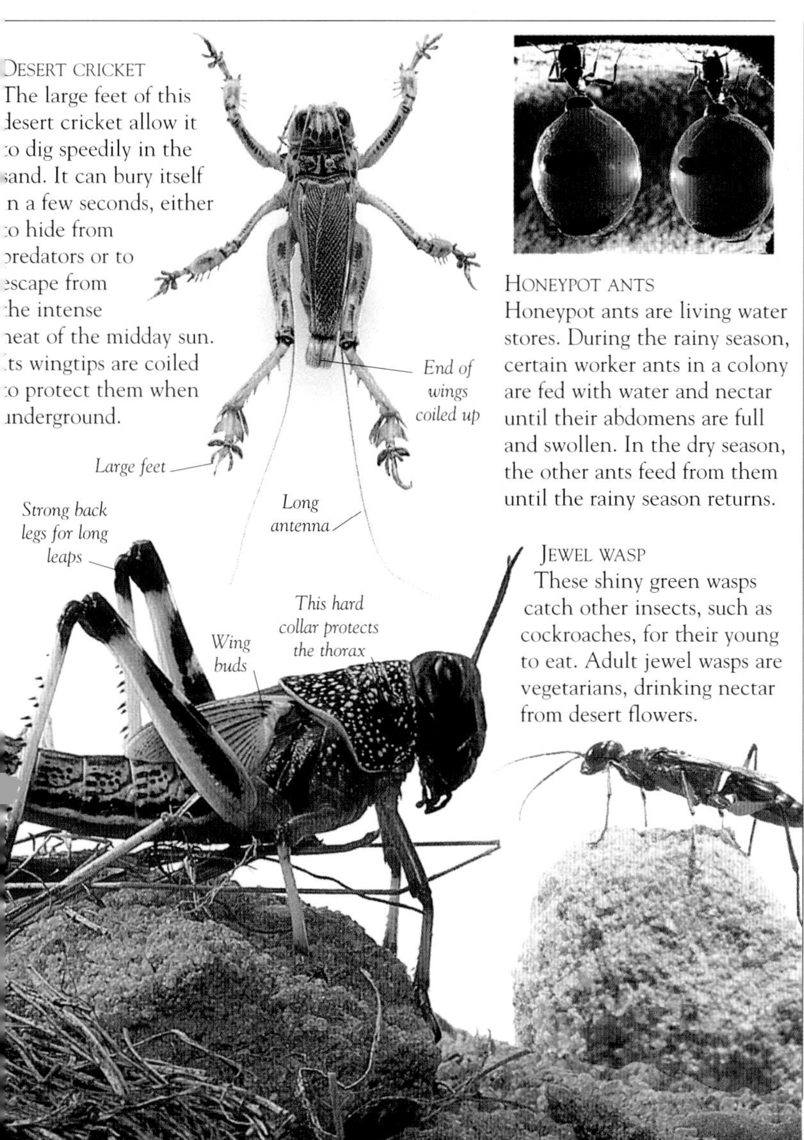

DESERT CRICKET

The large feet of this desert cricket allow it to dig speedily in the sand. It can bury itself in a few seconds, either to hide from predators or to escape from the intense heat of the midday sun. Its wingtips are coiled to protect them when underground.

HONEYPOT ANTS

Honeypot ants are living water stores. During the rainy season, certain worker ants in a colony are fed with water and nectar until their abdomens are full and swollen. In the dry season, the other ants feed from them until the rainy season returns.

JEWEL WASP

These shiny green wasps catch other insects, such as cockroaches, for their young to eat. Adult jewel wasps are vegetarians, drinking nectar from desert flowers.

CAVE INSECTS

ALL LIFE DEPENDS on the sun's energy. Plants change sunlight into food by a process called photosynthesis. In dark, sunless caves, nothing grows, and cave-dwelling insects must find food from outside. This food is sometimes washed in on floods, or dropped by bats and birds.

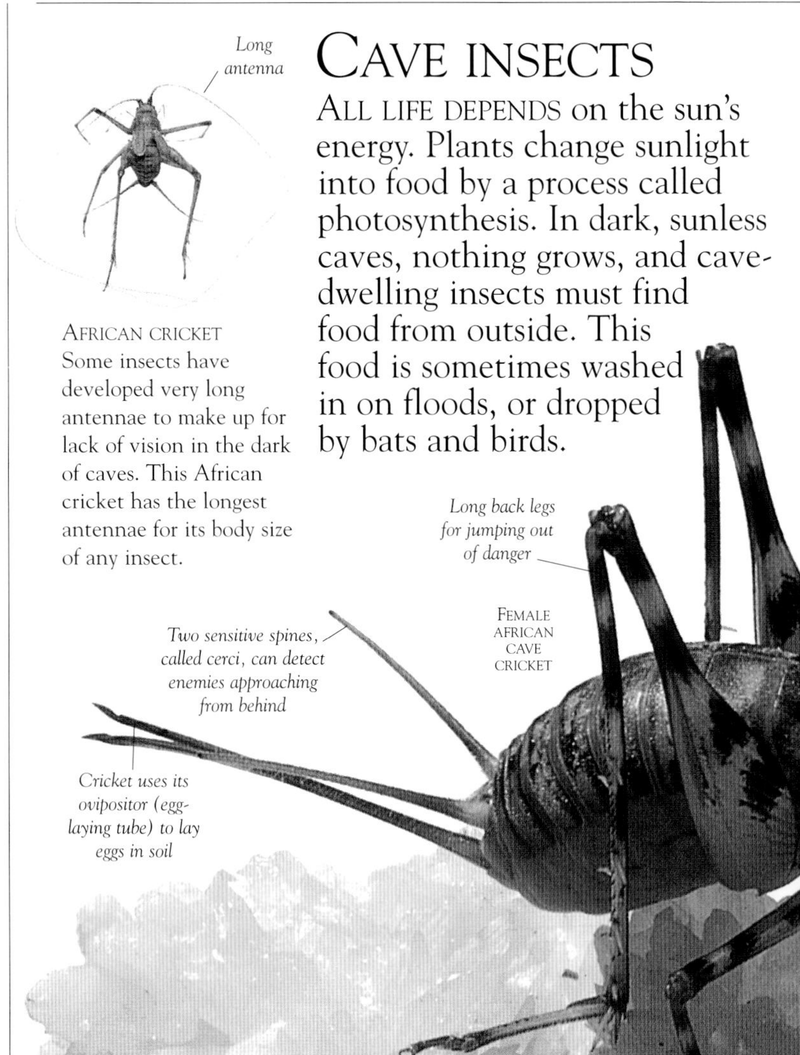
Long antenna
Long back legs for jumping out of danger
FEMALE AFRICAN CAVE CRICKET
Two sensitive spines, called cerci, can detect enemies approaching from behind
Cricket uses its ovipositor (egg-laying tube) to lay eggs in soil

AFRICAN CRICKET
Some insects have developed very long antennae to make up for lack of vision in the dark of caves. This African cricket has the longest antennae for its body size of any insect.

Dark underside of wings camouflages the peacock butterfly as it hibernates
Top of wings are brightly colored.
PEACOCK BUTTERFLY
SURINAM COCKROACH
Very long, sensitive antennae

PEACOCK BUTTERFLY
For some insects, caves provide shelter from the uncomfortable weather conditions. During cold northern winters, a cave is an ideal place for peacock butterflies to hibernate.

CAVE CRICKET
Crickets living in caves have smaller eyes and paler bodies than crickets living in sunlight. Cave crickets breed all year because the temperature and the amount of food in the cave stay constant.

COCKROACH
Cave-dwelling cockroaches eat bat droppings and bat carcasses, as well as mites and fungi. Cockroaches often eat each other, too. Caves make an ideal home for cockroaches since they love dark, damp places.

SOIL INSECTS

WHEN PLANTS and animals die, their remains usually get absorbed into the soil. Insects that live in soil are among the most important creatures on Earth because they help to recycle these remains, releasing their nutrients and so helping new crops and forests to grow. Soil insects are also an important food for many mammals and birds.

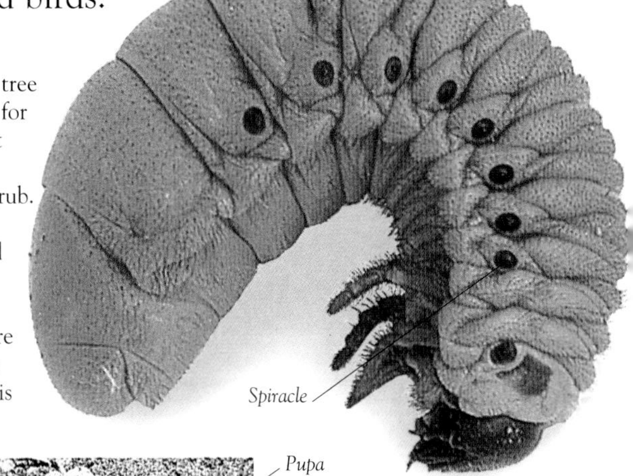

LAMELLICORN BEETLE GRUB

BEETLE LARVA
Roots and decaying tree trunks provide food for many types of insect larva, such as this lamellicorn beetle grub. The grub breathes through holes called spiracles, which are along the side of its body. Although there is not very much air underground, there is enough for insects.

Pupa

GOOD HABITAT
Living in soil has advantages. Insect are unlikely to dehydrate, and there is plenty of food in plant roots and decaying plants. This spurge hawk-moth pupa has sharp plates on its abdomen that help it climb to the surface just before the adult emerges

Legs for digging

Mole crickets are named after the mammals called moles. Like moles, these crickets spend their lives underground. They have small eyes and front legs modified for digging. Because they eat grass roots, they can be garden pests.

Leaf litter

Fallen leaves rotting into the ground contain nutrients that nourish the soil. Many insects, such as fly maggots and springtails, feed on this litter, and the larva of the devil's coach horse beetle feeds on these insects.

Click beetle larva

Wireworms get their name from their wiry appearance. They are not worms, however, but the larvae of click beetles. They crawl through the soil, feeding on the roots of plants.

Cicada grub

Some cicada nymphs live underground for many years before turning into adults. The nymphs suck sap from plant roots and have enlarged front legs for tunneling through the soil.

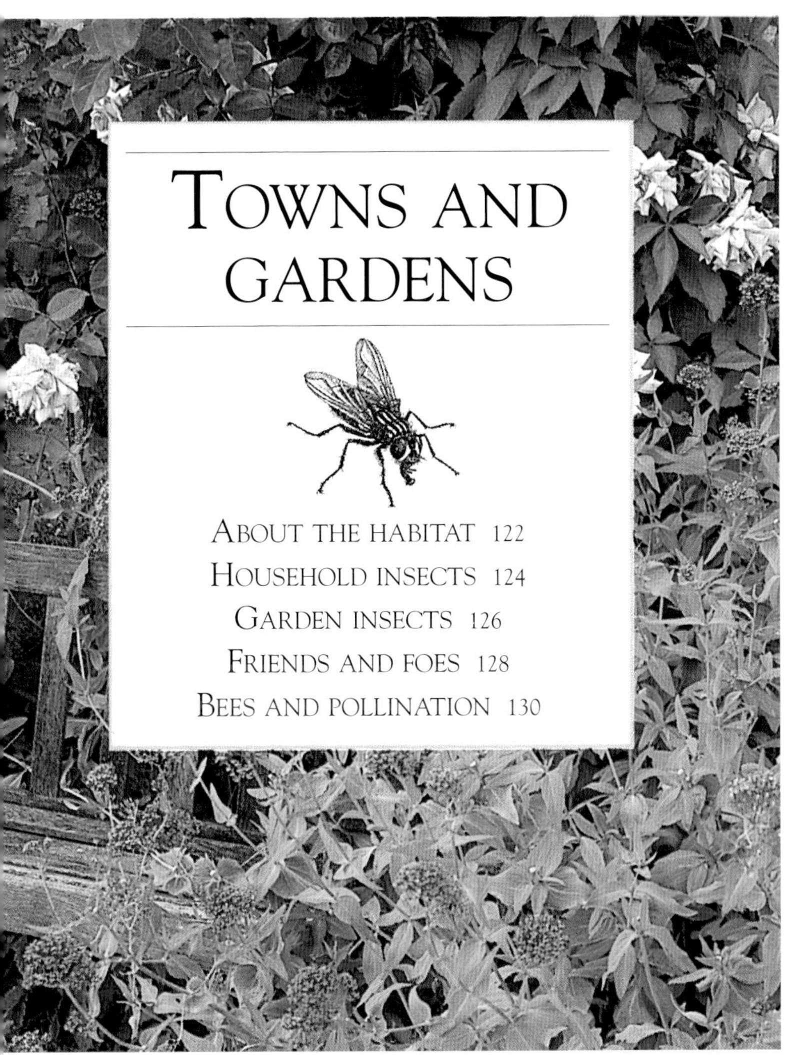

TOWNS AND GARDENS

ABOUT THE HABITAT

SINCE INSECTS HAVE managed to make homes for themselves in practically every natural habitat, it is no surprising that they have turned human habitats into their homes, too. Insects live in our houses, feeding in our furniture, clothes, foodstores, and garbage dumps. Our gardens and farms are also teeming with insect life, nourished by the abundance of flowers and vegetables.

Colorado beetle

Leaves of potato plant

Potato

POTATO PESTS
When potatoes were brought to Europe from South America, the Colorado beetle came with them. This insect eats potato plant leaves and can cause great damage to crops.

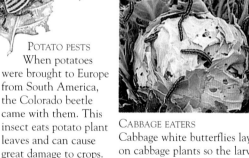

CABBAGE EATERS
Cabbage white butterflies lay eggs on cabbage plants so the larvae can eat the leaves. Farms provide acres of cabbages, and the butterflies become pests since they breed at an unnaturally high rate because of the abundance of food.

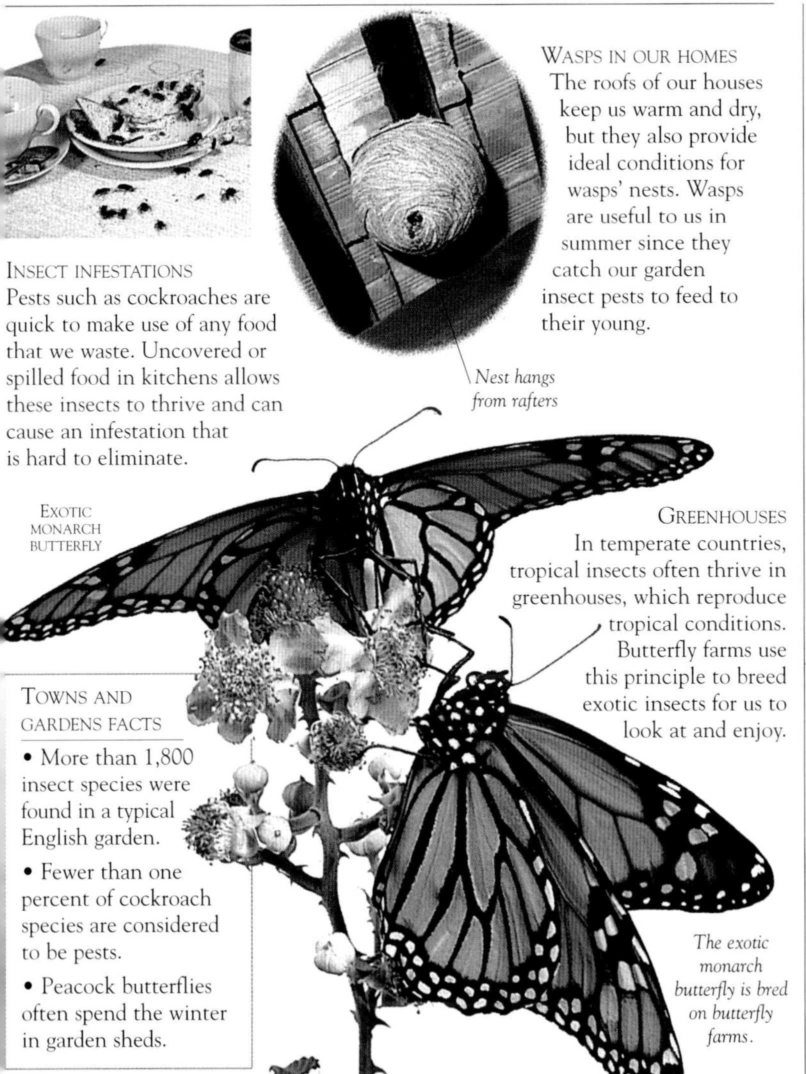

Wasps in our homes

The roofs of our houses keep us warm and dry, but they also provide ideal conditions for wasps' nests. Wasps are useful to us in summer since they catch our garden insect pests to feed to their young.

Nest hangs from rafters

Insect infestations

Pests such as cockroaches are quick to make use of any food that we waste. Uncovered or spilled food in kitchens allows these insects to thrive and can cause an infestation that is hard to eliminate.

Exotic monarch butterfly

Greenhouses

In temperate countries, tropical insects often thrive in greenhouses, which reproduce tropical conditions. Butterfly farms use this principle to breed exotic insects for us to look at and enjoy.

Towns and gardens facts

- More than 1,800 insect species were found in a typical English garden.
- Fewer than one percent of cockroach species are considered to be pests.
- Peacock butterflies often spend the winter in garden sheds.

The exotic monarch butterfly is bred on butterfly farms.

Household insects

SINCE PREHISTORIC times, insects have lived in human homes, attracted by warmth, shelter, and food. These insects eat our food, our furniture, and some even eat our carpets. Parasitic insects also live in our homes, feeding on the human inhabitants.

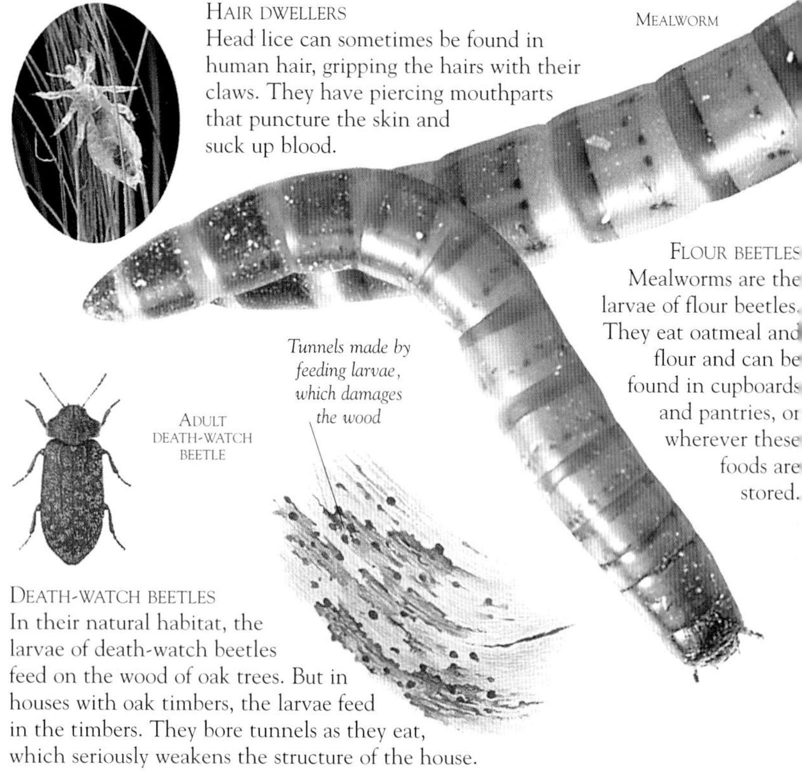

Tunnels made by feeding larvae, which damages the wood

Hair dwellers

Head lice can sometimes be found in human hair, gripping the hairs with their claws. They have piercing mouthparts that puncture the skin and suck up blood.

Flour beetles

Mealworms are the larvae of flour beetles. They eat oatmeal and flour and can be found in cupboards and pantries, or wherever these foods are stored.

Death-watch beetles

In their natural habitat, the larvae of death-watch beetles feed on the wood of oak trees. But in houses with oak timbers, the larvae feed in the timbers. They bore tunnels as they eat, which seriously weakens the structure of the house.

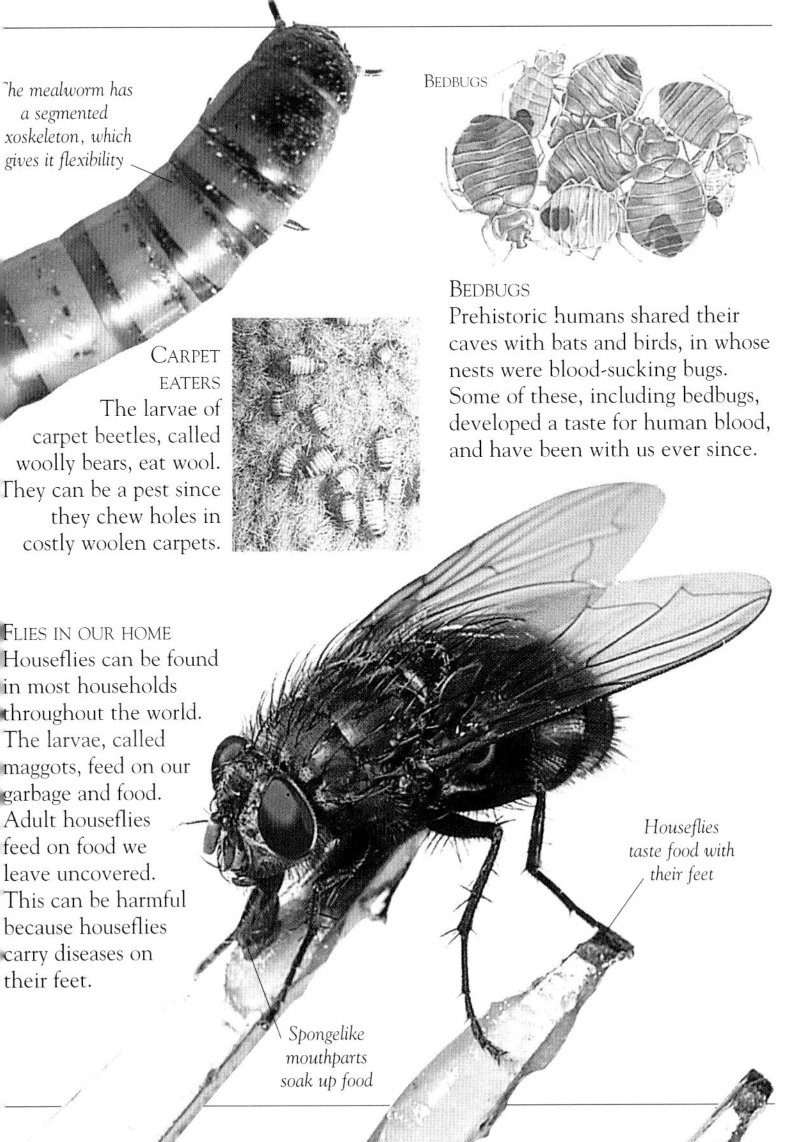

'he mealworm has a segmented xoskeleton, which gives it flexibility

CARPET EATERS
The larvae of carpet beetles, called woolly bears, eat wool. They can be a pest since they chew holes in costly woolen carpets.

BEDBUGS
Prehistoric humans shared their caves with bats and birds, in whose nests were blood-sucking bugs. Some of these, including bedbugs, developed a taste for human blood, and have been with us ever since.

FLIES IN OUR HOME
Houseflies can be found in most households throughout the world. The larvae, called maggots, feed on our garbage and food. Adult houseflies feed on food we leave uncovered. This can be harmful because houseflies carry diseases on their feet.

Houseflies taste food with their feet

Spongelike mouthparts soak up food

GARDEN INSECTS

A GARDEN IS a good place to watch and study insects. Many different insects are attracted into gardens to feed on the flowers, vegetables, and other plants. Som predatory insects come to eat the plant-eating insects. But most garden insects a just tourists, feeding on flower nectar as they pass through.

DEVIL BEETLES
Devil's coach horse beetles hunt at night, scouring the garden for insects to eat. These large beetles are common in compost heaps, scurrying away from the daylight when the compost is turned.

GARDENER'S FRIENDS
Hoverflies hover in front of flowers on hot, sunny days as they feed on nectar. They are particularly attracted to thistle flowers. Hoverfly larvae are the gardener's friends, feeding voraciously on plant-damaging aphids.

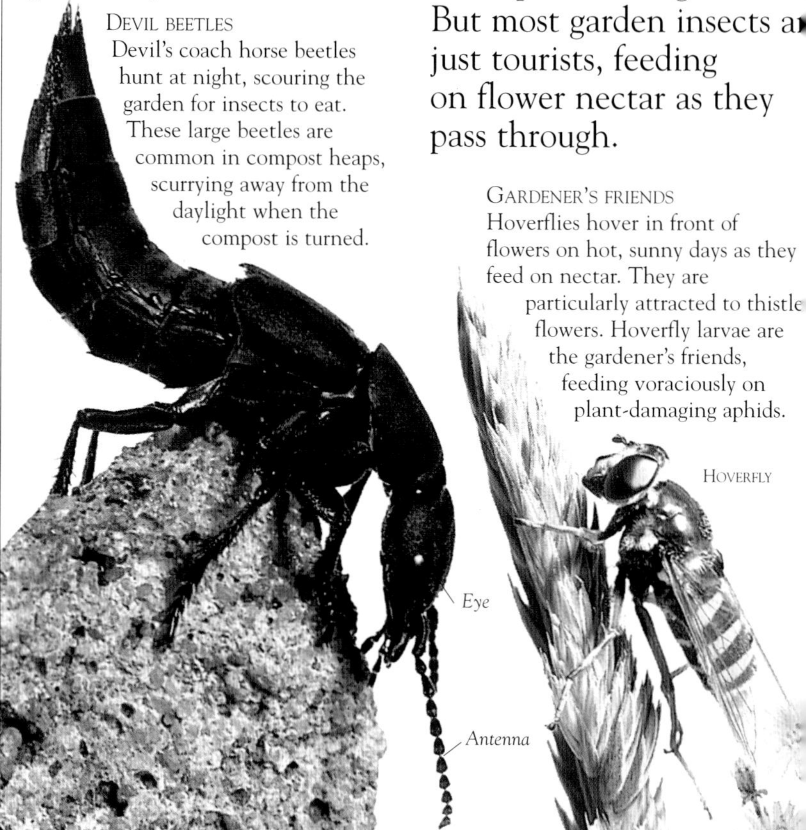

HAWK-MOTH

The caterpillars of hawk-moths can be recognized by their short, erect "tail." Most adult hawk-moths fly at night, hovering in front of flowers to gather nectar with their long tongues.

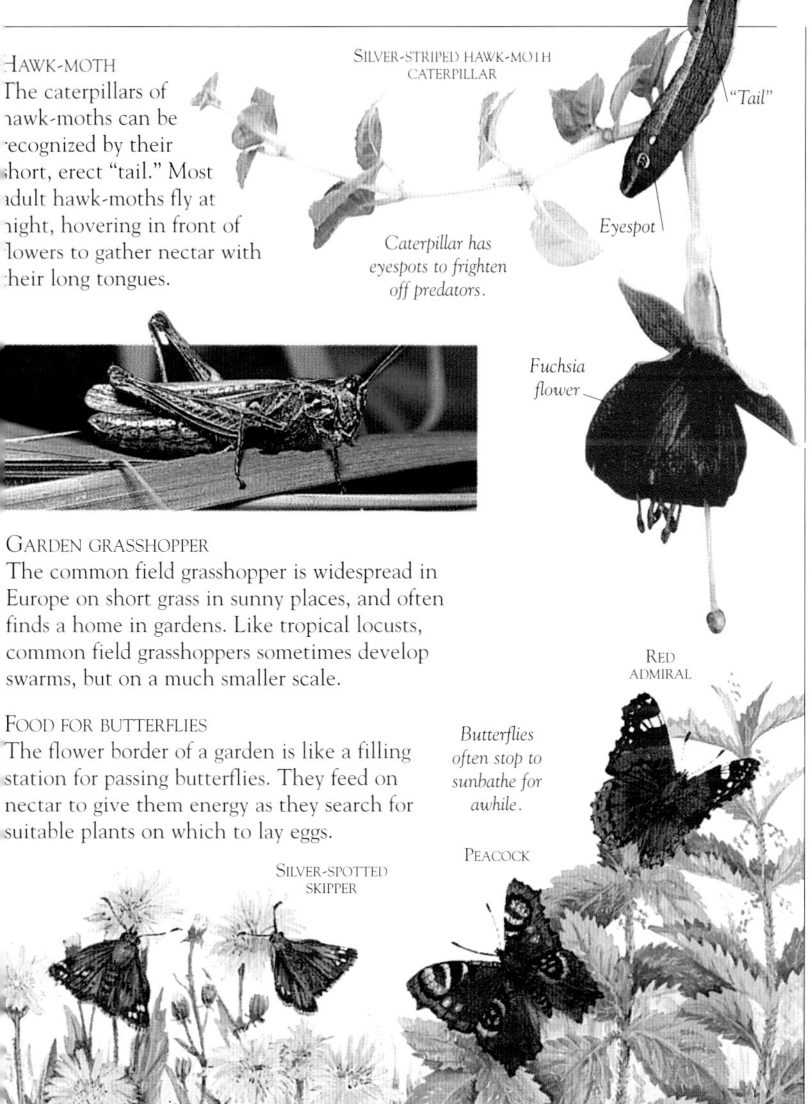

GARDEN GRASSHOPPER

The common field grasshopper is widespread in Europe on short grass in sunny places, and often finds a home in gardens. Like tropical locusts, common field grasshoppers sometimes develop swarms, but on a much smaller scale.

FOOD FOR BUTTERFLIES

The flower border of a garden is like a filling station for passing butterflies. They feed on nectar to give them energy as they search for suitable plants on which to lay eggs.

Friends and foes

The relationship between insects and humans is not always a good one. Many insects are useful to us, although others are pests. We enjoy seeing wild animals, but we destroy their habitats. This kills insects that other animals need as foo[d]. Ecology is about understanding the balance between our needs and the needs of other animals and plants.

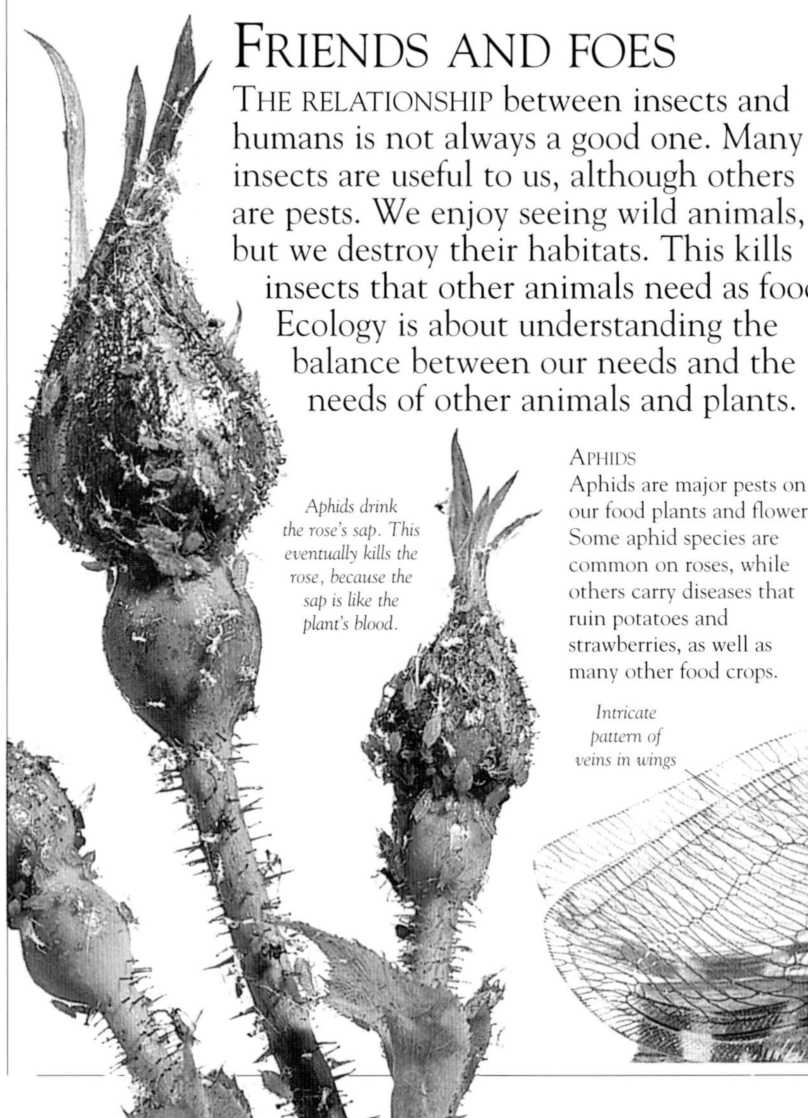

Aphids drink the rose's sap. This eventually kills the rose, because the sap is like the plant's blood.

Aphids

Aphids are major pests on our food plants and flower[s]. Some aphid species are common on roses, while others carry diseases that ruin potatoes and strawberries, as well as many other food crops.

Intricate pattern of veins in wings

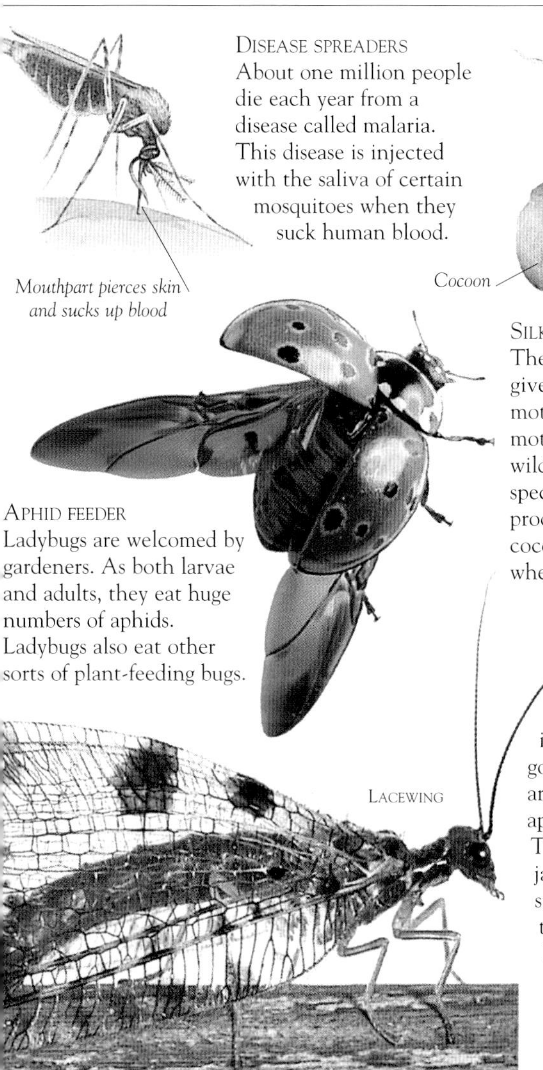
Mouthpart pierces skin and sucks up blood
LACEWING

DISEASE SPREADERS
About one million people die each year from a disease called malaria. This disease is injected with the saliva of certain mosquitoes when they suck human blood.

Moth

Cocoon

APHID FEEDER
Ladybugs are welcomed by gardeners. As both larvae and adults, they eat huge numbers of aphids. Ladybugs also eat other sorts of plant-feeding bugs.

SILK PROVIDERS
The silk we use in clothes is given to us by silk-worm moth caterpillars. Silk-worm moths no longer occur in the wild. Instead, they are bred in special farms. The caterpillars produce the silk to form cocoons that protect them when they pupate.

PEST EATERS
Lacewings are delicate insects, often with shining golden eyes. Their larvae are voracious predators of aphids and other plant lice. They have long, tubular jaws through which they suck the body contents of their prey. Lacewing larvae hide themselves from predators by sticking the remains of their prey onto small hairs on their back.

Bees and pollination

Bees and plants depend on each other. Plants need bees to carry pollen between flowers to produce seeds. Bees collect pollen and nectar from flowers to feed their larva Nectar in a hive is made into honey for winter food.

Bee-keeping

For thousands of years people have kept bees for their honey. Modern hives have racks of frames, each with a ready-made comb of cells. Individual frames can be removed and the honey drained.

Pollination

Other insects, such as butterflies, also pollinate flowers. Many flowers are a special color or shape to attract particular insects. These insects receive pollen and nectar in exchange for their work in carrying pollen to another flower.

Pollen baskets

Bees carry pollen back to their hive in special pollen baskets on their back legs. The baskets are made from curved bristles. A bee uses its front legs to comb pollen dust from its furry body and put it in the baskets.

Shape of dance shows bees direction of flowers
Pollen basket

Bee communication

When a bee finds flowers with nectar, it tells other bees in the hive by dancing. The bee conveys the distance of the flowers by how fast it shakes its abdomen, as well as the direction by the angle of its dance.

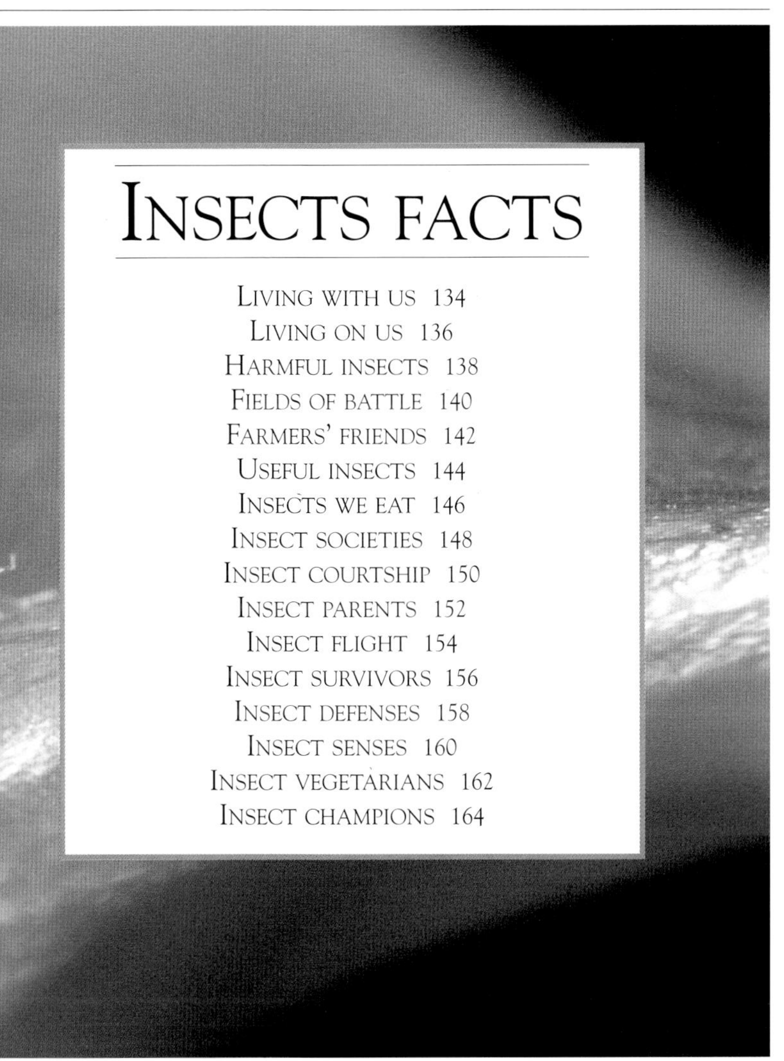

Insects Facts

LIVING WITH US

COCKROACHES

- Cockroaches eat anything and go anywhere. They are usually found in warm, humid places, such as kitchens.
- A cockroach's flat, brown body is coated with a layer of oil. This helps it to squeeze through floor and cupboard cracks as thin as a sheet of paper.

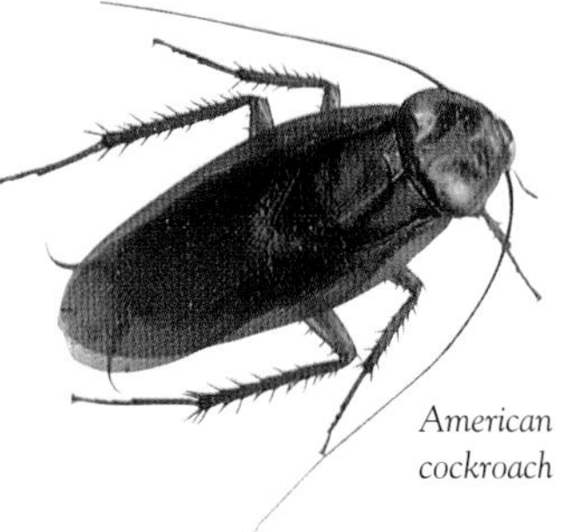

American cockroach

- Cockroaches hide by day and feed at night. They are not fussy feeders, and will eat anything from dried pasta to scraps of paper.
- A cockroach fouls whatever it feeds on and then spreads it when it walks around. Cockroaches also carry germs into the home from drains.
- The best way to get rid of cockroaches is to leave a window open – they dislike cool, fresh air.

IN THE KITCHEN

- Flour beetles are serious pests in flour mills and often spread into homes, too. They feed on cereals, beans, dried fruit, chocolate, and spices. Heavily infested foods take on a foul smell.
- One species of flour beetle, called the confused flour beetle, lays its eggs in flour. The eggs are coated with a sticky secretion, which helps them stick to packets and storage boxes.
- Saw-toothed grain beetles are one of the most common food pests. Their small, flat bodies mean that they can wriggle into damaged packages of pasta, sugar, nuts, bread, or cereal.
- When Indian meal moth caterpillars are feeding, they leave a telltale web of silk on the surface of their food. They are especially fond of powdered milk, seeds, cereals, and dried fruit.
- Hump-backed cigarette beetles love to eat dried plants. They feed on tobacco, dried flowers, spices, and even books or paper.

Red flour beetle

IN FURNITURE AND WOOD

- Deathwatch beetles are timber pests. They like to tunnel through old oak.
- Termites in the tropics can eat their way through an entire wooden house, hollowing out floorboards, doors, windowframes, and beams.

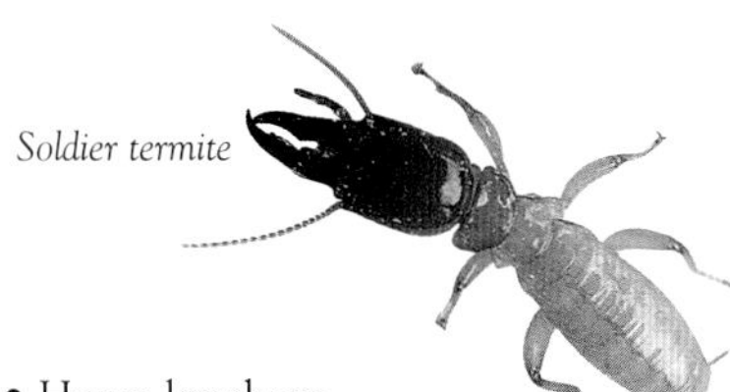
Soldier termite

- House longhorn beetle larvae spend several years eating roof timber before they emerge as adults and fly away.
- Woodworm beetles lay their eggs in wooden furniture or floors. You can see where the larvae have chewed their way out of the wood by the tiny exit holes they leave behind.

IN STRANGE PLACES

Scuttle fly larvae have been found living happily in tins of shoe polish. They have also been known to feed on latex paint.

Shoe polish

IN CARPETS AND CLOTHES

- Carpet beetles are sometimes known as wooly bears because they chew holes in woolen sweaters, blankets, and carpets. They also feed on silk, fur, feathers, and leather.
- The museum beetle feeds on stuffed animal exhibits, eventually reducing them to dust.
- The small, yellowish clothes moth feeds on clothing, rugs, and fur. It does the most damage to clothes that are soiled with sweat, oil, or spilled drinks.

IN DAMP OR DRY PLACES

- Slimy silverfish live in damp, dark corners, and they feed on wallpaper and scraps of fabric. They are so fast and slippery that it is almost impossible to catch them.
- Firebrats thrive in hot, dry places, such as cracks behind ovens. They feed on flour, starch, paper, and cotton.

Silverfish are often found in bathrooms.

LIVING ON US

FLEA BITES

- Fleas can jump up to 6 in (15 cm) high. That is about 65 times their own height – the equivalent of a human leaping 26 floors up the Empire State Building in one bound.
- On takeoff, a flea moves 20 to 50 times faster than a space rocket.
- A flea does not have teeth. Instead, it stabs skin with its sharp snout.

The strong hind legs of this cat flea help it to jump high.

- Humans cannot feel a flea bite as it happens. However, droplets of saliva in the bite soon set off a skin reaction. A small red puncture wound appears, surrounded by a red ring, and the skin starts to itch.
- A flea bites several times a minute and keeps biting even when it is full.
- Fleas bite because they live on their prey's blood. Most fleas feed on blood from mammals, but about 5 percent feed on blood from birds.
- Fleas can wait up to a year for their next victim. As soon they sense heat, noise, or even breathing, they leap on board and start to feed.

ITCH MITES

- Itch mites dig burrows into the place where they lay their eggs – human skin.
- Only female mites do the burrowing. Male mites stay on the skin's surface.
- As she digs, the female itch mite bites into human skin cells and sucks out the fluid inside.
- The female mite lays about three eggs a day. In eight weeks, she lays more than 150 eggs under the skin.
- When the young mites hatch, they climb to the skin's surface.
- Juices from the itch mite leave human skin covered with welts and blisters, making it extremely sore and itchy. This condition is called scabies.
- Itch mites, like all mites, are not true insects. Mites have eight legs – insects only have six.

BLOODTHIRSTY BEDBUGS

- During the day, bedbugs hide in mattress seams, bed frames, or behind wallpaper. At night, they head straight for the warmth and fragrant smell of the nearest sleeping human.

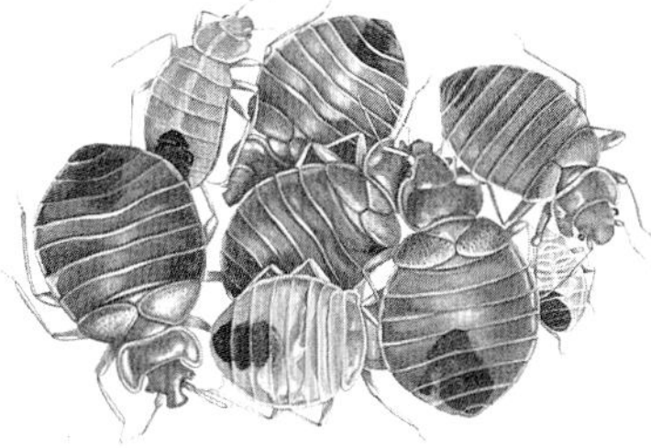

Bedbugs are 0.25 in (6 mm) long.

- When they find a patch of bare flesh, bedbugs puncture the skin with their sharp beaks and start feeding on human blood.
- A bedbug can sip blood nonstop for ten minutes.
- In one meal, a hungry bedbug can drink up to six times its weight in blood. That's the equivalent of a young human gulping down 400 lb (180 kg) of potatoes.
- When bedbugs are frightened, they leak a sweet, oily liquid that smells like rotting raspberries.

STABBED BY MOSQUITOES

- Only female mosquitoes attack humans. Male mosquitoes sip nectar.
- A female mosquito does not bite. Instead, she stabs the skin with her mouthparts and slips a thin needle (called a stylet) into the tiny hole.
- As the mosquito drinks, saliva flows into the wound to stop the blood from clotting. If the blood did clot, it would block the mosquito's mouth-parts, and the mosquito would starve.
- Mosquito saliva reacts with human skin and makes it swell into a welt that we call a mosquito bite.
- Some mosquitoes transmit diseases, such as malaria. They spread the disease by feeding on the contaminated blood of one person. When they bite the next person, the disease is passed on to him or her through the mosquito's saliva.
- Malaria kills around one million people every year.

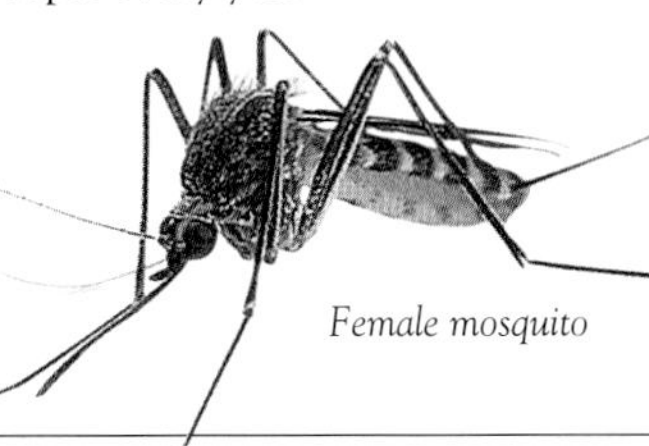

Female mosquito

HARMFUL INSECTS

TSETSE FLIES

- The African tsetse fly spreads sleeping sickness, a serious disease for people and animals. Each year, around 40,000 people die from sleeping sickness. It also kills millions of cattle, goats, and sheep.
- The tsetse fly homes in on its prey by the smell of carbon dioxide on its breath and by the odor from its urine.
- The flies have long stabbing mouthparts tipped with teeth. They pierce their victim's skin and feast on a meal of blood.
- The flies themselves pick up sleeping sickness by biting an infected animal.

Both male and female tsetse flies drink blood, which is unusual among biting flies. More often just the female drinks blood.

- They pass the sickness along in their saliva to their next victim.
- Sleeping sickness starts with headaches, fevers, and chills. It can be treated early with drugs. However, if it is left too long, it leads to coma and death.

RAT FLEAS

- The fleas that infest black rats carry a deadly disease called plague.
- Plague is a bacterium – a microscopic form of life. When it gets into rats or humans, it attacks the immune system and swiftly brings on death.

Black rat, a carrier of disease

- As a flea bites an infected rat, it sucks up plague germs. The germs are passed along the next time the flea bites another rat or a human.
- Plague has been attacking humans for thousands of years.
- In the 1300s, when it was known as the Black Death, one outbreak of plague killed half of all the people in the cities of Italy. In China, about 35 million people died from it.

BOTFLIES

- A botfly is a tropical fly with a nasty way of laying its eggs. The female catches a mosquito, or another biting insect, and glues her eggs to its body.
- When the mosquito bites a warm-blooded mammal, the botfly eggs sense the mammal's warmth and hatch out immediately. The newly hatched maggots (larvae) jump ship and burrow into the mammal's skin.
- The maggots live and feed in the skin. They pop out when they are ready to become pupae.
- Digging out a maggot can make it burst and cause a nasty infection.

ATTACKING ONE CROP

- A tiny aphid called the grape phylloxera attacks the roots and leaves of grape vines.
- The aphid causes so much damage to roots that it reduces harvests and even kills the vines.
- In the late 1800s, this tiny bug wiped out two-thirds of French vineyards after it arrived from North America. Many people wondered if French wine would vanish forever.
- Then somebody noticed that hardy root stocks from American vines could resist phylloxera. They were planted in the French vineyards, and the aphid was eventually brought under control.

ATTACKING MANY CROPS

Every year, insects destroy between 10 and 50 percent of planted crops.

INSECT	THE CROP IT ATTACKS
Potato leafhopper	Alfalfa
Colorado beetle	Potatoes
Cereal leaf beetle	Oats
Corn earworm	Corn
Japanese beetle	Leaves and fruits of 275 different plants
Vegetable leafminer	Cucumbers, squash, tomatoes
Cabbage butterfly	Cabbages, cauliflowers
Seedcorn maggots	Soybeans, beans, peas
Armyworm	Wheat
Mole cricket	Sweet potatoes
Boll weevil	Cotton

Leafhoppers

FIELDS OF BATTLE

LOCUST SWARM

- In 1957, in Africa, a giant swarm of locusts ate its way through 163,660 tons (167,000 tonnes) of grain. That is enough grain to feed about a million people for a year.
- A single locust is only about the size of a human thumb, but it eats its own weight in grass and leaves each day.
- A swarm of locusts can strip a field of grain in a couple of hours.
- A large swarm might contain 50 billion locusts spread over an area of 400 sq miles (1,000 sq km).
- By the time the swarm has gone, every shrub and field will have been stripped bare.
- Locust swarms can fly downwind for hundreds of miles over many weeks. They finally come to a halt and die out when they have exhausted all food supplies.

A locust can leap up to ten times its body length.

BEETLE BATTLE

- The greatest potato pest in the world is the Colorado beetle. This fat little beetle looks like a ladybug but with stripes instead of spots.
- Colorado beetles once lived only in the western US. When potatoes began to be planted more widely, the beetles spread. By 1871, they had crossed the US to reach the East Coast.
- By 1900, Colorado beetles had hitched a ride to Germany in sacks of potatoes. The beetles became such a menace to potato farmers there that the army was called in. Soldiers used poison, oil, and fire to stop the beetle but had little success.
- Colorado beetles also spread farther east. By 1940, they reached Russia. They have since spread all over Europe.
- Adults and larvae feast on the leaves of potato plants in large numbers and can wipe out an entire crop. Farmers now isolate infected fields to stop the beetle from spreading further.

BILLION-DOLLAR BUG

In 1991, a tiny bug called the silver-leaf whitefly caused billions of dollars' worth of damage to farmers in the southern US. It erupted like a plague in fields of cotton, melons, tomatoes, and other important crops, sucking all the sap from the plants. Whitefly resist chemicals and spread very fast.

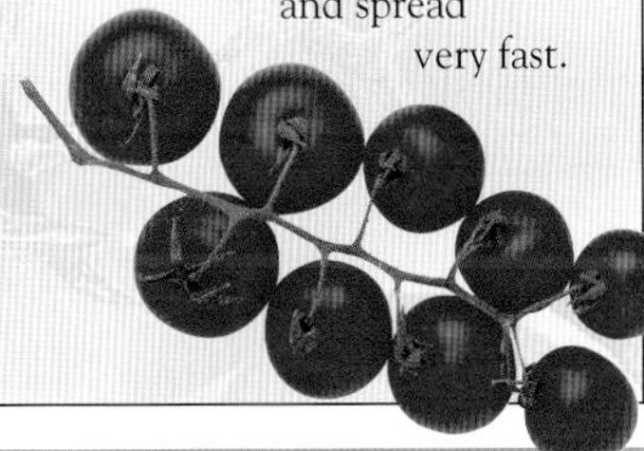

GRAIN DRAIN

- Grain weevils are tiny insects that feed on wheat, oats, barley, and rice.
- The female grain weevil drills into a kernel, drops an egg inside, and plugs up the hole.
- Young weevils hatch in the grain and feed and grow until they become adults. Then they cut an exit hole and climb out.
- Grain weevils ruin stored grain, especially if it has been lying undisturbed for some time.

COTTON WAR

- A little beetle called the boll weevil feeds on just one crop – cotton.
- The weevil is easy to recognize. It has a long snout almost half as long as its body.
- The weevil lays its eggs in unripe seedpods, or bolls, of cotton. When larvae hatch and eat their way out, they destroy the precious cotton fibers around the seeds.
- Boll weevils arrived in the US from Mexico in 1892. Since then, they have caused an incredible $14 billion worth of damage to US cotton growers.
- In the town of Enterprise, Alabama, a ruined cotton crop led local people to find other ways of making a living. The new ventures were so successful that the town put up a statue of a boll weevil to show their gratitude.
- Eventually, farmers learned to plant rows of cotton farther apart so that the sun's heat killed the weevils. They also picked and burned infested plants, and doused their fields with insecticides.
- Today, smart farming methods have beaten back boll weevils in many parts of the southern US.

FARMERS' FRIENDS

POLKA-DOT KILLERS

- An adult ladybug eats about 50 aphids every day – that's about 5,000 during its lifetime.
- Ladybugs don't just control aphids. They also eat scale insects, mealy bugs, and whitefly, making them the gardener's (and farmer's) friends.
- Some growers rear ladybugs in large quantities to prevent mealy bugs and whitefly from running amok in their greenhouses.
- In parts of the US, seven-spot ladybugs are used to control potato aphids. In large numbers, ladybugs can save a whole crop from destruction.
- If there is not enough food, ladybugs turn cannibal and start to eat their young.
- To protect themselves from being eaten by predators, ladybugs leak nasty-tasting chemicals from their knee joints. Their bright warning color also deters birds from eating them.

Seven-spot ladybug

ANT ATTACK

- One large colony of wood ants can kill and eat 100,000 other insects, such as caterpillars, in a single day.
- In Italy, wood ant nests are sometimes dug up and moved to tree plantations. The ants swarm up the tree trunks and branches to catch caterpillar pests. They protect the growing trees, which would otherwise be damaged.
- Every morning, wood ants fan out along regular hunting routes, searching for scents or vibrations made by likely prey.
- The ants overcome their victims with a bite from their pincerlike jaws, or with a puff of formic acid from glands at the back of their bodies. The acid is so strong that an attack by an ant colony can turn bluebells pink.
- Each wood ant brings back about one-and-a-half times its own weight in food every day.

WONDERFUL WASPS

- Wasps are farmers' friends because so many are parasitic. This means that they lay their eggs in or on other insects.
- The yellow braconid wasp is a parasite that lays its eggs on the caterpillar of the sugarcane stem borer moth. This moth is a pest that destroys valuable sugarcane plants.

Parasite braconid wasp larvae feeding on a sugarcane stem borer caterpillar.

- Once the braconid wasp eggs hatch, the larvae feed on the body of the caterpillar. The caterpillar cannot get rid of the larvae, and it dies.
- The yellow braconid wasp was introduced into Barbados in 1971, to control the sugarcane stem borer moth population. As a result, damage to valuable sugarcane crops fell by two-thirds.
- The cabbage apanteles wasp is another parasite, laying its eggs on the caterpillar of the cabbage white butterfly.
- The larvae of the cabbage apanteles wasp hatch out and feed on the caterpillars, eventually killing them.
- Cabbage growers often find this wasp a cheaper alternative to chemicals.

WEED CONTROL

- The prickly pear cactus can grow unchecked, like a weed.
- When this cactus was transplanted from Central America to Australia in the 1800s, it began to spread like wildfire. Eventually it covered an area about the size of Great Britain.
- Farmers were losing their livelihoods as valuable farmland was taken over by the cactus. Then the cactoblastis moth was introduced in 1925.
- The caterpillars of this moth feed on the thick leaf pads of the cacti in such numbers that the pads turn yellow, rot, and die. By 1933, the prickly pear plague in Australia had been brought under control.

Prickly pear cactus

USEFUL INSECTS

SILKWORMS

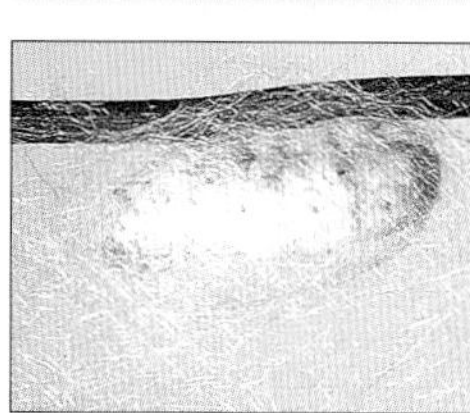

A silkworm spinning its cocoon.

- The larvae of the silkworm moth feed on mulberry leaves and other vegetation. When they are ready to turn into pupae (the final stage before adulthood), they spin a cocoon of silk.
- Each silkworm wraps itself in about 0.57 miles (a kilometre) of silken thread.
- Silkworm farmers breed the larvae and harvest the cocoons for their silk. They bake the cocoons in hot ovens, and then soak them in boiling water to loosen the threads. The end of the silk strand is placed on a winding bobbin, and the cocoon is slowly unrolled.
- It takes 1,000 silkworm cocoons to produce enough thread to weave a single silk shirt, and up to 2,000 cocoons to make a dress.

DUNG BEETLES

- Dung beetles recycle dung about as fast as animals produce it. They produce good compost for farmers.
- The beetles head for steaming fresh dung as soon as it hits the ground. Within days, the dung is buried by the busy beetles.
- Researchers studying elephant droppings found over 7,000 dung beetles busy taking apart a single giant pat of dung.
- Some beetles prefer the dung of one variety of animal. Others are less fussy, feeding on anything they find.
- Some beetles roll dung into a ball and knead it before laying their eggs in it.
- Dung beetles always lay their eggs in fresh dung. When the eggs hatch, the larvae find themselves with all the nutritious food they need to grow.

Dung beetle rolling ball of dung

HONEYBEES

- In its lifetime, a single honeybee collects enough nectar to make about 1.5 oz (45 g) of honey.
- A busy and successful colony will gather as much as 15 lbs (7 kg) of nectar in a summer's day.
- Bees gather nectar from flowers and take it back to their hive or nest. There they pack the nectar into tiny cells to feed growing larvae.
- Thick, sweet honey forms when water evaporates from nectar.
- Bees are kept for honey and also for beeswax, which bees use to construct cells. Beeswax is used to make candles and polish.

SCALE INSECTS

- One species of the scale insect, called the lac insect, oozes sticky goo (called lac) as it feeds. The goo helps to protect it from its enemies.
- People gather the goo, mash it, wash it, and bleach it. Finally, they dissolve it in alcohol to make a substance called shellac.
- Shellac is a shiny liquid that sets hard when dry. It is used to varnish wood, and as a coating for drug tablets and sweets.
- The female of another scale insect – the cochineal – stores a deep maroon pigment in its body fluids and tissues.
- The cochineal is crushed and the brilliant red color of its pigment is used as a colorant in food dye and makeup.

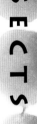

POLLINATORS

Humans rely on ants, bees, beetles, butterflies, moths, wasps, and other insects to pollinate many of the plants we grow so that the plants will produce fruit and flowers.

KINDS OF PLANTS	CROPS POLLINATED BY INSECTS
Fruit	Apples, grapes, pears, plums, oranges
Vegetables	Onions, peas, carrots, cabbages, cucumbers
Field crops	Cotton, clover, alfalfa
Garden flowers	Buttercups, carnations, orchids, sweet peas

INSECTS WE EAT

IN AFRICA

- Humans eat over 1,400 different kinds of insects. However, only about 500 are food that we choose to eat. The rest are hidden in flour, bread, fruit, and vegetables.
- By the shores of Lake Victoria, in east Africa, clouds of midges swarm so thickly that local people gather them by the handful and press them into cakes. The cakes are baked over a fire and eaten with relish.
- In Algeria, north Africa, people once collected great quantities of desert locusts. They cooked the locusts in salt water and dried them in the sun. This preserved them, like dried dates.
- In many parts of Africa, termites are so plentiful that they are a good source of food. The termites' wings are snapped off and their bodies are usually fried.
- In Botswana and South Africa, insects including the caterpillar larvae of many species of butterfly and moth are sold as canned food.
- In parts of Nigeria, Africa, people like to eat a very large insect called the palm weevil. They collect the weevil's fat, fleshy larvae from the trunks of palm trees and then panfry them.

ACCIDENTAL SNACKS

It is almost impossible to grow and harvest crops in open fields without harvesting insects, too. See what may be in your pantry...

TYPE OF FOOD	INSECTS
Chocolate	Assorted fragments
Canned sweet corn	Larvae
Canned mushrooms	Maggots
Peanut butter	Fragments
Tomato sauces	Eggs or maggots
Flour (wheat)	Fragments

Raspberries and other berries may contain larvae and adult insects.

IN THE PACIFIC

- Farmers in the Philippines flood their fields to catch burrowing mole crickets. They sell the insects to restaurants at a good price.

Mole cricket – a delicacy in the Philippines.

- In Bali, in the Pacific Ocean, dragonflies are either roasted or boiled with ginger, garlic, onions, chili peppers, and coconut milk.
- In parts of central Australia, rich-tasting witchety grubs (larvae) are considered a great delicacy. They are said to taste like almonds.

IN JAPAN

- In Japan, if you are offered *sangi* at a restaurant, you will be served a dish of fried silk-moth pupae.
- Fried cicadas are another Japanese delicacy. The cicadas are usually harvested as they molt into their adult stage.
- Mealworms are fried and roasted and added to rice dishes in Japan. They are said to have a pleasant nutty taste.
- Canned wasps, complete with wings, are sold in some some Japanese stores. They are usually served with rice.
- Fried wasps mixed with boiled rice were said to be a favorite dish of Emperor Hirohito of Japan.

Grasshoppers are eaten in many countries, providing a crunchy, nutritious snack.

ARE INSECTS GOOD FOR YOU?

Can you stay alive by eating insects, if you have nothing else available? It is surprising how nutritious they are compared to the things we generally eat.

INSECT	PROTEIN PER 4 OUNCES*	FAT PER 4 OUNCES*
Small grasshopper	0.82 oz	0.24 oz
Giant water beetle	0.79 oz	0.33 oz
Dung beetle	0.69 oz	0.17 oz
Red ant	0.56 oz	0.14 oz
Ground beef	1.1 oz	0.85 oz

* (100 g)

INSECT SOCIETIES

WASP NESTS

- In spring, a common wasp queen starts a nest by herself. By fall, she will have raised thousands of wasps – but with plenty of help.
- The queen starts by building a tough paper nest with half a dozen pockets.
- She lays an egg in each pocket (cell) and raises the grubs to adulthood. This takes about five weeks.
- When the first wasps emerge, they take over the hard work of nest-building and hunting for food.
- The queen turns herself into an egg factory, while her workers care for and feed the next generation of eggs and grubs.

Common wasp

TERMITE TOWERS

- If you could weigh all the termites in the world, they would be twice as heavy as all the human beings.
- A nest has a single queen (who lays all the eggs) and a king who fertilizes them. Both can live for 15 years. There are also soldier termites to guard the colony and workers to gather food, care for the young termites, and keep the nest clean.
- Below ground is the cellar of the termite tower. The cellar can stretch to 10 ft (3 m) across with nurseries for young termites and a queen's chamber.
- Termites communicate in the colony by giving off a scent. Each colony has its own odor. If an intruder enters, the termites can identify them by their different scent, and will raise the alarm.
- Some soldiers and workers bang their heads against the tunnels in the termite tower to warn the colony that they have been invaded.
- If a termite finds a new source of food, it lays a chemical trail for the colony to follow.

Some termite mounds are so well made that they can last more than 40 years.

ANT COLONIES

- Ants' nests range in size from a dozen or so ants to several million.
- Sometimes, several ant nests will flourish together. One super-nest of Japanese ants spread over 45,000 connecting nests and contained more than 300 million ants.
- Most ants in a colony are wingless female workers. They find food, build the nest, and care for the young.
- A single queen lays all the eggs. She is many times bigger than a worker ant.
- Some ant nests are built underground. Others are mounds of earth above ground.

Jewel wasp ant

GUESTS IN THE NEST

- Some kinds of beetles live in ant nests. Some eat their hosts' eggs and larvae. Others steal the ants' food.
- Other guests are more welcome. Some species of caterpillar live peacefully alongside ants and provide them with food. In return, the ants protect the caterpillars from predators.
- Wax moths lay their eggs in bees' nests. When the wax moth larvae are growing, they feed on the wax that holds the cells together in the nest and destroy it.
- The larvae of many flies and bugs often live in termites' nests to avoid being eaten by predators.

BEE HIVES

- A large bee hive may contain more than 60,000 female workers, as well as several hundred male drones to guard the workers and the queen.
- The queen keeps control of the hive by a special scent that comes from her head. The scent stops workers from laying their own eggs and sends them out to hunt for food.
- Early in spring, the queen starts to lay eggs so that the hive will have plenty of workers to gather nectar when flowers start to bloom. In the summer, she lays more than 1,000 eggs a day.
- In the winter, honeybees live on stores of honey they have made in their hive.

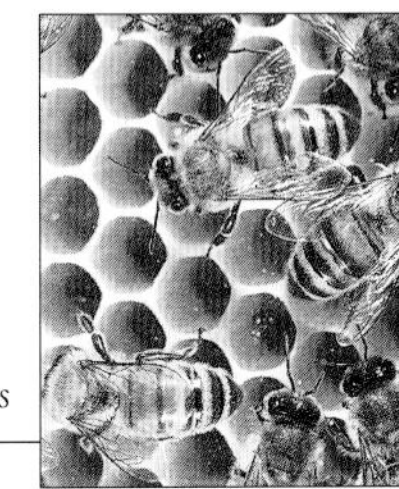

Worker bees

INSECT COURTSHIP

FINDING A MATE

- Some butterflies use perfumed powder to find a mate. They fly past a female and scatter her with sweet-smelling dust. The scent makes the female land and sit still, ready for the male to approach.
- The perfume of a female emperor moth is so alluring that it attracts males from several miles away.
- Male bumblebees mark out their territory with spots of scent. Any female that comes across this trail finds it irresistible and lands. She then waits there until the next time the male bumblebee passes on patrol.
- A male firefly flashes light signals from its abdomen as it flies around at night. If a female flashes back, she is interested in mating. The time between the flashes of light indicate the firefly's sex.

Firefly

- If a scorpion fly wants to mate, he brings his intended female a little gift – a blob of saliva.

FIGHTING A RIVAL

- A male stag beetle defends his section of branch – and a female – by rushing up to any rival, grabbing him with giant jaws. and pushing him off the edge.
- Male fighting-flies in Malaysia battle for supremacy in staring contests. The two males line up head to head and stare until one or the other backs off.
- The first male atlas beetle to find a female fights off any rivals that show up later, attacking them with its long horns.

Male atlas beetle

- Male bottlebrush weevils fight by waving their bushy snouts like tiny swords.
- A golden dung fly grabs a female that lands beside him. However, any male coming along will try to wrestle her away.

SONG AND DANCE

- When a male black-dance fly sees a female, he starts to loop and weave through the air with her. If the dance goes well, they will mate.
- When a male cicada wants to attract a female, he starts to sing. He vibrates a set of organs on either side of his abdomen. The sound is amplified by air sacs. At full throttle, it is as loud as a vacuum cleaner.
- A male deathwatch beetle taps on wood with its head to let a female know he is available. If a female hears, she taps back a reply.
- A male mosquito finds a female by the whirr of her wings, which beat at a different speed from his.

DAMSELFLIES

Most insects mate for a few seconds and then scoot away. Damselflies, however, take their time. The male damselfly grips the female's neck while they mate and she lays her eggs – sometimes for up to ten hours.

The male damselfly's grip prevents other males from mating with the female.

FEROCIOUS FEELINGS

- Some female insects gobble up their male partner after they have mated. This is because the male's body gives her and her eggs extra nutrition – and therefore a better chance of survival.
- A female praying mantis is much bigger than a male. She may grab and bite off the male's head if he is not careful when approaching her.
- Hanging flies are fierce killers of other insects. A male will therefore only approach a female if he can offer her a juicy snack. That way, he avoids ending up as her next meal after they have mated.
- Firefly females do not always mate with the males they attract when flashing their lights. If the male that approaches is from a different species, the female grabs and eats him.

INSECT PARENTS

PARENTS THAT PROTECT THEIR EGGS

- A stinkbug protects her eggs by gluing them in a tight bunch on a plant stem. She then guards them until they hatch out. If anything attacks, she puffs a vile-smelling scent at it.
- Some water bugs protect their eggs by hiding them inside the stems of plants. That way, predators swimming by will not notice the eggs.
- Many female grasshoppers hide their eggs in a small burrow dug in the soil.
- The female carpenter bee tunnels into wood to make a nest. She builds several cells, stocks them with pollen for food, then lays an egg in each one. The bee guards the nest and buzzes at anything that gets too close.

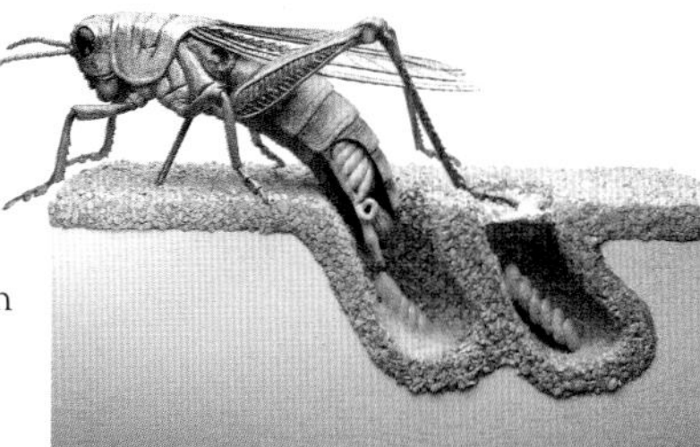

Cross-section model of a grasshopper laying eggs

PARENTS THAT PROTECT THEIR YOUNG

- A female earwig digs a small hole under a stone, and lays up to 50 eggs inside. She cleans the eggs regularly. When they hatch, she feeds the young for around two weeks, until they are big enough to leave the nest.
- The female tsetse fly produces a single egg, which hatches inside her body. The young larva feeds on special juices there, and only emerges when it becomes a pupa and falls to the ground.
- Female thrips from Panama stay with their young after they hatch. By day, they take them to feed on fungus. At night, they herd them to safety beneath the bark of trees.
- Male and female burying beetles work together to bury the dead bodies of small animals, such as mice. The female lays her eggs in the flesh and stays with the eggs until they hatch. Afterward, she cleans her young and feeds them partly digested meat.

PARENTS THAT PROVIDE FOOD

- Lots of insects lay their eggs near food so that their young have something to eat as soon as they hatch.
- Bluebottle flies lay their eggs on rotting meat, such as a dead mouse or bird. The maggots feed on the meat once they hatch.
- The acorn-eating weevil uses its long snout to drill a hole into a fresh acorn. It then lays an egg in the hole. When the weevil grub hatches, it is surrounded by a ready supply of food.
- The female hunting wasp makes sure her young have food and shelter. First she catches an insect, paralyzes it with a sting, finds a small burrow, and hides the victim inside.
- Then the hunting wasp lays her eggs on top of the insect. After hatching, the larvae can feed and hide out in safety.
- Cabbage white butterflies search out cabbages by the mustard smell of their leaves. They lay their eggs on the cabbage leaves, providing the caterpillars with their favorite food as soon as they hatch.

STICK INSECTS

Some insects seem to do little to take care of their eggs. Some stick insects, for example, sprinkle their eggs around like confetti – where they land is where they hatch. In fact, laying lots of eggs makes it harder for hunters to find them all, so some will survive.

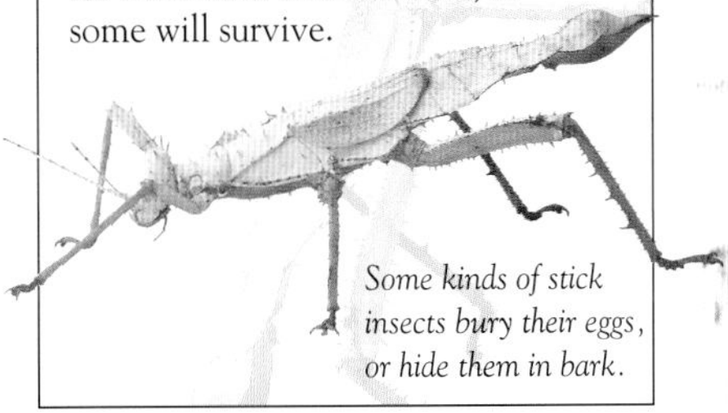

Some kinds of stick insects bury their eggs, or hide them in bark.

GIANT WATER BUG

Few insect males put any effort into being fathers. One exception is the giant water bug. The male allows the female to lay a sticky batch of eggs on his back. He then carries them around until they hatch and are old enough to care for themselves. He can carry 150 eggs on his back for up to a month.

Male giant water bug

INSECT FLIGHT

INSECT WINGS

- Most insects have wings. Usually, they have four – a pair in front and back.
- Flies have only one pair of flapping wings. The other pair are thin wings used for balance.
- Beetles spend more time on the ground than in the air, and are weak fliers. Their front wings act as tough outer coverings for the delicate back wings underneath. In flight, beetles hold their front wings up and out of the way while their back wings beat up and down.
- Many insects link their front and back wings together in flight so that they only have to flap two flight surfaces instead of four. The wings of bees and wasps are joined by a row of hooks.
- Dragonflies can glide, fly backward as well as forward, and even hover. The one thing they cannot do is tuck their wings neatly away when they land.
- Butterflies and moths rest with their wings in different positions. Moths are mostly active at night and rest by day. They fold their wings flat so they can hide in narrow crevices.

FIRST FLYERS

- The biggest insect ever found was an ancient dragonfly fossil in the US. It had a wingspan of about 24 in (60 cm). This giant bug lived during the Triassic period, 248–213 million years ago.
- Insects began to fly about 300 million years ago. They were the first creatures to take to the air.
- At first, these insects only used their wings to jump and glide, much as grasshoppers do today. They could not fly long distances.
- Most early insects had two pairs of wings that flapped separately and did not fold back – rather like today's dragonflies.

Resting butterfly with wings folded upward.

Resting moth with wings folded flat.

Flight feats

- During the mating season, male horseflies race about in short bursts at up to 90 mph (145 kmh). Over a longer distance, however, the fastest fliers are hawk-moths, which reach speeds of around 33 mph (53 kmh).
- Swarms of monarch butterflies regularly migrate distances of up to 1,800 miles (2,900 km) from Canada to Mexico to find warmth and food.
- Migrating locusts sometimes ride updrafts of wind that lift them up to 1.2 miles (2 km) high. Then they travel huge distances as they glide down.
- Damselflies swoop and soar with such skill that they can pluck midges out of the air or lift spiders off their webs without touching the sticky silken threads.

Monarch butterfly

FLAPPING WINGS

- Some insects flap their wings faster than others. Bees buzz along at 200 beats per second. Some tiny midges beat their wings over 1,000 times a second. The housefly beats its wings over 20,000 times a minute.
- One of the slowest wing flappers is the swallowtail butterfly. Its wings stir the air barely five times a second.
- When a butterfly launches itself into the air, it brings its wings down so hard that they slap together beneath its body.
- Some moths flap their wings several times before takeoff to warm up their flight muscles.

NOT JUST FOR FLIGHT

- Male crickets use their front wings to sing as well as fly. They scrape a file on the base of one wing against a drumlike area on the other wing. The loud sound attracts nearby females.
- The male South American forest butterfly uses its wings to scatter scent that attracts females. The butterfly has long hairs on the underside of its front wings. As the butterfly flaps its wings, the hairs brush against the back wings, pick up tiny grains of scent, and scatter them around.
- Bees shiver their wing muscles while keeping their wings still. The exertion generates heat to warm the hive.

INSECT SURVIVORS

SURVIVING IN HEAT

- Surface temperatures in the Sahara Desert may soar to 140°F (60°C), yet there are desert ants that can move around even in this blistering heat.
- Most desert insects do not drink. They get all their moisture from food.
- The larvae of one species of African midge shrivel up when the pools they live in evaporate. The larvae can remain in this deathlike state for months or even years. When it rains, they soak up moisture and revive.
- Desert beetles collect moisture from the air in their wings as they fly. When they land, their hard wing cases close over their wings and trap the moisture.
- The wing cases of the Namib Desert darkling beetle contain no pigment (color), and reflect the Sun's heat.

The darkling beetle's long legs enable it to run quickly and keep its body off the hot sand.

SURVIVING IN COLD

- Insects are cold-blooded, so the only way they can survive winter weather is by hibernating until warmer weather returns.
- Rock crawlers are cousins of crickets. They can live in their cold snow-covered mountain habitat in China because their blood contains chemicals that stop it from freezing.
- The carabid beetle that lives in the Arctic can survive temperatures as low as –112°F (–80°C). It has a special chemical in its blood called glycol, which acts like the antifreeze in a car engine.
- Another insect with antifreeze chemicals in its body is a tiny, wingless midge. It is just 0.5 in (12 mm) long, yet it is the biggest land animal in the Antarctic. Most of the year the midge is frozen stiff. It thaws out when the weather warms up in the spring.
- The only other insects that live in Antarctica are lice that cling to the fur and feathers of seals and birds, which keep them warm.

Safety in numbers

- The female oil beetle lays 3,000 to 4,000 eggs at a time. Even if nine out of ten do not survive, the rest live long enough to lay the next batch of eggs.
- If every egg laid by the world's insects survived, the entire planet would be waist-deep in creepy crawlies in less than a year.
- In one soil study in Iowa, scientists found 100 million tiny springtail insects in 11 square feet (a single square meter) of farmland.
- Some scientists believe that if you weighed all the animals living in the Amazon region of South America, a third of the total would be made up of ants.

SURVIVING IN THE WATER

- Salt water normally kills insects because the salt draws water out of their bodies. However, brine fly larvae can survive in water that is almost five times saltier than the sea. The larvae survive by sucking dissolved oxygen from the water into their gills.
- The larvae of some midges live in water about 4,300 ft (1,300 m) below the surface of Lake Baikal, in Russia. They absorb oxygen from the water and store it in their bodies.
- Some fly larvae survive in hot springs in Iceland, where the water temperature can reach 120°F (49°C).

SURVIVING IN THE DARK

- Cave crickets have poor eyesight, but they can detect the slightest movement in the darkness. The crickets wave their long antennae backward and forward to sense any approaching predators.
- Cave crickets are usually brown or gray, which helps them blend in with their surroundings.
- The roofs of many caves in New Zealand glimmer with tiny, twinkling, blue lights. The lights are the larvae of a type of gnat that glows to attract prey. Insects that fly too close bump into sticky feeding lines, get caught, and are eaten.

A cave cricket has the longest antennae for its body size.

INSECT DEFENSES

WARNING COLORS

Black domino beetle

- The black domino beetle of northern Africa has white spots – a warning that it can squirt stinging acid at a predator.
- The bright yellow and black coloring of cinnabar moth caterpillars warns predators that the caterpillars have an unpleasant taste, which comes from eating poisonous ragwort. Any bird that grabs one spits it out immediately.
- The postman caterpillar eats passionflower leaves that are full of cyanide poison. The poison is stored in spikes on the caterpillar's back. The caterpillar's bold colors and patterns warn potential predators that eating it would be a deadly mistake.

SURPRISE!

- Many insects try to escape by startling their attackers. This may give them a few precious seconds in which to get away.
- Screech beetles squeak loudly if grabbed by a predator. This sometimes startles the predator into letting the insect go.
- Giant cockroaches in Madagascar frighten anything that seizes them by making a sudden loud hissing noise.
- Many butterflies have large eyelike patterns on their hind wings. If attacked, the butterfly flashes the "eyes" at its predator, fooling the predator into thinking it has attacked a larger animal, such as a cat or an owl.
- Some weevils outwit a would-be attacker by playing dead. They pull up their hind legs and fall to the ground in the hope that the hunter will lose interest and go away.

Banana-eating butterfly with large eyespots on its hind wings

MIMICRY

- Many insects mimic the warning colors of deadly insects in order to fool their enemies. For example, harmless black and yellow hoverflies are left alone because they look so similar to common wasps that sting.
- The elephant hawkmoth caterpillar has big snake eyes on its body. If disturbed, it rears up so that it looks like a poisonous snake about to strike.
- A weevil in New Guinea mimics the way spiders walk – spiders have far fewer enemies than weevils.
- Thorn bugs disguise themselves to look like poisonous thorns. They are left alone by even the hungriest birds.
- Giant leaf insects resemble dried leaves. They even have holes in their wings to make them look as though another insect has been eating them.
- Stick insects look just like twigs, and rock gently to and fro to mimic swaying in a gentle breeze.

Thorn bug on tree branch

CAMOUFLAGE

- Many insects are colored in a way that blends into their background. This makes them almost impossible to see. Many grasshoppers have green bodies, perfect for hiding in meadow grasses.
- Some Central American flatid bugs have see-through bodies. As they rest on a tree, enemies see only the bark, not the insect sitting on top.
- Several species of moth have wing markings similar to the brown and white lichen that grows on tree trunks. As the moths rest on the bark, they seem to melt from view.
- Flower mantids are brightly colored in pink, yellow, or green so that they blend with the flowers on which they rest. Some also have extensions on their legs that resemble leaves.

INSECT SENSES

SIGHT

- Up to 80 percent of an insect's brain is used to understand what its eyes see and its antennae sense.
- A common wasp has five eyes – two large ones on either side of its face, and three tiny ones on top of its head. The smaller eyes can only sense light and dark, and are used mainly to help the insect balance.
- Human eyes have one light-gathering lens in the center. Dragonflies have almost 30,000 lenses per eye, helping them to detect tiny movements of prey.
- Unlike humans, insects can see ultraviolet light. Ultraviolet helps them to find nectar in flowers. The light causes a chemical reaction in the flowers, changing their color. This guides the insects to them.

SMELL

- Most insects do not have noses. They smell by using their antennae.
- Many insects that feed on fresh blood can smell the carbon dioxide gases that their prey breathes out. This helps them to track down their victims.
- Male butterflies use scent to stake out a territory and then chase out any trespassing males.
- An injured honeybee gives off a scent that acts like an alarm. Other bees smell it and buzz furiously around the hive, looking for intruders.
- Most moths fly at night. It is difficult to see in the dark, so they rely on scent to find each other. A male silk moth has such a good sense of smell that it can smell a female up to 2.5 miles (4 km) away.

The feathery antennae of this brown-headed moth detect scent.

TASTE

- Some insects run the tips of their antennae over their food before they eat it, to find out what it tastes like.
- Flies can taste food with special hairs on their feet.
- The cabbage white butterfly makes sure she has landed on the right plant for her eggs by stamping on its leaves with her feet to taste them. If a leaf tastes like mustard oil, she will lay her eggs on it.

Damselfly nymph feeding on a water flea

TOUCH

- Insects have tiny hairs all over their bodies, each with a small nerve at its base. The hairs are so sensitive that they can pick up the weak vibrations of air made by something moving around in a room.
- Insects' finely tuned sense of touch tells it whether an attacker is coming closer or moving farther away.
- One type of grasshopper can feel air currents that are moving at less than 0.1 mph (0.16 kmh). That is about the speed of a slowly moving snail.
- Ants have bristles on their body. These help the ant when it is above ground to detect tiny movements of potential prey in the soil as far down as 5 cm (2.5 in) below the surface.

HEARING

- Cicadas make the loudest sounds in the insect world. They set off a racket that can be heard half a mile (over 1 km) away.
- Crickets don't have ears. Instead, they "hear" through large swellings on each of their front legs.
- Some male crickets have three different songs: one for calling to other crickets, one for finding a mate, and one for challenging other males.
- Moths and some lacewings have ears on their wings.

"Ear"

Swellings on a cricket's legs can detect the mating calls of other crickets.

INSECT VEGETARIANS

LEAF MUNCHERS

- Many insects are strict vegetarians, living on a diet of crunchy leaves and shoots. Caterpillars eat vegetation nonstop to store up enough food to last them into adulthood. Their mouthparts slice up leaves like scissors and mash them into a pulp.
- The caterpillar of a swallowtail butterfly can eat a large leaf in just a few hours.
- The tiny larvae of some flies and beetles eat leaves from the inside out. They leave a trail of tunnels as they munch through the leaf's layers.
- Instead of fresh leaves, many beetles and springtails prefer to eat dead leaves that are coated with nutritious fungi and bacteria.
- Leaf-cutter ants carry bits of snipped-off leaves back to their nest and chew them into a mushy compost. They feed on fungus that grows on the compost.

Swallowtail butterfly caterpillar

SAP SUCKERS

- True bugs have mouths that look like needles. They use them to stab flowers, stems, leaves, or roots, to reach the sugary juices inside.
- A bug's long mouthpart, or rostrum, contains two tubes. One carries saliva to the plant to digest the sap, and the other sucks up the liquid meal.
- Aphids pierce plant stems where the sap flows strongest, so that they hardly need to suck at all. They leave droppings of sap, known as honeydew – the sweet syrup that is devoured by ants.
- Aphids spread diseases that attack the plant they feed on. Peach aphids carry more than 100 harmful viruses.
- Aphids swarm in large numbers, and cause damage to crops. They are the most destructive plant-eating insects.

GOING WITHOUT

An adult mayfly eats nothing at all. This is because it only lives for a day. In this short time, it is so busy mating and laying eggs that it does not have time for food.

BORING EATERS

- Many moths and beetles lay their eggs inside plant stems. When the young hatch out, they can feed in safety, hidden within the stem.
- Bearded weevil grubs bore in the stems of banana plants. The stems are so badly damaged that they sometimes collapse under the weight of the growing bananas.
- Dying or fallen trees attract many beetles. Longhorn beetles like to lay their eggs in rotten wood where there is plenty of fungus for their young to feed on when they hatch.
- If they can't find any dead wood, beetles sometimes gnaw bark off a branch to kill it.

Longhorn beetle

FRUIT FEEDERS

- Many moths lay their eggs in fruit that is full of sugars and easy for their larvae to eat after they hatch out.
- Fruit flies lay their eggs in rotting fruit that contains the yeasts preferred by their larvae.
- Yeast in rotting fruit often forms alcohol. Although fruit fly maggots can drink it, it is poisonous to most other insects.

Overripe bananas are a breeding ground for fruit flies. Their larvae feed on them once the bananas have fallen to the forest floor.

NECTAR SIPPERS

- To produce seeds, plants rely on insects to carry pollen from one flower to another. Bees, wasps, and ants are the most important pollinators. Next come flies, then beetles, then butterflies and moths.
- Butterflies and moths have a long tongue called a proboscis, which is rolled up under the head like a hose. The proboscis is uncoiled, then dipped into a flower to reach the sugary nectar inside.
- The tongues of some kinds of bee-fly are long and rigid. As a bee-fly sips nectar, it has to hold its tongue outstretched like an unsheathed sword.

INSECT CHAMPIONS

REPRODUCING

- The Australian ghost moth lays more eggs than any other insect – about 29,000 at a time.
- An aphid gives birth to 50 young in a week. If they and their young survived, within a year the planet would be 93 miles (150 km) deep in aphids.
- Fire brats go through 60 molts (the shedding of old skin for new skin) as they grow from youngsters to adults – more than any other insect.
- Some scientists believe that there are about 1.6 billion insects for every single human being in the world.
- Although we know of about a million kinds of insects, each year some 8,000 new species are discovered.

Ghost moths drop their eggs on the ground one at a time, around the plants their young will feed on.

HEROIC FEATS

- The oldest insect on record is a wood-boring beetle. It spent 51 years as a larva in the timber of a building before it emerged as an adult.

Wood-boring beetle

- Many insects can easily cling to windows and hang upside down. The champion gripper is a tiny blue beetle with yellow feet that can hang on despite a tug that's 80 times its body weight. The secret of its grip is its big feet, which have hairs moistened with oil.
- A housefly cannot fly upside down, so how does it land on a ceiling? By flying below it, raising its front legs, and grabbing hard. Then it swings its four back legs forward and lands solidly on the ceiling's surface.
- Ants can carry loads 50 times their own weight. The honeybee can carry 300 times its weight.

MOVING

- Cockroaches have special brain cells to help them run at high speed – that's about 40 body lengths a second, 10 times faster than humans.
- Size for size, grasshopper muscles are 1,000 times stronger than human muscles. That's why grasshoppers can jump up to 10 times their body length.
- Like all insects, a caterpillar only has six real legs. The rest, called prolegs, are muscles that stick out from the sides of its long body. The caterpillar uses its prolegs to move around and its real legs to hold its food.
- The painted lady butterfly travels approximately 4,000 miles (6,440 km) from North Africa to Iceland, giving it the longest migration of all insects.
- Locusts have enough energy to fly up to 20 hours without stopping to rest. Few other insects can match this.

FEEDING

- Colobopsis ants hunt inside pitcher plants. They catch their prey by diving into the sticky fluid at the bottom of the pitcher where insects are trapped. Then they work as a team to haul their prey to the rim of the pitcher, where they feast on it.
- Some flesh-eating flies can smell the scent of a rotting corpse 1 mile (1.6 km) away.
- The diving beetle larva stabs its prey with pointed fangs, and then squirts juices into it to dissolve the prey into a mushy soup in order to slurp it up. It mainly attacks underwater prey.
- The insect with the longest proboscis is a hawk-moth. It unrolls into a 10 in (25 cm) straw – exactly the right size for the hawk-moth to sip nectar from the flowers of the star orchid of Madagascar.

Pitcher plant

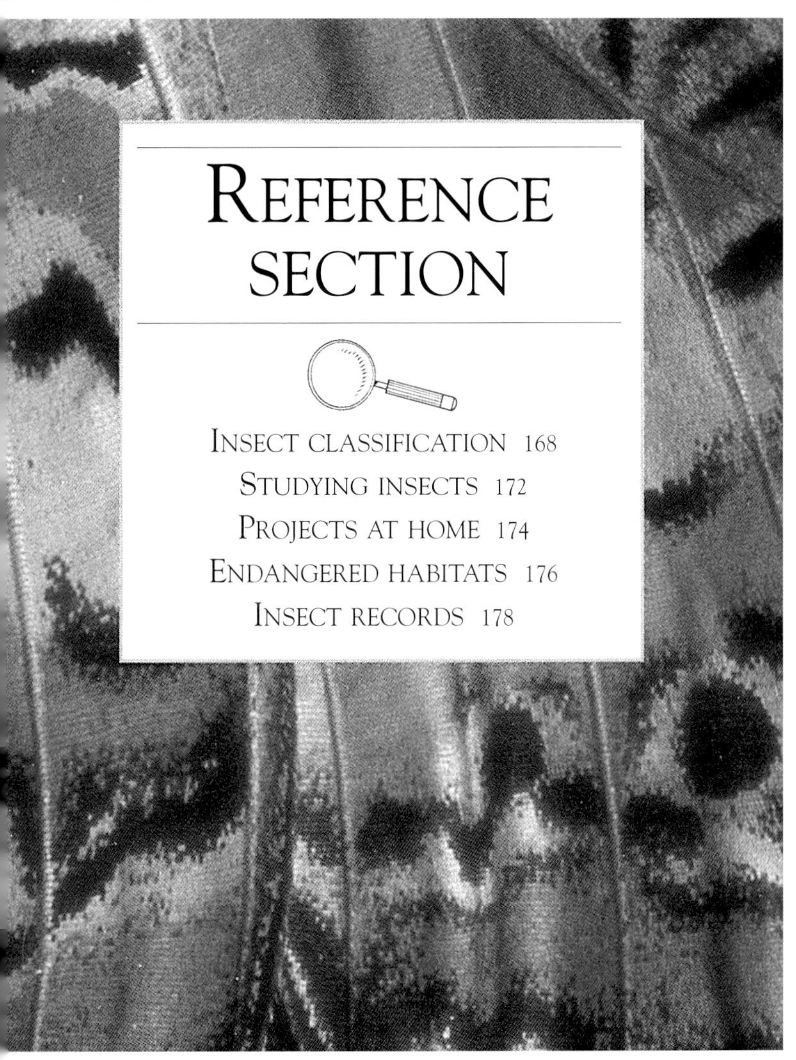

Reference Section

INSECT CLASSIFICATION

THE FIVE million or so insect species are part of the animal kingdom, which includes every other animal species. In order to discuss the different species, we classify them into a series of categories according to the features they have in common. The largest category is the kingdom, which includes all animals. The kingdom is divided into smaller categories, which are further divided until individual species are reached.

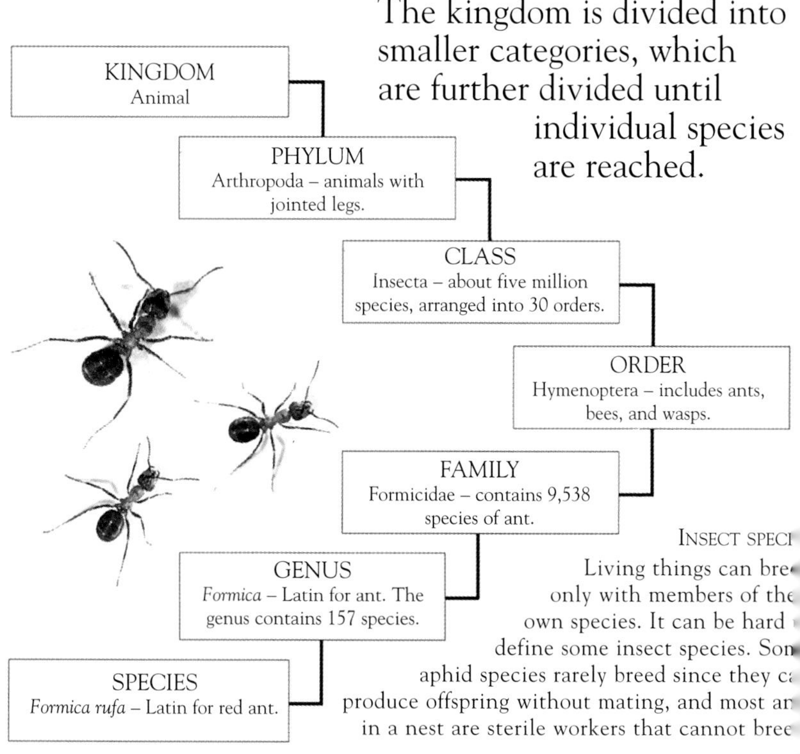
KINGDOM
Animal
PHYLUM
Arthropoda – animals with jointed legs.
CLASS
Insecta – about five million species, arranged into 30 orders.
ORDER
Hymenoptera – includes ants, bees, and wasps.
FAMILY
Formicidae – contains 9,538 species of ant.
GENUS
Formica – Latin for ant. The genus contains 157 species.
SPECIES
Formica rufa – Latin for red ant.

INSECT SPECI
Living things can bre
only with members of the
own species. It can be hard
define some insect species. Son
aphid species rarely breed since they c
produce offspring without mating, and most ar
in a nest are sterile workers that cannot bree

ORDER	SPECIES	CHARACTERISTICS
COLLEMBOLA	Springtails	Primitive wingless insects, often found on soil in vast numbers; incomplete metamorphosis
THYSANURA	Silverfish	Primitive wingless insects, found in caves and damp houses; incomplete metamorphosis
EPHEMEROPTERA	Mayflies	Larvae found in fresh water, adults have no feeding apparatus and live only a few days; incomplete metamorphosis
ODONATA	Dragonflies and damselflies	Generally large insects found worldwide, either carnivorous or herbivorous, larvae are predators in fresh water; incomplete metamorphosis
PLECOPTERA	Stone-flies	Adults are either herbivorous or do not feed at all and usually live along riverbanks, larvae live in fresh water; incomplete metamorphosis
BLATTODEA	Cockroaches	Omnivorous (eating both animals and plants) insects, often scavengers, found worldwide; incomplete metamorphosis
ISOPTERA	Termites, also known as white ants	Social insects that live in vast colonies, each with one queen who lays all the eggs, most species feed on wood; incomplete metamorphosis
MANTODEA	Mantids	Predatory insects with large eyes and grasping front legs, found mostly in the tropics; incomplete metamorphosis

ORDER	SPECIES	CHARACTERISTICS
DERMAPTERA	Earwigs	Omnivorous insects with fan-shaped hind wings and pincers on the tail; incomplete metamorphosis
ORTHOPTERA	Grasshoppers	Grass-feeding insects with jumping back legs; incomplete metamorphosis
PHASMATODEA	Leaf insects, stick insects	Leaf-feeding insects with camouflaged, flattened, or very slender bodies; incomplete metamorphosis
PSOCOPTERA	Book lice	Small chewing insects feeding on tree bark, in packs of food, and in book bindings – hence their name; incomplete metamorphosis
PHTHIRAPTERA	Parasitic lice	Parasites of birds and mammals, live on skin and feed on feathers, skin, or blood, wingless; incomplete metamorphosis
HEMIPTERA	Bugs	Insects with piercing and sucking mouthparts, feed on plants, insects, or mammals; incomplete metamorphosis
THYSANOPTERA	Thrips	Tiny insects with fringed wings, herbivorous with sucking mouthparts; incomplete metamorphosis
MEGALOPTERA	Alderflies, dobson flies	Larvae are aquatic and carnivorous, adults have long antennae; incomplete metamorphosis

ORDER	SPECIES	CHARACTERISTICS
NEUROPTERA	Lacewings, ant-lions	Predatory as larvae, adults are either carnivorous or herbivorous; incomplete metamorphosis
COLEOPTERA	Beetles	Very varied insects, with a hard front pair of wings covering the second pair, found worldwide; complete metamorphosis
MECOPTERA	Scorpion flies	Small predatory insects with biting mouthparts, found in woodlands, caterpillar-like larvae; complete metamorphosis
SIPHONAPTERA	Fleas	Wingless insects with jumping hind legs, parasites of birds and mammals feeding on blood with piercing and sucking mouthparts; complete metamorphosis
DIPTERA	Two-winged flies	Adults feed on plants and animals and in rotting vegetation, found worldwide in all habitats, larvae (maggots) are legless; complete metamorphosis
TRICHOPTERA	Caddis flies	Larvae live in fresh water and build a protective case around their body, adults either feed from flowers or do not feed at all; complete metamorphosis
LEPIDOPTERA	Butterflies and moths	Larvae (caterpillars) feed mainly on plants but colorful adults drink nectar, adults of some species feed very little; complete metamorphosis
HYMENOPTERA	Wasps, ants, and bees	Mainly carnivorous insects although some are herbivorous, some species live in highly ordered societies; complete metamorphosis

OAK LEAF WITH WASP GALLS

STUDYING INSECTS

ONE OF THE BEST ways to learn about an insect is to study it up close, either by observing the insect in its natural habitat or by capturing a specimen for a short time to examine it even more closely. Keep a record of when and where the insect was found, its appearance, behavior, and habitat.

MAKE AN INSECT TRAP

Even a small garden may contain hundreds of different types of insect. Setting up a series of pitfall traps is a good way of catching several insects for a closer look. You will need a trowel, plastic cups, large stones, and flat, square pieces of wood.

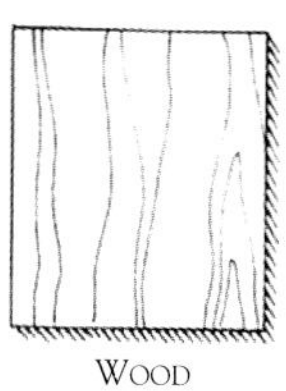
WOOD

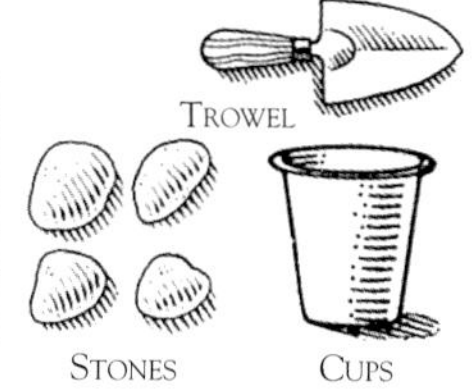
TROWEL

STONES

CUPS

1 Dig a hole for a cup. The top of the cup must be at ground level. Put one cup inside another. You can remove the inner cup to examine your catch.

2 Put cups in different places around the garden: under trees, on bare soil, among herbs, next to a pond, or in the middle of the lawn.

3 Place the wood on stones over each trap to form a protective cover. Inspect the traps regularly and record which insects you find.

JAR AND BRUSH

Most insects are small and move quickly. To get a better look at an insect, carefully use a paint brush to knock one into a jam jar. Make sure to keep the insect cool, and after examining it, let it go in the same place it was caught.

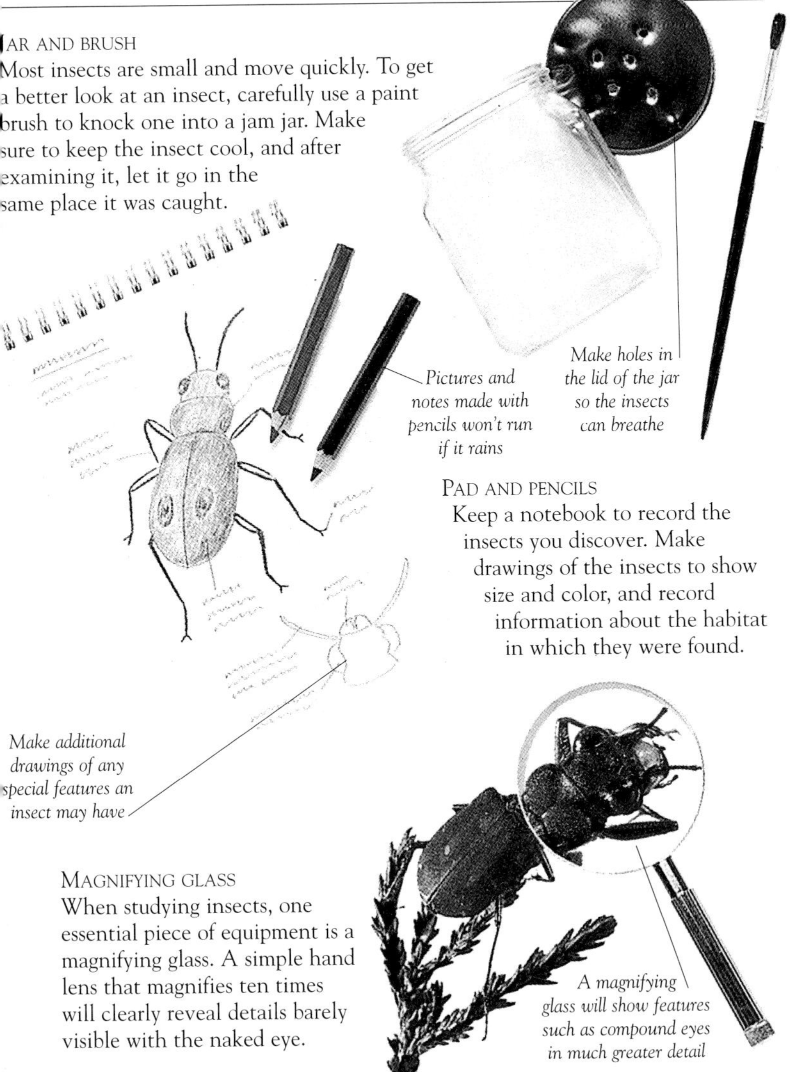

Make holes in the lid of the jar so the insects can breathe

Pictures and notes made with pencils won't run if it rains

PAD AND PENCILS

Keep a notebook to record the insects you discover. Make drawings of the insects to show size and color, and record information about the habitat in which they were found.

Make additional drawings of any special features an insect may have

MAGNIFYING GLASS

When studying insects, one essential piece of equipment is a magnifying glass. A simple hand lens that magnifies ten times will clearly reveal details barely visible with the naked eye.

A magnifying glass will show features such as compound eyes in much greater detail

PROJECTS AT HOME

A CATERPILLAR is an ideal subject for observing an insect's life cycle. In captivity, it will grow, pupate, and finally emerge as an adult. Keep a community of pond insects in an aquarium, to study the way they live – both above and below the surface of the water.

Caterpillars are soft and should be handled gently. Avoid handling caterpillars with hair – these may sting and cause a rash.

CATERPILLAR BOX

When you have found a caterpillar, put it in a box with plenty of leaves from its feeding plant. Keep the box clean and dry and replace the leaves as they are eaten or begin to shrivel. After the caterpillar pupates and becomes a butterfly or moth, release it in the place the caterpillar was found.

INSECTS AND SAUCERS

Use three saucers of food to see how different food scents attract different insects. Place fruit in one saucer, gravy in another, and water in the third. Use a white saucer and a yellow saucer for the water, to see if color attracts insects.

Butterflies and wasps are drawn to feed on the sugary fruit.

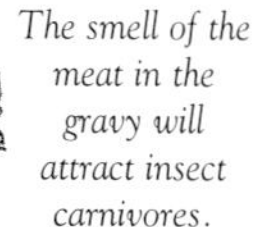

The smell of the meat in the gravy will attract insect carnivores.

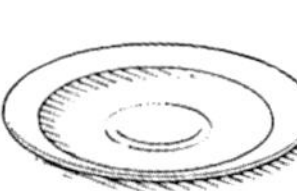

Clean water has no smell – but a colored plate may draw insects

How to make your own insect aquarium

Set up an aquarium to observe pond insects in a habitat like their own. You will need a plastic aquarium, some gravel, a few large stones, some dead sticks, and a few water plants.

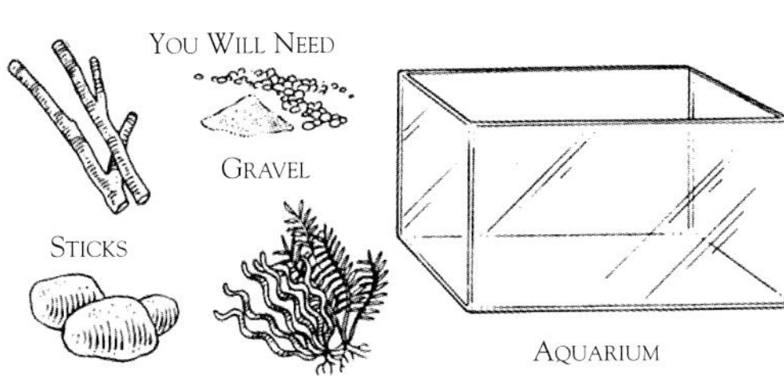

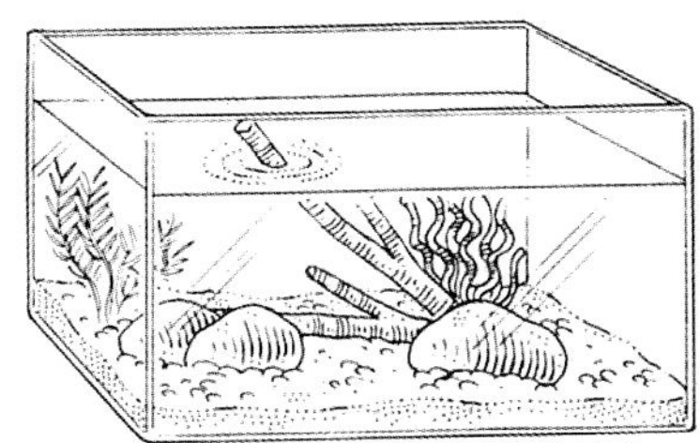

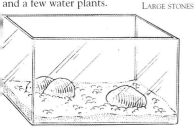

1 Cover the bottom of the aquarium with about 2 in (5 cm) of gravel and dot the large stones around. The gravel will provide a home for microscopic animals that will help to keep the water clean.

2 Fill the aquarium by pouring water over an upside-down bowl. In this way you do not disturb the gravel. Next root the water plants into the gravel and put in the sticks so that they poke out above the water.

3 Using a pond net, catch some insects and snails from a local pond, place them in your aquarium, and watch what they do. You can buy live waterfleas in a petshop. They help to keep the water clean and provide a good source of food for the predators.

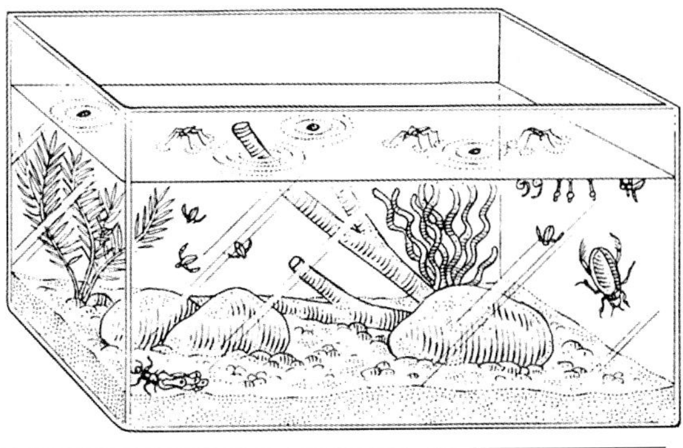

ENDANGERED HABITATS

ALL OVER THE WORLD the natural environment is shrinking as people exploit and destroy natural habitats. The threats come from agriculture, forestry, mining, road building, the spread of towns, and pollution. Even nature reserves can have problems with increasing numbers of visitors. As habitats disappear, so do the communities of plants, insects, and other animals that live there.

HABITAT	REASONS FOR DESTRUCTION	INSECT EXAMPLES
RAIN FOREST	Species-rich forests felled for timber or replaced by grasslands for cattle or crops. These support few insect species and are plagued by pests because all the natural predators have gone.	Hercules beetle; Queen Alexandra's birdwing butterfly; 8-spotted skipper butterfly; Wallace's giant bee
BIG TREES	Large trees in forests felled for timber. Access roads in forest encourage farmers to settle, who then clear more trees. Some trees and the insects associated with them threatened with extinction.	Periodical cicada; Giant carrion beetle; Sugarfoot moth fly; European wood ant; Frigate island giant tinebrionid beetle
SEMIDESERT AREAS	Domestic livestock over-grazing leads to erosion of topsoil. Heat quickly evaporates irrigation water, resulting in salts building up in soil. Fewer plants can grow leading to expansion of deserts.	St. Helena earwig; Belkin's dune tabanid fly; Avalon hairstreak butterfly; Ravoux's slavemaker ant

HABITAT	REASONS FOR DESTRUCTION	INSECT EXAMPLES
TROPICAL DRY FOREST AREAS	Leaves fall off trees in dry season. Trees are destroyed by burning to produce grasslands for cattle. Fires are allowed to burn out of control. One of the most threatened habitats.	Giant wetas; Small hemiphlebia damselfly; Lord Howe Island stick insect; Australian nothomyrmecia ant
PRAIRIES	Natural grasslands rich in wild flowers and insect species get plowed up and drenched in fertilizers and insecticides to produce cereal crops and "improved" grasslands for cattle.	Delta green ground beetle; Dakota skipper; Wiest's sphinx moth
LAKES AND RIVERS	Water is polluted by fertilizers running off fields. Pollution from sewage and industrial waste, and metal pollution from mine wastes. River channels are straightened and dredged.	Large blue lake mayfly; Freya's damselfly; Relict Himalayan dragonfly; Florida spiketail dragonfly; Tobias caddis fly
GRASSLANDS	Drainage of water meadows and plowing of grasslands for crops destroys natural plants. Addition of fertilizers results in domination by aggressive species of grass with fewer wild flowers and insects.	Pygmy hog sucking louse; Large blue butterfly; Bay checkerspot butterfly; Uncompahgre fritillary butterfly
BOGS AND PEATLANDS	Land is drained for agriculture, such as planting of timber trees for commercial forestry. Cutting and extraction of peat for use in gardens or as fuel for power stations.	Ohio emerald dragonfly; Flumiense swallowtail butterfly; Harris' mimic swallowtail butterfly

INSECT RECORDS

INSECTS ARE the most numerous animals on Earth. Their success is due mostly to their small size and remarkable adaptability. The following are some of the more amazing insect record-breakers.

SIZE

- Bulkiest: goliath beetle – 4⅓ in (110 mm) long weighing 3½ oz (100g)
- Smallest: mymarid wasp – 0.0067 in (0.17 mm) long
- Largest wingspan: Australian hercules moth – 11 in (28 cm) wide
- Largest water insect: giant water bug from Venezuela and Brazil – 4½ in (11.5 cm) long
- Most numerous insect: springtails – about 5,000 per sq ft (50,000 per sq m) in grassland

FLIGHT

- Fastest ever: a giant prehistoric dragonfly probably had to fly at least 43 mph (69 km/h) to stay airborne
- Fastest-flying living insects: hawk-moths – reach top speed of 33⅓ mph (53.6 km/h)
- Fastest wingbeat: the midge *Forcipomyia* – 62,760 beats per minute
- Slowest wingbeat: swallowtail butterfly – 300 beats per minute
- Farthest migration: painted lady butterfly – 4,000 miles (6,436 km) from North Africa to Iceland

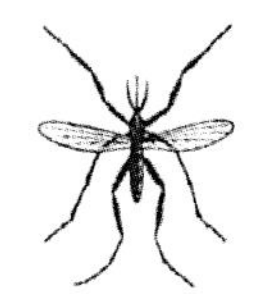

PESTS

- Most fatalities: more than half of all deaths since the Stone Age are due to malaria-carrying mosquitoes. Rat fleas carry a plague that killed 20 million people in 14th-century Europe
- Most poisonous: about 40,000 people are killed each year by wasp or bee stings
- Most disease-ridden: the housefly transmits more than 30 diseases and parasites
- Most destructive: a locust swarm can eat 20,000 tons (tonnes) of crops per day

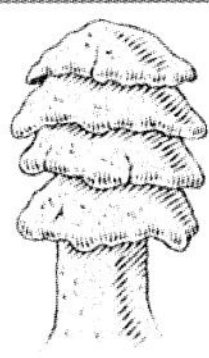

Nests

- Largest: Australian termite nests – up to 23 ft (7 m) high and 100 ft (31 m) in diameter at the base
- Tallest: nests of African termite – 42 ft (12.8 m) high
- Deepest: nests of desert termite – 131 ft (40 m) below ground

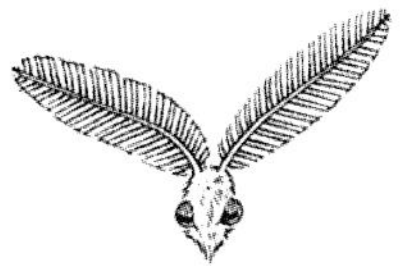

Communication

- Loudest: cicada – its song can be heard by humans from a distance of ¼ mile (400 m).
- Most sensitive sense of smell: Indian moon moth – can detect pheromones of a mate from a distance of over 6¾ miles (11 km)

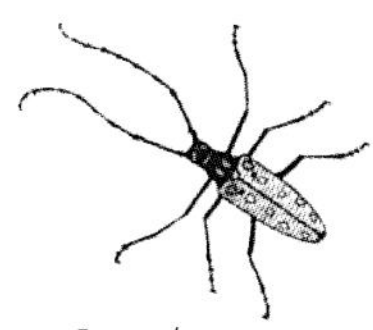

Legs/Antennae

- Longest: giant stick insect – 20 in (51 cm)
- Longest antennae: New guinea longhorn beetle – 7½ in (20 cm)
- Longest jump: Desert locust – 19½ in (50 cm), which is ten times its own body length

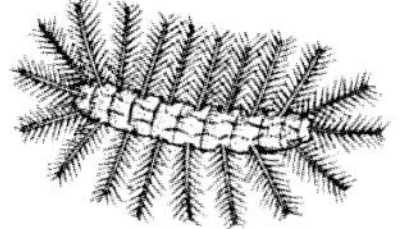

Toughest

- Larvae of ephyrid flies live in the waters of hot springs at 140° F (60°C)
- The snow flea remains active at temperatures of 5° F (-15°C)
- Larvae of the midge *Polypedilum* can survive years without water and three days in liquid nitrogen (-321° F, -196° C)

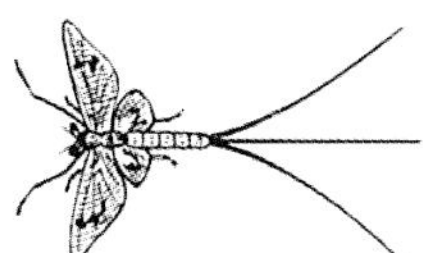

Lifestyle

- Longest lifecycle: periodic cicada – 17 years
- Longest-lived larva: wood-boring beetle – can survive for up to 45 years
- Shortest-lived insect: housefly – can complete its entire lifecycle in 17 days

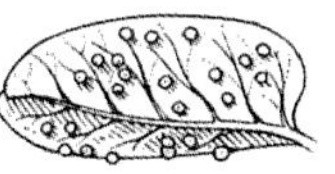

Eggs

- Largest: ⅖ in x ³⁄₂₀ in (10.2 mm x 4.2 mm) laid by cerambycid beetle, *Titanus giganteus*
- Longest time in the egg stage: 9½ months by the cerambycid beetle *Saperda carcharia*
- Most eggs laid: the queen *Macrotermes* termite can lay 40,000 eggs per day

Glossary

ABDOMEN
Segmented section of arthropod's body behind thorax that contains the digestive and reproductive organs.

ANTENNAE
Two long and thin appendages on the head of insects and other arthropods used mainly for touching and smelling.

ARTHROPOD
An invertebrate with jointed limbs and a hardened exoskeleton.

BROOD CELL
A space or structure in a bee or wasp nest where a single egg is laid and the larva develops until it becomes an adult.

CAMOUFLAGE
The means of disguising the body in order to go unnoticed by predators or prey.

CARNIVOROUS
Flesh-eating.

CASTE
In social insect societies, a group containing individuals that perform specialized tasks, such as "workers" in wasp nests or "soldiers" in ant nests.

CATERPILLAR
Any wormlike insect larva, but usually refers to the larva of moths and butterflies.

CERCI
Two spine-shaped sensory growths at the end of the abdomen of some arthropods.

CHRYSALIS
The pupa of a moth or butterfly, sometimes enclosed in a silk cocoon.

CLASPERS
Two pincerlike appendages on the abdomen of male insects that grasp the female during mating.

COCOON
Protective silk casing that the larvae of many insects weave around themselves prior to pupation.

COLONY
A group of social insects living and working together and sharing a nest.

COMPLETE METAMORPHOSIS
Where an insect's development from egg to adult has distinct stages including a pupal stage; usually the larva looks very different from the adult and also has a different diet.

COMPOUND EYE
An eye composed of many separate eyes called ommatidia. Each ommatidium is capable of vision.

COURTSHIP DANCE
Dancelike movements, often performed in flight, between two insects before mating.

CUCKOO SPIT
Frothy liquid produced by certain plant bugs in which they hide from predators and which stops them from dehydrating.

DISRUPTIVE COLORATION
A combination of colors and patterns on

the body that disrupt the body's shape, making it hard to recognize.

Elytra
The front wings of beetles that are hardened and protect the body.

Entomology
The scientific study of insects.

Exoskeleton
The external skeleton of an arthropod.

Eyespots
Markings on an insect's body that look like eyes for frightening or distracting predators.

Fossil
The remains of something that once lived, preserved as stone.

Fungus
A simple plant, usually growing on other plants and animals and often causing decay and disease.

Fungus garden
Fungus cultivated in a nest as food by leaf-cutter ants and certain species of termite.

Gall
An abnormal growth on a plant caused by the presence of an insect's egg or its feeding activities.

Gills
Outgrowths on an aquatic insect's body by which it breathes underwater.

Grub
An insect larva, especially of beetles, that lives underground or in rotting wood.

Halteres
The hind wings of two-winged flies that have been modified into clubbed stalks and are used as balancers in flight.

Herbivorous
Plant-eating.

Honeydew
A sweet, sticky liquid secreted by aphids and treehoppers, derived from the sap of plants on which they feed.

Honey guides
Lines on the flower petals of certain plants that reflect ultraviolet light and direct insects to the pollen and nectar.

Host
Animal or plant on which a parasite feeds and lays its eggs.

Incomplete metamorphosis
The development of insects where the nymphs hatch looking like small versions of the adults and there is no pupal stage.

Invertebrate
An animal without a backbone.

Larva
The stage in an insect's life from when it hatches from the egg to when it pupates. The young stage of insects that do not pupate is called a nymph.

Leaf miner
Insects that live and feed inside a leaf, creating a mine, or tunnel, as they feed.

Mammal
A warm-blooded animal that drinks its mother's milk when it is young.

Mating
The reproductive act between a male and female of the same species where the male puts sperm in the female in order to create young.

METAMORPHOSIS
The process of insect growth from egg to adult where the body shape metamorphoses, or changes, as it grows.

MIMICRY
The process whereby one insect species copies the coloration and behavior of another species, usually for the purpose of protection from predators.

MOLTING
The shedding of old skin to be replaced by a new skin.

MUD PUDDLING
The habit of butterflies, usually in the tropics, of gathering in groups to drink from muddy puddles in order to obtain essential minerals and salts.

NECTAR
A sugary fluid found in plants.

NOCTURNAL
Being active by night and resting by day.

NYMPH
See LARVA.

OCELLI
Simple eyes that have a limited function, probably only detecting light and shade.

OMMATIDIUM
A single part of a compound eye capable of detailed vision.

OMNIVOROUS
Having a diet of both animal and plant food.

OVIPOSITOR
The egg-laying tube of insects.

PARASITE
An animal that completes its development on, or in, the body of another animal without benefiting its host in any way.

PALPS
Sensory feelers beside the jaws of some insects.

PHEROMONES
Chemicals produced by insects of both sexes that act as a sexual attractant to members of the opposite sex.

POLLEN
A flower's male sex cells that fertilize the female sex cell (ovule).

POLLINATION
The process by which the pollen of one flower is transported, usually by insects or by the wind, to the female part (ovary) of another plant of the same species to produce seeds.

PREDATOR
An animal that hunts other animals for food.

PROLEGS
Also known as false legs, fleshy growths on the abdomen of some insect larvae, especially caterpillars, that function as legs.

PUPA, PUPAL STAGE
The inactive, non-feeding stage of insects that undergo complete metamorphosis, when the larva transforms into an adult.

ROSTRUM
The piercing and sucking, beaklike mouthparts of true bugs.

SALIVA
A liquid secreted into the mouth that begins the process of digesting food. In some insects, the saliva is deadly and is injected into prey, killing the prey and dissolving its insides.

SCALES
Modified hairs that

have become flattened, especially found in butterflies and moths.

Simple eye
See Ocelli.

Social
Living in groups.

Soldier
A caste member from a termite or ant colony which has an enlarged head and jaws used in a defensive role to protect the other nest members.

Solitary
Living alone.

Species
A group of animals or plants that can breed only with each other and produce fertile offspring.

Sperm
A male cell that is put inside a female during mating to join with her egg-cell, which creates a new individual.

Spiracles
External openings of the tracheae on the body of an insect through which the insect breathes.

Sting
The modified ovipositor of certain wasps, bees, and ants that has lost its egg-laying function and is used to inject venom into prey or enemies.

Stylet
A piercing needlelike organ, usually a mouthpart of bugs and certain blood-sucking insects.

Swarming
Any huge group of insects traveling together, but usually the behavior of honeybees when the queen and a large number of workers leave their nest to set up a new nest elsewhere.

Tarsus
The insect's "foot," consisting of between one and five segments and one or two claws for gripping surfaces.

Temperate regions
Parts of the Earth between the tropical and the polar regions, with moderate temperatures.

Thorax
The part of an arthropod's body between the head and abdomen that carries the legs and wings.

Tracheae
Tubes in the body of an insect that transport oxygen around.

Tropical regions
Parts of the Earth around the equator with hot temperatures all year.

Ultraviolet
Beyond the violet end of the light spectrum, ultraviolet is invisible to most mammals, but visible to most insects.

Venom
A poison that is often deadly, produced by many predatory insects for injecting into prey or enemies.

Warning coloration
Bright, conspicuous body coloring used by many insects with weapons or poisonous bodies; predators learn to avoid these insects.

Worker
A member of an insect colony that is sterile (cannot breed) and whose duties include caring for the larvae, maintaining the nest, and foraging for food.

Latin name index

INDEX

Acknowledgments

Dorling Kindersley would like to thank:
Sarah Goulding for editorial assistance, Helen Corrigan for consulting on additional material, and Hilary Bird for compiling the index.

Photographs by:
Julie Anderson, Jane Burton, Peter Chadwick, Neil Fletcher, Frank Greenaway, Colin Keates, Dave King, Andrew McRobb, Oxford Scientific Films, Tim Ridley, Bill Sands, Kim Taylor, Jerry Young.

Illustrations by:
John Davis, Ted Dewan, Nick Hall, Brian Hargreaves, Nick Hall, Nick Hewetson, John Hutchison, Mark Iley, Richard Lewington, Ruth Lindsay, Tommy Swahn, Simon Thomas, John Woodcock, Colin Woolf.

Picture credits: t=top b=bottom c=center l=left r=right
Beth Chatto 145br; Bruce Coleman/Eric Crichton 58cl, 60-61; Gerald Cubitt 59br, 90-91; Geoff Doré 59bc, 82-83; P.A. Hinchcliffe 38tr; Eckart Pott 123tc; Dr. Sandro Prato 129tr; Hans Reinhard 81tl; Kevin Rushby 41tl; Dr. Frieder Sauer 57br; Kew Gardens 165bl; Kim Taylor 29tr, 68cr, 76cr, 123tl; Norman Tomalin 92c; Natural History Museum 136cr, 164bl; Natural History Museum/Frank Greenaway 80cr; Natural Science Photos/M. Boulard 119bc; P. Bowman 72cl; M. Chinery 125cl; Carol Farneti 92bl; Adrian Hoskins 77cr; Richard Revels 72tr, 122cr; P.H. & S.L. Ward 39cr, 127c; David Yendall 85tr. Oxford Scientific Films/Kathie Atkinson 35tr; G.I. Bernard 85cl; Raymond Blythe 118bl; Densey Clyne 115tr; C.M. Collins 46bl; J.A.L. Cooke 57c, 124tl; Michael Fogden 113tl; Peter Gathercole 45tr; Mantis Wildlife Films 10cl; Peter O'Toole 46cr; James Robinson 54cr, 83br; Harold Taylor 63c; Steve Turner 59cr, 110-111, 113tr; P & W Ward 112cr. Premaphotos/K.G. Preston-Mafham 37tr, 45br, 49br, 51cl, 52br, 58br, 74-75, 92br, 96bl, 109t, 109cr. Dr. Bill Sands 48cr. Science Photo Library/J.C. Revy 100cr. Tony Stone Images/Mike Surowiak 85bc; Jerry Young 147br, 160br.

Every effort has been made to trace the copyright holders and we apologize in advance for any unintentional omissions. We would be pleased to insert the appropriate acknowledgment in any subsequent edition of this publication.